strategies *and*
tactics *for*
effective
instruction

Bob Algozzine

Jim Ysseldyke

Judy Elliott

ISBN #1-57035-119-8

Edited by Lynne Timmons
Text layout and design by Susan Fogo
Cover design and illustrations by Eye for Design

Printed in the United States of America
Published and Distributed by:

Sopris West

4093 Specialty Place • Longmont, Colorado 80504
(303) 651-2829 • http://www.sopriswest.com

Bob Algozzine, Ph.D., has taught students labeled educable mentally retarded, disabled readers, and emotionally handicapped. He has been a teacher in a vocational institution and center for disturbed students as well as an educational diagnostician in a large school system. He taught at the University of Florida for 12 years and has been a faculty member at the University of North Carolina, Charlotte, since 1987. For five years, he was a research associate at the University of Minnesota's Institute for Research on Learning Disabilities. Dr. Algozzine has been on the editorial review board of more than 15 professional journals dealing with special education and educational research. He currently is the co-editor of *Exceptional Children*.

Jim Ysseldyke, Ph.D., is Professor of Educational Psychology and Director of the National Center on Educational Outcomes at the University of Minnesota, Minneapolis. He has been a classroom

teacher and school psychologist. He received his doctorate from the University of Illinois. Dr. Ysseldyke is nationally recognized for his research and writing on assessment and effective instruction.

Judy Elliott, Ph.D., is a former special education teacher and school psychologist with 14 years experience in public schools, elementary through secondary levels. She is a national consultant and staff development professional to school districts, education organizations, and state departments of education in both the South Pacific and the United States. Dr. Elliott has trained thousands of staff, teachers, and administrators in linking assessment to classroom intervention, effective instruction, teacher assistance teams, authentic assessment, curriculum-based evaluation, instructional enviroment evaluation, behavior management, and other relevant areas. Currently, she is a senior researcher at the National Center on Educational Outcomes at the University of Minnesota.

This book represents a collaborative effort. It would be very difficult to write a book like this alone. First, developing the components and principles of a model for effective instruction is a challenge not to be taken lightly. The task of compiling and organizing tactics is formidable as well. Most of the material presented in this resource came from effective teachers. Many contributed tactics as part of our early efforts to use the model in inservice workshops and they were acknowledged in the first edition of *Strategies and Tactics for Effective Instruction*. At workshops and conference presentations that we attended across the country, others knowingly, and unknowingly, contributed ideas that were later converted to tactics to fit within the model we were developing. Still others contributed generally by their associations with us and our work.

We have worked with many outstanding teachers, administrators, students, and just plain wonderful people over the years, and we are grateful that they have touched us with their wisdom along the way. A few individuals require specific thanks and acknowledgment: Peter Allen, Carol Bement, Charlie Carbone, Margaret Dolan, Ron Gentile, Cathy Hays, Bill Heller, Bill Jenson, Mary Ann LoVullo, Walter Majewski, Thomas McCully, Susan Pilarski, Katherine Sacca, John Salvia, John Sutherland, Martha Thurlow, Donald Tiburzi, and Gloria Weinstein. We are also indebted to the folks at Sopris West for providing the support, encouragement, and continuing interest that has made the production of this work more of a joy and less of a chore than it might have been.

Having trouble deciding what to teach and how to teach? Running into difficulties figuring out the best ways to use time productively and establish a positive classroom environment? Concerned about how to present, monitor, and adjust your instruction? Are evaluation, record keeping, and instructional decision making tough and time consuming?

Don't worry, "Bob" is here. He's here to help you plan, manage, deliver, and evaluate your instruction in new and effective ways. "Bob," the *STEI* guy, will lead you to hundreds of very specific tactics to help you plan, manage, deliver, and evaluate instruction for even the most difficult-to-teach students. This highly organized resource will help you identify specific tactics to use to accomplish your instructional goals.

In an accompanying resource, *Time Savers for Educators*, "Bob" will direct you to ready-to-use black line masters of worksheets, record-keeping forms, practice sheets, and other tools to use with the tactics described in this book. The clock icon ⏲ in *STEI* identifies the tactics that have supplemental tools in *Time Savers for Educators*.

Follow "Bob" throughout *STEI* and *Time Savers* to get specific ideas about how to improve your teaching and how to get even the most resistanct learners to be responsive. Follow "Bob," and learn to use this second edition of *Strategies and Tactics for Effective Instruction* to give your colleagues ideas about what to do. Follow "Bob," and let him make your life just a little easier.

Bob Algozzine
Jim Ysseldyke
Judy Elliott

planning   15

managing   61

o v e r v i e w

Teachers are confronted daily with an increasingly diverse group of students, and they are expected to assist these students in meeting increasingly high standards. They want to know specifically what to do with those students, and they do not have time to dig through journals and textbooks for specific teaching ideas. They need a structured and organized way to get to specific ideas.

There are empirically demonstrated principles of learning, and there are principles of teaching. Theoretically, teachers systematically apply these principles of learning and teaching to planning, managing, delivering, and evaluating instruction for students who are experiencing difficulties. That's the theory. Reality is quite another matter. To date, actual practice looks something like this:

 Students in preservice college or university courses learn long lists of principles of learning and principles of teaching. They recite Anderson, Berliner, Bloom, Brophy, Carroll, Good,

Hull, Skinner, and Thorndike. Yet, they soon forget the memorized lists, and they have incredible difficulty applying the principles to the day-to-day instruction of students. Application is assumed rather than taught, and the link between principles of effective instruction and actual teaching practice is obscure. Connections between theory and practice are not clear.

 Students in college and university special education courses learn characteristics of specific types or categories of exceptional learners, often under the presumption that if they can profile characteristics they can intervene. Things have not changed much since Bateman (1967) said …

> *Teachers in practice do not walk around reciting principles of learning and principles of teaching; nor do they think about how these principles apply to teaching children and youth.*

Rather, they have a set of (usually their own) strategies and tactics that they apply. They learn the strategies and tactics through experience, or often by being told by other teachers what to do. For example, a teacher may prompt correct responses with associated signals. If a student is having difficulty remembering a word, the teacher may say the word repeatedly, each time tapping the desk with a pencil. As the student reads along in the passage, when he/she comes to the difficult word, the teacher taps the desk with the pencil to prompt the correct response and prevent an error from occurring. (p. 25)

Other teachers teach students to manage their own behavior by reinforcing decision-making behavior. When students "choose" to follow rules, the teacher rewards their behavior with statements such as, "You have chosen to complete your assignment on time. That was a good decision." These teachers have learned that the tactic is especially helpful with students who are prone to breaking rules. It is effective to point out to these students that following the rule is a better decision and that the decision to do so is under their control. These teachers encourage development of personal responsibility.

Effective teachers have procedures for times between activities that occur before, during, and at the end of the school day. Some teachers start each day with a news item of interest, a short story, a riddle, or a "brain teaser" to stimulate thinking and help students settle into school. Others begin the day with "administrative tasks" (e.g., attendance, lunch count, school events, daily schedule). Still others combine interesting activities with school business to start or end the day. Many teachers also find procedures valuable in controlling room entry and exit behaviors of students; they help minimize disruptions that commonly occur when students make bathroom, library, or extra-curricular trips.

Teachers all have specific strategies and tactics that they use to make their instruction effective. Yet, the connections between principles of learning, principles of teaching, and strategies and tactics are not clear. What often results ends up looking very much like hodgepodge.

The authors have long been trying to change the focus of assessment and intervention so that interventions make a difference for students—and ultimately for school systems and society. They have concentrated their efforts in special education, challenging assessment and intervention practices (Ysseldyke, 1973; Algozzine & Ysseldyke, 1981, 1982, 1986; Ysseldyke, Algozzine, & Mitchell, 1982; Ysseldyke & Thurlow, 1984), and have developed measures of the instructional environment (Ysseldyke & Christenson, 1987, 1993). Christenson, Ysseldyke and Thurlow (1989) developed a way to think about instruction at the principle level. They specified four components of effective instruction: Planning, Managing, Delivering, and Evaluating. These are shown in Figure 1.

A problem remains. Teachers report that they know the components of effective instruction, know the principles of effective instruction, have a few strategies and a collection of tactics, but that they do not know how to conceptualize instruction and think systematically and in a structured, organized way about planning, managing, delivering and evaluating instruction. They ask, "How do I make clear connections between theory and practice?"

In the first edition of *Strategies and Tactics for Effective Instruction* (STEI) the authors demonstrate how to link principles of learning and principles of teaching to strategies and tactics for effective instruction (Algozzine & Ysseldyke, 1992). This process was developed by:

1 Organizing empirically demonstrated principles of learning and principles of teaching into the four major components of instructions: planning, managing, delivering, evaluating.

2 Reviewing the research literature to identify all of the major strategies of effective instruction, and specifically for empirically demonstrated strategies of effective instruction.

3 Organizing strategies within principles, so that for each principle there are a set of strategies.

4 Collecting representative tactics from teachers then designing additional new tactics. The tactics were organized within strategies, and additional tactics were written for each strategy.

Figure 2 is a conceptual model of instruction. Within the model the four components of effective instruction are identified, as well as specific principles for

components of effective instruction	
Planning Instruction	The degree to which teaching goals and teacher expectations for student performance and success are stated clearly and are understood by the student
Managing Instruction	The degree to which classroom management is effective and efficient
	The degree to which there is a sense of positiveness in the school environment
Delivering Instruction	The degree to which there is an appropriate instructional match
	The degree to which lessons are presented clearly and follow specific instructional procedures
	The degree to which instructional support is provided for the individual student
	The degree to which sufficient time is allocated to academics and instructional time is used efficiently
	The degree to which the student's opportunity to respond is high
Evaluating Instruction	The degree to which the teacher actively monitors student progress and understanding
	The degree to which student performance is evaluated appropriately and frequently

Figure 1
Components of Effective Instruction

each component, and specific strategies for each principle. The figure is used to illustrate the fact that, for example, in planning instruction one must decide what to teach, decide how to teach, and communicate realistic expectations. Specific strategies for deciding how to teach include: setting instructional goals, establishing performance standards, choosing instructional methods and materials, establishing grouping structures, pacing instruction appropriately, monitoring performance, and replanning instruction.

a conceptual framework for effective instruction		
Component	Principle	Strategy
Planning Instruction	Decide What to Teach	Assess to Identify Gaps in Performance Establish Logical Sequences of Instruction Consider Contextual Variables
	Decide How to Teach	Set Instructional Goals Establish Performance Standards Choose Instructional Methods and Materials Establish Grouping Structures Pace Instruction Appropriately Monitor Performance and Replan Instruction
	Communicate Realistic Expectations	Teach Goals, Objectives, and Standards Teach Students to Be Active, Involved Learners Teach Students Consequences of Performance
Managing Instruction	Prepare for Instruction	Set Classroom Rules Communicate and Teach Classroom Rules Communicate Consequences of Behavior Handle Disruptions Efficiently Teach Students to Manage Their Own Behavior
	Use Time Productively	Establish Routines and Procedures Organize Physical Space Allocate Sufficient Time to Academic Activities
	Establish Positive Classroom Environment	Make the Classroom a Pleasant, Friendly Place Accept Individual Differences Establish Supportive, Cooperative Learning Environments Create a Nonthreatening Learning Environment

Figure 2
The Algozzine-Ysseldyke Model of Effective Instruction

a conceptual framework for effective instruction

Component	Principle	Strategy
Delivering Instruction	Present Information	**For Presenting Content** Gain and Maintain Attention Review Prior Skills or Lessons Provide Organized, Relevant Lessons
		For Motivating Students Show Enthusiasm and Interest Use Rewards Effectively Consider Level and Student Interest
		For Teaching Thinking Skills Model Thinking Skills Teach Fact-Finding Skills Teach Divergent Thinking Teach Learning Strategies
		For Providing Relevant Practice Develop Automaticity Vary Opportunities for Practice Vary Methods of Practice Monitor Amount of Work Assigned
	Monitor Presentations	**For Providing Feedback** Give Immediate, Frequent, Explicit Feedback Provide Specific Praise and Encouragement Model Correct Performance Provide Prompts and Cues Check Student Understanding
		For Keeping Students Actively Involved Monitor Performance Regularly Monitor Performance During Practice Use Peers to Improve Instruction Provide Opportunities for Success Limit Opportunities for Failure Monitor Engagement Rates
	Adjust Presentations	Adapt Lessons to Meet Student Needs Provide Varied Instructional Options Alter Pace

Figure 2 (continued)
The Algozzine-Ysseldyke Model of Effective Instruction

a conceptual framework for effective instruction		
Component	Principle	Strategy
Evaluating Instruction	Monitor Student Understanding	Check Understanding of Directions Check Procedural Understanding Monitor Student Success Rate
	Monitor Engaged Time	Check Student Participation Teach Students to Monitor Their Own Participation
	Keep Records of Student Progress	Teach Students to Chart Their Own Progress Regularly Inform Students of Performance Maintain Records of Student Performance
	Use Data to Make Decisions	Use Data to Decide if More Services Are Warranted Use Student Progress to Make Teaching Decisions Use Student Progress to Decide When to Discontinue Service

Figure 2 (continued)
The Algozzine-Ysseldyke Model of Effective Instruction

The second edition of *STEI* retains the conceptual framework presented in the first edition, but provides new and expanded tactics to use in planning, managing, delivering, and evaluating instruction.

Strategies and Tactics for Effective Instruction is not a textbook or inspirational work. Connected text has been kept to a minimum in an attempt to provide kernels of knowledge that can be applied to improve teaching. The authors have not personally tested every tactic that is presented, but each is grounded in a principle or strategy from teacher effectiveness research.

The best way to improve instruction is to decide which principles are most important and work on them first. Doing this necessarily involves selecting a component of instruction (i.e., planning, managing,

delivering, or evaluating) and working on principles within it first. This decision can be based on formal evaluations or on informal bases (e.g., personal interest in improving management). By working on one component and selected principles within it, the task of improving instruction becomes more manageable.

What STEI is Designed to Do

Grounded in the findings of educational research, *STEI* identifies and helps you apply the strategies and tactics used by effective teachers. *STEI* is a flexible instructional improvement tool that can be used in several different ways:

Individual Student Interventions—*STEI* is primarily designed to help school personnel plan instructional interventions for individual students. The system provides ideas on how to accomplish specific objectives and effective instruction. It provides tips and tactics to use in planning, managing, delivering and evaluating instruction.

Individualized Education Programs—*STEI* is also useful in writing Individualized Education Programs (IEPs) for students with disabilities. Educators are required by law to develop and have on file an IEP containing a statement of instructional goals and methods for achieving those goals for all students with disabilities. *STEI* is useful in helping teachers and other professionals generate the strategies and tactics that will be used to meet students' special needs.

Prereferral Intervention—Most states require that teachers engage in prereferral interventions before they formally assess students. The prereferral intervention process consists of systematic alteration of instruction and careful evaluation of the effects of instructional modifications on student learning. Teachers may vary instructional approaches, pacing, feedback procedures, or other factors; students accomplish instructional goals. STEI gives school personnel a catalog of alternative tactics to use in prereferral intervention.

Teacher Assistance Teams—Many schools now use Teacher Assistance Teams, Intervention Assistance Teams, or Problem Solving Teams. These are groups composed of regular classroom teachers and/or related services personnel whose job it is to help teachers solve instructional problems, usually with individual

students who experience difficulty. *STEI* is especially useful in reviewing with teachers those strategies and tactics they have already used, and in identifying additional tactics to try.

Instructional Consultation—*STEI* strategies are useful in instructional consultation. Instructional consultants are charged with the task of identifying students' instructional strengths and weaknesses, and designing interventions to teach to those strengths or weaknesses. It is virtually impossible for a consultant to be mindful of the myriad of strategies and tactics that promote effective instruction. *STEI* is a useful organization of the instructional enterprise, and includes a large number of tactics representative of those that could be used to achieve goals related to the four key components of effective instruction.

Training Teachers and Related Services Personnel— *STEI* is useful in training teachers and related services personnel. The empirically demonstrated principles of effective instruction have been systematically organized to give teachers a way to think about instruction and a systematic approach to use. Those who train teachers will find *STEI* useful in training teachers in how to proceed and in giving them concrete suggestions of tactics to use in instruction. This resource is especially useful in linking theory of effective instruction to actual classroom practice.

Levels at Which STEI Can Be Used

STEI has been designed for use primarily with elementary age students, though many tactics are included that are applicable to all students, and some that are applicable specifically to secondary students. *STEI* can be used at three levels:

Individual Student Level—*STEI* is most useful at the level of the individual student. Teachers and related services who must develop interventions can use the system as a springboard for instructional ideas. Often teachers know what they want to accomplish, but lack concrete ideas or strategies or tactics to reach their goals and objectives. *STEI* gives school personnel those ideas.

Classroom Level—*STEI* also is useful at the classroom level. Teachers often know what they want to accomplish instructionally with a class, but run short of ideas on planning, managing, delivering, or evaluating instruction. *STEI* is loaded with ideas on tactics to use in teaching effectively.

Building or District Level—*STEI* also can be used at the school building or school system level. Schools or districts engaged in or entering into site-based management can use this system as a resource bank and in planning inservice training. *STEI* contains strategies and tactics necessary to promote effective instruction at the building or district level.

Where to Begin Using STEI

This system may be used either informally or formally. When professionals use the system in an informal manner they browse through the components in order to spot strategies and tactics they may want to use to meet their instructional needs. Such browsing usually results in identification of some "neat" teaching tactics, or more often gives the reader ideas of additional tactics or ways in which those in the book can be modified to meet specific needs. There are several ways to enter the system if a formal approach is desired. Each is described briefly in the sections that follow.

Traditional Norm-Referenced Assessment

Traditional norm-referenced tests (like intelligence tests or reading or mathematics achievement tests) are useful in making decisions about what to teach; they tell the user the skills that students do and do not have. They are, however, of limited use in making decisions about how to teach. When norm-referenced tests are used, the teacher gains information about those content areas a student has already mastered. In fact, the component on planning illustrates how norm-referenced tests can be used in planning to provide the professional with information on subject matter mastery.

STEI is useful for making decisions about how to teach and provides the teacher with specific tactics to use in instructional interventions. The strategies and tactics suggested for the four components (planning, managing, delivering, and evaluating instruction) will work regardless of the subject matter being taught.

Curriculum-Based Assessment or Curriculum-Based Measurement

Curriculum-based assessment (Tucker, 1987) provides professionals with an analysis of specific skills a student has mastered within a specific content area. Curriculum-based measurement (Fuchs & Deno, 1991) provides professionals with data on general educational outcomes. Either approach tells the educator what skills are already present and those that must be developed. STEI can be used to derive methods or tactics to use to teach the skills. Again, the resource is more helpful in making decisions about how to teach than in deciding what to teach.

Assessment of Instructional Environments

The Instructional Environment System-II (TIES-II) (Ysseldyke & Christenson, 1993) is a system that enables professionals to assess the extent to which components of effective instruction are evidenced in students' instructional environments and the extent to which home environments are supportive of what is occurring in school. Data are collected by means of classroom observation, student interview, teacher interview, and parent interview, and judgments are made about the extent to which components of effective instruction are: (1) present; and (2) important in students' instructional programs. On the basis of assessment findings, individuals or teams decide that

specific kinds of instructional interventions are necessary. *TIES-II* and *STEI* are based on the same model of effective instruction. *STEI* provides suggestions of intervention strategies and tactics in the areas assessed by *TIES-II*. Linking assessment of instructional environments to instructional interventions is a relatively straightforward process.

Collaborative Intervention Planning

The authors strongly recommend that those who use *STEI* engage in collaborative intervention planning. This is a process in which many school personnel meet as a group (sometimes the group is comprised entirely of teachers, sometimes it includes teachers and related services personnel) to share information and plan an intervention to address the teacher's concern for the student. Ysseldyke and Christenson (1993) describe a nine-step process of collaborative intervention planning. Activities at each step are as follows:

Step 1: Describing the Teacher Concern—A referring teacher describes the nature of his or her concern about the student's performance, stressing the discrepancy between actual and desired performance. Team members work to state concerns in specific, observable, and measurable language, and to describe the student's performance relative to that of peers (this process is often called normative peer comparison).

Step 2: Sharing Information—Team members share what they know about the student's behavior and academic performance. Data may be derived from observation, testing, interviewing, or inspection of student records. The information shared may be based on informal data collection methods, or preferably on formal methods like *TIES-II*.

Step 3: Arriving at Consensus—It is important for team members to arrive at consensus about the student's instructional needs. Ysseldyke and Christenson (1993) suggest that team members list all instructional needs and then prioritize these in terms of immediacy for intervention. The classroom teacher should play the major role in deciding what is and is not important.

Step 4: Describing Home Support for Learning—It is easier to achieve desirable instructional outcomes when parents and school personnel work together. Thus, it is important to think about the extent to which there is support at home for the interventions school personnel want to implement. As part of *TIES-II*, Ysseldyke and Christenson (1993) provide a methodology for assessing home support. They provide a way to look at five components of home support (Expectations and Attributions, Discipline Orientation, Home Affective Environment, Parent Participation, and Structure for Learning). It is a good idea to use the Home Support for Learning Form provided with *TIES-II* to document the extent to which there is home support for school interventions, and then to select interventions taking this into account.

Step 5: Identifying Ways to Involve Parents—It is important to think systematically about the ways in which parents can be involved in instructional interven-

tion for students. Team members should discuss ways in which parents can be involved and should consider parents' statements about how they want to be involved.

Step 6: Brainstorming Ideas/Options—Team members should identify all possible interventions. The framework of the Algozzine-Ysseldyke Model of Effective Instruction illustrated on pages 4-6 of this manual should be helpful in identification of areas of intervention need.

Step 7: Selecting an Intervention—The use of *TIES-II* enables professionals to identify areas of effective instruction that are not present and that are important for individual students. It enables relatively rapid identification of areas of need.

Step 8: Sharing Resources—This is where *STEI* comes in. Rather than having to start from scratch or generate intervention ideas off the tops of their heads, team members can use this resource as a way to generate ideas and as a starting point in identifying interventions. Additional resources are listed in the Appendix.

Step 9: Addressing Other Questions—It is important to include as a final step in intervention planning an opportunity for team members to address questions not directly related to instructional intervention. As team meetings take place, inevitably there are tangents to discussions of interventions. There must be an opportunity for team members to put those tangential issues "on the back burner," and to then discuss them at the end of the meeting.

Summary

Effective teaching is a complex process. Researchers have shown that effective teachers plan, manage, deliver, and evaluate instruction differently than their less effective peers. *Strategies and Tactics for Effective Instruction* is a resource based on the components and principles that guide the efforts of effective teachers. A **component** is a main part of the process of effective teaching. For example, researchers have shown that effective teachers plan their instruction. Planning instruction is a component of effective instruction. A **principle** is a fundamental teaching activity on which more specific strategies and tactics are based. For example, these principles are related to planning instruction: deciding what to each, deciding how to teach, and communicating realistic expectations. They are the basis for more specific strategies and tactics. *Strategies and Tactics for Effective Instruction* is a compendium of strategies and specific tactics for use in improving classroom teaching. A **strategy** is a plan of action for use in implementing effective teaching principles. For example, to effectively decide what to teach, teachers must assess to identify gaps in performance, establish logical sequences of instruction, and consider contextual variables. Strategies are steps that should be taken; they are the "what" rather than the "how" of effective teaching. A **tactic** is an action that a teacher can take to influence learning. It is the lowest level that a component can be broken into for training and implementation purposes; it is a specific behavior or teaching activity. Relations between components, principles, strategies, and tactics of effective instruction are illustrated in Figures 4 and 5.

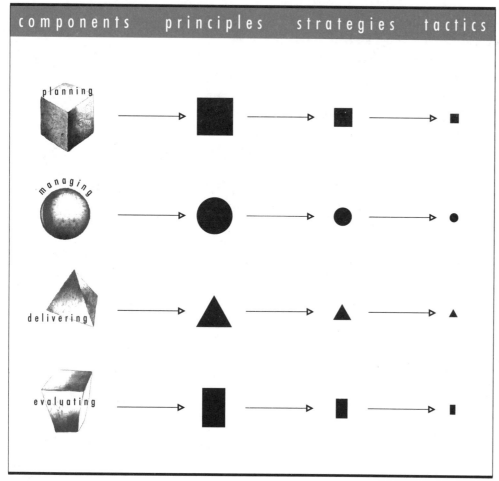

components	principles	strategies	tactics	example

Figure 4
Four Components of Effective Teaching

	example
Effective Teaching Component	**Delivering Instruction**
Teaching Principle	**Providing Relevant Practice**
Teaching Strategy	**Provide Students With Help** A goal of independent practice is high rates of accurate responding. Effective teachers want to avoid having students practice errors when engaged in independent practice. They should provide feedback during independent work sessions.
Teaching Tactic	**Use Signals to Request Help** Develop a signal for each student to use when assistance is needed during an independent practice session. Circulate through the room when students are practicing and look for signs that someone needs help. Provide help as quickly as possible so that students can continue to work.

Figure 5
Example Illustrating the Organizational Relations in STEI

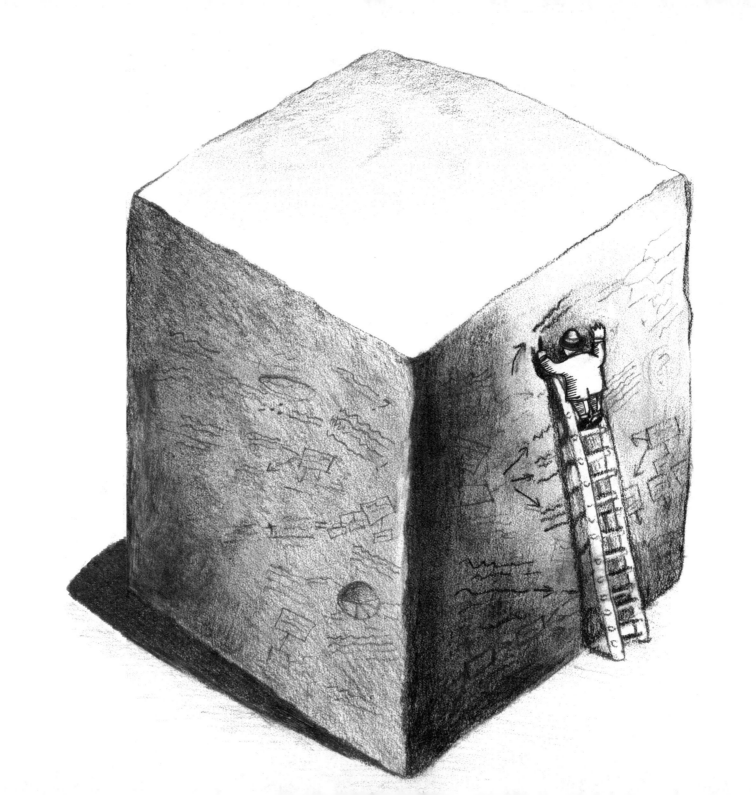

planning

If everyone in a class was at the same instructional level, and if schools had clearly prescribed goals and instructional objectives that were the same for all students, then teaching would consist simply of doing the same things with everybody, being certain to do them in the right order and at the right time. Of course, all students are not alike and the goals, objectives, or methods of schooling are not the same for everybody. This is why planning is a key component of effective teaching.

Effective instruction requires planning. This means that effective teachers make decisions before they start teaching. They make decisions about what content to present, about what materials or activities to use and how to present the content, and about how to

planning

encourage students to approach learning in positive ways. There are three principles of effective planning:

1 Decide what to teach

2 Decide how to teach

3 Communicate realistic expectations

Component	Principle	Strategy
Planning Instruction	Decide What to Teach	Assess to Identify Gaps in Performance Establish Logical Sequences of Instruction Consider Contextual Variables
	Decide How to Teach	Set Instructional Goals Establish Performance Standards Choose Instructional Methods and Materials Establish Grouping Structure Pace Instruction Appropriately Monitor Performance and Replan Instruction
	Communicate Realistic Expectations	Teach Goals, Objectives, and Standards Teach Students to Be Active, Involved Learners Teach Students Consequences of Performance

Figure 6
Three Principles of Effective Planning

Each of these principles implies a set of strategies that teachers use when planning (see Figure 6).

Decide what to teach involves accurate assessment of student characteristics (e.g., skill levels, motivation), task characteristics (e.g., sequence, cognitive demands), and classroom characteristics (e.g., instructional groupings, materials). Using this information, effective teachers plan their instruction to produce logical lessons that best match student, task, and classroom characteristics to the instructional demands of the content they are teaching. The goal when deciding what to teach is accurately determining the appropriate content to present based on what is known about individual students and their learning needs.

Decide how to teach involves making decisions about instructional performance standards, methods and materials, and instructional pace. Based on information available for students in their classes, effective teachers set instructional goals and performance standards. They select instructional methods, including grouping structures and pace, and materials to help them achieve their goals. And, they identify monitoring procedures that will assist in determining the extent to which their instruction is matching learner skills with intended outcomes. The goal of effective teachers in deciding how to teach is to find the best way to present the desired instructional content.

Communicate realistic expectations means being sure that students understand the goals, objectives, and standards of instruction, getting students to be active and involved learners, and getting them to understand the consequences of success and failure. Effective teachers know that communicating realistic expectations is an important part of planning because active student engagement and motivation have long been seen as critical parts of learning. Trying to achieve goals, objectives, or standards that are too high or too low causes frustration or boredom, and, too often, misbehavior. The goal in communicating realistic expectations is to ensure that "everybody is on the same instructional page" and that nobody's needs are ignored, overlooked, or missed.

These three planning principles are addressed in this section. An overview is provided for each, illustrating how the principle relates to effective planning, and describing a set of specific strategies that effective teachers use when focusing on the principle. The main content of the unit is a set of tactics that illustrate specific ways to actively address each principle and strategy when providing effective instruction.

planning

principle

Decide What to Teach

Planning instruction involves making decisions about what to teach. Teachers decide what to teach for entire classrooms and for individual students. Sometimes these decisions are made centrally in school districts, and teachers are required to adhere to district mandated instructional content and sequences. More often, teachers are given the flexibility they as professionals deserve.

There are three strategies involved in deciding what to teach. Effective teachers assess students' current levels of skill development and analyze skills carefully to determine gaps in performance that form the basis for instruction. Often this takes the form of task analysis: breaking complex skills down into subskills and assessment of the extent to which the student demonstrates the subskills. Teachers also carefully consider the content of their instruction to identify logical sequences for teaching. Effective teachers also consider contextual variables (like instructional groupings in the classroom, how the student interacts with other students, and availability of materials) that have a direct influence on what is taught and what can be taught.

Component	Principle	Strategy	Page
Planning Instruction	**Decide What to Teach**	Assess to Identify Gaps in Performance . . . . . 20 Establish Logical Sequences of Instruction . . . 23 Consider Contextual Variables 28	

planning

Assess to Identify Gaps in Performance

Results of learning are improved when instruction is matched to students' ability. Effective instruction moves students from current levels of instruction to desired levels based on age and grade expectations. Students experience learning difficulties when instruction is not aligned with their levels of skill development. Effective teachers assess students' skills and identify discrepancies in specific content areas, then adjust instruction to meet learner needs and progress toward desired learner competencies.

Tactic: Use Norm-Referenced Tests Effectively

To identify discrepancies the current level of skill development must be assessed. There are number of ways to do this. Norm-referenced tests are used to measure skill development in basic academic areas. Performance on them provides an indication of what students know in broad content areas like science, social studies, and mathematics. Most group-administered norm-referenced achievement tests take from two to five hours to administer. Brief, individually administered norm-referenced tests are also available. There are a few considerations that make efforts to use norm-referenced tests more effective:

- If group tests are used, the smaller the group the better.

- If a large group administration is necessary, bring in additional assistance (paraprofessionals, other teachers, parent volunteer).

- Students with disabilities may need additional assistance and/or testing accommodation. Plan ahead to ensure that accommodations written on the student's Individualized Education Program (IEP) are provided.

- Tests must be administered exactly according to directions. Departure from the standardized procedures can destroy the meaning of the test scores. Review the instructions before administering any test.

- As a rule of thumb, the length of sitting should not exceed 30 minutes for primary grades, 40 to 50 minutes in intermediate grades, and 90 minutes in middle and secondary grades. These times may vary for individual students, especially students with disabilities.

- Testing environments should be free of distractions.

Tactic: Use Curriculum-Based Measures Effectively

Curriculum-based measurement directly assesses a student's skill and progress within the actual content being taught. It provides information on the student's mastery of curriculum content. The benefits to this approach include: assessment is completed in natural settings; assessment is completed in the materials

planning

with which the student is familiar; assessment can take on many forms and allows for frequent, direct measurement of student performance. Tied to the student's curriculum, this type of assessment is sensitive to the improvement of student achievement over time. Knowledge of student performance via curriculum-based measures is especially helpful in identifying gaps in skill development and designing instructional interventions to address them. Typically a teacher makes a list of skills that the student needs to acquire as the result of instruction. Test samples commonly called probes are then directly developed and administered to the students. These probes are administered frequently throughout the year or unit of instruction and student performance is recorded (and often graphed).

Curriculum-based measures are inexpensive to produce in terms of both time and development. Although there are commercially-available curriculum-based achievement tests, many are teacher-constructed. Reading (fluency and comprehension), written expression, mathematics, and spelling are the major skill areas easily assessed using curriculum-based evaluation.

Tactic: Pretest Skills You Teach

Although pretesting can be completed with norm-referenced tests, it is usually more effective to use curriculum-based measures. The purpose of a pretest is to assess the extent to which students have the component skills necessary to perform a more complex skill. Sample performance by asking students to read aloud from their books, read silently and answer comprehension question orally, spell the words on their spelling lists, or complete the kinds of math problems that are in their math texts. Keep records of these performances and use them as a basis for later comparisons.

Most reading and mathematics series now include unit mastery tests. These can also be used as pretests to measure the extent to which students have mastered the content to be taught. Teachers may use this information gained from pretesting to make judgments about where and at what level instruction should begin as well as the extent to which instruction has been effective.

Tactic: Conduct Environmental Inventories

Environmental inventories allow teachers to evaluate the skills a student needs in order to be successful in a specific environment. Sometimes called a functional analysis, information is gathered via skills inventories of the kinds of competencies that are necessary to function successfully in working and learning situations. Once identified discrepant, required skills are directly taught to the student with the ultimate goal, of course, being fluent and accurate skill performance in the natural environment. Environmental inventories are especially useful for those students who present challenging behaviors and/or evidence more severe disabilities.

planning

Tactic: Use Portfolio Assessment Effectively

Portfolios are collections of products used to demonstrate what a student has done and, by inference, what a student is capable doing. They go beyond a simple display of student work. Portfolios usually consist of collections of students' work over a relatively long period of time. Portfolios are intended to facilitate judgment about student performance by examining progress over time and by the quality of work done. Portfolio assessment serves several purposes:

- To document student effort
- To document student growth and achievement
- To enhance information from other assessments
- To provide public information about the quality of educational progress.

Six elements define portfolio assessment:

1 Targeting valued student competencies for assessment

2 Using tasks that mirror work in the real world

3 Encouraging cooperation among students and between teacher and students

4 Using multiple dimensions to evaluate student work

5 Encouraging student reflection

6 Integrating assessment and instruction

Portfolios need to be tailored for a specific purpose to avoid the collection of piles of papers placed in a folder. For example, depending on its purpose, a portfolio could include classroom assignments, rough drafts, audio tapes, a list of books read, tests, checklists, journal entries, videotapes, response logs, completed projects art work, and reading logs.

Student participation is an important part of the process of developing a portfolio. For example, sometimes students select a product they think is particularly good or of which they are particularly proud and then present it as such in parent-teacher conferences. Othertimes, students select a product they do not like and make reflective statements about it (e.g., self-evaluation). Decisions about what to include in a portfolio are made in collaboration with students, teachers, and sometimes parents.

One of the challenges of using portfolio assessment is the scoring procedure for evaluating student work. Scoring rubrics are carefully articulated scoring systems that often have accompanied work samples that testify, for example, less than satisfactory, satisfactorily strong, and excellent work. Typically rubrics are developed by teachers or assessment committees and reflect a range of acceptable student performance for identified valued learner competencies.

Tactic: Assess Frequently and Informally

Similar to curriculum-based measurement, informal, direct, and frequent assessment means daily or weekly checks of student performances on instructionally relevant tasks. This type of assessment has high content validity because you measure exactly what you expect to do in current, appropriate instructional material. Information gained from frequent, informal assessments provides instructionally relevant data for planning instruction. Additionally, it provides information on the extent to which students are able to apply what they learn in their daily lessons.

Informal assessment should occur frequently, be direct, and be designed to evaluate precisely what students need to learn or have been learning. To select tasks for informal assessment, have students:

- Use the work you are assigning on a daily basis

- Use the work you expect them to complete over the next week or two or for a specific project or unit of instruction

As a general rule, informal reading assessments like these should be administered at least several times initially and at least once per week after instruction has begun.

Tactic: Use Informal Reading Inventories

Informal reading inventories (IRIs) are collections of short reading passages written at different reading levels. Typically they include at least two passages at each reading level, preprimer through sixth grade, one of which is to be read orally and one to be read silently. The student reads passages of increasing difficulty until a frustration level is reached. Frustration level is that level at which a student has to struggle considerably with word recognition or comprehension. Based on the student's word recognition accuracy and comprehension accuracy at various reading levels, an instructional reading level is determined. Using the information about the level at which the student can read comfortably, instruction and/or remediation can be effectively planned.

Establish Logical Sequences of Instruction

Complex skills are learned by teaching subskills in a sequence, but there is nearly always more than one way to learn a skill. Factors to consider are the extent to which a given method is being used, the degree to which the student is profiting from it, and the instructional techniques employed in delivering instruction.

Tactic: Consider What Is Needed and Essential

The breadth and depth of a curriculum can be overwhelming when one thinks about the actual days of instruction within which learning is to occur. Given this reality, it is important to identify and prioritize desired learner competencies to be acquired. Some skills are critical to learning other skills. Therefore, teach these skills early in the instructional sequence. Give top instructional priority to those skills that are

planning

necessary and essential to the performance of more complex skills. Often developers of instructional materials slice tasks into smaller and smaller pieces. It is usually possible to combine smaller related tasks for instructional purposes. In other words, group related tasks instead of teaching small pieces of tasks.

Tactic: Consider What the Student is Ready to Learn

Using results from assessment and information about skill development, establish goals and objectives and make decisions about those that need top priority. Consider what the student already knows and is ready to learn. Don't make students back track because the scope and sequence of the course dictates it. Rather, move them on to the material/skills they are ready to learn. Most teachers' manuals include a description of the scope and sequence for the content to be taught. Refer to the description in the manual in deciding how to sequence instruction, but do not simply accept the sequence as law. Make teaching decisions based on the kinds of students you are teaching and their learning priorities as well as their instructional needs and levels of skill development.

Tactic: Consider Type of Curriculum

There typically are two general types of curriculum that are used in schools today—functional curriculum and developmental curriculum.

A functional curriculum is one that provides the latitude to teach the skills a student needs for success in the immediate future. Typically, this curriculum focuses on life skills, vocational skills, and any others a student needs. A funtional curriculum is especially critical for older students approaching graduation.

A developmental curriculum can be viewed as the traditional scope and sequence of instruction. Typically hierarchical in nature, the student progresses through curriculum as laid out in text books or by curriculum plans developed by school content departments or the state education department.

There are a number of variables to review before deciding which curriculum to pursue with a student. This decision is not necessarily mutually exclusive; there may be a melding of both. The key to deciding which curriculum and how to apply it should be based on several student-based factors. A functional curriculum should be considered for adoption if:

- The student has significant difficulty acquiring new skills, either hierarchical or nonhierarchical in nature.

- The student has not been able to keep pace with his/her peers in the total number of skills acquired.

- The student participates in relatively few instructional activities throughout the day. That is, the student may participate in a vocational education or alternative program that requires the stu-

planning

dent to be in another setting conducive to the respective curriculum.

- The student is approaching graduation.

A developmental curriculum should be considered if:

- The student acquires new skills at a relatively rapid rate.

- The student is able to maintain rate of acquisition of skills commensurate with his/her peers.

- The student spends a substantial part of the school day in classroom instructional activities.

- The student has a number of years of school before graduation.

Adapted from: Schloss, P., & Sedlak, A. (1986).

⏱ Tactic: Modify Instruction for Students Who Need It

Students are all unique in different ways, and these differences often result in splintered skill development with knowledge and acquisition of some advanced skills, but gaps in others. In planning instruction, consider the extent to which this splintering affects delivery of instructional material. Within a curricular scope and sequence you may need to enrich or expand learning activities for some students while extending learning opportunities for others. Extension activities are for those students who master

the material or skills and would benefit from meaningful activities while perhaps other students are working to master or are engaged in corrective activities. The purpose of extensions are to allow for opportunities for individualized instruction, more in-depth study of an objective or skill, and creative problem solving at higher levels of thinking. Correctives, on the other hand, are alternate teaching strategies designed for students who have not achieved success from initial instruction and need an alternate strategy for learning the skill. This may simply be more opportunities to practice. It is often a good idea to present correctives using formats not used during initial instruction. For example, if lecture was the mode of delivery, engage students using different methods such as flashcards, charts, bulletin boards, computer, etc. But remember, gaps in skill acquisition may not be eliminated simply by providing enrichment and extension learning opportunities. Use direct and frequent assessment to guide instruction.

⏱ Tactic: Identify Knowledge Demands of Instructional Tasks

There are three basic types of knowledge that students are required to engage in to make progress in school—factual, conceptual, and strategic knowledge (Howell, Fox, & Morehead, 1993). Each has its own distinct set of characteristics:

- Factual knowledge involves the rote learning of specific information like simple facts ($25 \div 5 = 5$), verbal chains (saying the alphabet, telephone

planning

numbers), and discriminations (identifying differences between letters, numbers, geometric shapes). Factual knowledge can involve a student knowing a correct answer without knowing how to figure it out or apply it.

Factual Knowledge	
Simple Facts	5 x 2 = 10 Washington was the first U.S. president H_2O is chemical symbol for water Holá is "Hello" in Spanish
Verbal Chains	Singing the ABCs Counting aloud Reciting address and phone numbers Repeating nursery rhymes

Anything involving rote learning without necessarily requiring procedural awareness or how to use information can be considered factual knowledge.

■ Conceptual knowledge involves understanding meaning and recognizing critical attributes. For any concept to exist, critical attributes or essential and nonessential information must be identified. Critical attributes are the defining feature of a concept. Conceptual knowledge allows students to sort or categorize items as well as identify examples and nonexamples of things. For example, when teaching the concept "under" to

a group of students, one might ask, "What is an object that is always under? Never under? Sometimes under?" Another example of teaching a concept could be, "What are the critical attributes of a rectangle?" (two sets of equal sides, equal angles, parallel sides, enclosed space ...) "What are the noncritical attributes of a rectangle?" (space orientation, size, color ...) "Look around the room and find some rectangles. Find some shapes that are not rectangles and tell why."

Conceptual Knowledge
■ Ideas and meaning associated with an object, event, behavior, or situation
■ Categorization and/or sorting
■ Critical attributes and noncritical attributes of objects, events, behaviors, or situations
■ Same or different
■ Examples and nonexamples

■ Strategic knowledge involves using a procedure, plan, or rule to solve problems, perform tasks or find answers. For example, solving a mathematic equation, or how to find the capitol of Alaska. Strategic instruction involves teaching students how to find or arrive at an answer.

planning

Strategic Knowledge

Involves the procedure, plan, or rule used to solve problems, perform tasks, or find answers:

- Steps or procedures for solving problems or completing a product

- Rule relationships

- Often embedded in instructional tasks

Example: Kerri will write answers to addition facts with 100% accuracy using a repeat-addition strategy.

levels of proficiency*			
	Accuracy	**Mastery**	**Automaticity**
Definition	Identifies or produces information accurately at a preset percentage level	Identifies or produces information accurately and quickly at a preset rate.	Identifies or produces information accurately and quickly in context and/or different settings
Content of Instruction	Example: Produce the correct quotients to division problems 100% of the time.	Example: Produce the correct answer to multiplication facts at a rate of 75 digits per minute.	Example: Produce the correct answers to addition facts completed in a checkbook.

*Student behaviors usually fall into two domains: "identify" or "produce."

Adapted from: Howell, Fox, & Morehead (1993).

Figure 7

Effective teachers take into account the extent to which students are required to engage in these knowledge types when presented with instruction. While some students demonstrate the ability to correctly produce answers to simple questions (factual knowledge), they may not have the ability to explain how they arrived at it (strategic knowledge). Identifying the types of knowledge required for specific tasks does not mean that tasks involve only one type of knowledge exclusively. For example, teaching three digit by one digit multiplication involves using facts, the concept of multiplication, and the strategy of putting them together.

Source: Howell, Fox, Morehead (1993).
Adapted: Workshop materials, Sacca & Elliott (1994a).

Tactic: Consider Alignment of Learning and Instruction

To effectively plan any lesson, it is good practice to identify the proficiency level of instruction and the current level at which the student is performing. Before teaching, consider what level of proficiency the task demands (Accuracy, Mastery, or Automaticity; see Figure 7). If a student lacks knowledge of a task, he/she may be at the initial phase of learning called acquisition. Perhaps another student is able to perform a task but is too slow to effectively complete quality work on time. This student needs fluency instruction (e.g., rapid drill and practice) that facilitates

planning

mastery—accurate and fast. All instruction aims to have students use a skill independently and apply it automatically whenever needed. In order to gain automaticity of a skill students need to be taught how to generalize or apply learned skills in larger, novel contexts.

Consider Contextual Variables

Learning does not occur in a vacuum. Each student brings to the instructional environment a set of individual characteristics and a learning history. And, each student responds differently to teachers' instructional efforts. There is a reciprocal relationship between students and instructional environments. Learning occurs when the learning environment is modified to elicit an appropriate response from the student. Variables such as student population, class size, noise levels, physical configuration of the classroom and furniture, to mention just a few, must absolutely be taken into account when planning instruction. It is also important to consider the context of the home environment. Home/school collaboration is an important component for achievement. In considering the instructional needs, both in the context of the classroom and home, the primary goal is to create an instructional environment that facilitates and encourages students to successfully achieve to their maximum potential.

 ## Tactic: Use Sociometric Scales Effectively

Sociometric methods are effective ways to gather information about classmates from classmates. This method helps gain an understanding of how students are perceived by their respective class peers. There are several ways to do this. For example, each student in the class may be given a sheet that has all the class students' names or pictures on it. Then simple questions can be asked such as "Who would you most like to sit next to during lunch?"; "Name two other students who you would also invite to sit at your table."; "Who would you least like to sit next to at lunch?"; "Name two other students you would not invite to sit at your lunch table." Students write their answers independently. Responses are private and are not shared. Given this information teachers can proactively manage effective instructional groups or provide opportunities to build social skills or classroom relationships.

Tactic: Consider Group Size and Structure

Some kinds of instruction are best taught in large groups, while others in small groups. Consider the types of knowledge and proficiency levels of tasks and students, respectively. For example, when students are at the acquisition stage of learning, it is helpful to have students work in small groups. In doing so individuals can be given attention and errors or acquisition of skills can be better monitored. Frustration levels of students should also be considered. If the group task requires fast and fluent responding, some students may not be as quick to produce information

planning

as others. They may still need more opportunities for drill and practice.

Tactic: Match Groups With Specific Tasks

Student skills in any classroom differ considerably for any particular task. For example, students may exhibit different kinds of skills in oral reading or written expression. Instructional tasks differ in the types of knowledge and levels of proficiency required, and therefore in the demands they place on students. Build a matrix or grid on which you rank your students in terms of the level of competency they demonstrate (see Figure 8). Rank the instructional tasks by skill demand. Then group students who have comparable skills and instruct them at the appropriate level. For example, a reading task could be divided into three areas of competence: decoding and word analysis, word recognition, and comprehension. Students showing competencies in each area are listed, thus providing a variety of ways students could be grouped according to the presented task demand.

note: any time students are grouped for any instructional task or activity there must be frequent and ongoing evaluation of skill progress. Frequent, direct assessment of skills not only provides information for instructional remedition, but allows for students to fluidly move in and out of groups when they demonstrate skill proficiency.

Reading Skill Competency Matrix*			
Student	Decoding and Word Analysis	Word Recognition	Reading Comprehension
Bill	3	2	3
Ted	4	3	2
Carol	7	6	5
Alice	8	8	7
Mark	1	1	2
John	2	1	2
Jean	5	5	6
Shaheena	6	7	8

*grade level skill

Figure 8

planning

principle

Decide How to Teach

There is a fundamental myth that most teachers are taught in their teacher preparation programs. It is the belief that the way to decide how to teach individual students is to give them a test. This approach forms the basis for another common misconception. Teachers are told that they simply must identify specific learner strengths and weaknesses (using a test), and then remediate or compensate for weaknesses. There is little research support for this practice.

The best way to decide how to teach is to teach. Effective teachers first set instructional goals and

performance standards. Next they identify and try alternative methods and materials until they find an approach or combination of approaches that works best in moving students toward accomplishment of instructional goals. In making decisions about how to teach, effective teachers make an "educated guess" about the kinds of instructional grouping structures and pacing alternatives that will work best, then try them and monitor the results before replanning instruction.

Component	Principle	Strategy	Page
Planning Instruction	**Decide How to Teach**	Set Instructional Goals	32
		Establish Performance Standards	34
		Choose Instructional Methods and Materials . .	36
		Establish Grouping Structure	38
		Pace Instruction Appropriately	45
		Monitor Performance and Replan Instruction .	47

planning

Set Instructional Goals

How do teachers decide if what they do is successful? The logical answer, of course, is that their students learn. The next question would be what is it that they expect their students to learn? (Answer: specific and defined content.) Curriculum is defined as a set of goals that reflect this content. Effective teachers map out both the goals of instruction as well as the specific skills or behaviors they want students to acquire and demonstrate. Failure to do so results in poor student performance and scattered instruction. A prerequisite to instruction is the writing of goals, defining precisely what students will acquire or accomplish as a result of a lesson, chapter, or content course. Instructional goals specify what learners will do, under what conditions, and the criteria that will be used to determine progress and performance.

Tactic: Review Goals Periodically

To maintain a high level of instruction, effective educators continually review and revise exactly what they want their students to accomplish. Be assured that the more precise and exact your instructional objectives the better the learning results. Why? Because both you and your students will know exactly what is expected and consequently will understand what must be accomplished to receive a certain grade or mark. As the instructor, you will be better able to tailor and monitor students' learning and progress because you will know what it is they are working toward.

More and more educators are moving away from simple adoption of textbook or curriculum guide objectives to developing those that are a result of a collective effort of parents, teachers, students, and administrators. Regardless of what instructional objectives are used, be sure they reflect the needs of individual learners in classroom and the expected outcomes of learning.

Tactic: Write Acceptable Objectives

Once you have determined what the goals of instruction are, it is time to write the corresponding objectives. Instructional objectives must be clearly expressed so that they are understood by all (including other teachers, substitutes, students , parents, administrators, and paraprofessionals). They should be observable, measurable, student-centered, and include products of learning. Here are four desired characteristics of acceptable objectives:

1 Content—What the student will be learning (e.g., functional math)

2 Behavior—What the student will be doing to learn the content (e.g., completing addition facts)

3 Conditions—Circumstances under which the student be performing the behavior (e.g., in a checkbook)

4 Criteria—Expected level of performance (e.g., rate of 40 correct per minute

planning

Example: Martha will write the answers to addition facts in a checkbook at a rate of 40 correct per minute.

Be sure you can identify each of the essential components of the objective whenever you write one.

Tactic: Consider Levels of Learner Proficiency

Prior knowledge and the learning history each student brings to the table may be quite different. As a general rule, when writing goals, selecting instructional content, and developing objectives, arrange to teach in such a way that lessons contain 75% known and 25% unknown material.

Effective teachers identify the types of knowledge demands of instructional materials and the appropriate proficiency level for each objective. That is, what type of knowledge (fact, concept, strategy) and level of proficiency does the task or objective demand. Finally, what level is the student performing (acquisition/accuracy, fluency/mastery, or automaticity/generalization). All students reach proficiency levels at different rates thorough the curriculum. Not all students will learn the same thing in the same way or at the same time. This is especially true considering the types of content being delivered (facts, concepts, or strategies). Proficiency levels tell how to measure student performance, so considering task demands and current levels of performance or proficiency should guide effective instruction (see Figure 9).

types of knowledge		
Facts	Concepts	Strategies
Simple awareness of facts $(2 + 2 = 4)$	Awareness of meaning, can provide examples and nonexamples.	Knowledge of steps or procedures to complete a task or solve a problem.

Levels of Proficiency: Accuracy, Mastery, Automaticity

Adapted from: Howell, Fox, & Morehead (1993).

Figure 9

Tactic: Consider Knowledge Demands

In general, three types of knowledge are typically taught: factual, conceptual, and strategic. Instruction for any objective may include all three types of knowledge. In identifying different components of a task, one can identify which type of knowledge is being demanded and can plan accordingly for groups or individual students. For example, some students have difficulty problem solving, identifying a rule or procedure to solve a particular problem. In knowing this, a teacher can provide prompts, mnemonics, or learning strategies to aid the student. While other students may be able to produce the strategic knowledge to solve this same task, they may be weak in their ability to define and identify characteristics or attributes

planning

needed to actually put problem solving into motion. It is not uncommon for students, when working with mathematical word problems, to know how to solve them but be unable to identify essential facts in order to correctly complete the task. With this in mind, effective teachers plan accordingly using a lesson format that takes into consideration prior knowledge needed for the lesson and the types of knowledge and teacher actions required to teach the skills. (See Planning: What to Teach; Identify Demands of Instructional Tasks.)

Tactic: Modify Objectives When Appropriate

Often it is necessary to adapt instructional objectives to meet a wide range of learning needs. This can be done without rewriting new objectives. By modifying the behavior and/or criteria, it is possible to alter an objective and provide instruction that is very close to the original one without rewriting a new one. For example, notice how the following objective is modified to meet the needs of Trish, a student with learning problems.

Class Objective—Students will write at least one paragraph about butterflies that includes a topic sentence, at least two facts, a concluding sentence, and no more than two errors in mechanics.

Trish's IEP Goal—Trish will move from speaking in incomplete thoughts to communicating ideas around a topic using complete thoughts.

We can modify the original classroom objective for Trish by changing both the behavior and criteria as follows:

Trish's Objective—After drawing a picture of a butterfly, Trish will orally tell two supporting facts about butterflies.

There are many ways to modify an original classroom objective to meet a wider range of learner needs in the classroom. The point is not to take on the arduous task of creating new ones until the original ones prove to be ineffective. Be creative with behavior, conditions, content, and criteria. Be sure that you are modifying for a reason and to specific performance standard. Modify for a purpose.

Adapted from: Howell, Fox & Morehead (1993).

Establish Performance Standards

In today's bustle of educational standards one thing is very clear—one primary goal for all of us is to improve our schools. Although this has most often been viewed in a national perspective, many educators are beginning to see this as a challenge at the local school level. What should all children learn during their years of schooling? How will their learning be assessed? And, what part do educators play in setting this agenda in motion? Within the planning component, educators must establish instructional goals and

planning

objectives for students. Within the larger context of educational reform, the planning and developing of these components of effective instruction more clearly than ever shed light on the formidable task faced by educators—teaching all students to learn to even higher levels of performance. The thoughtful writing of instructional goals and objectives allows educators the opportunity to impact this reform by creating learning environments sensitive to student needs and performance.

There are many terms tossed about that relate to the standards movement. As a point of clarification, the National Council on Education Standards and Testing's recommended components of standards are:

Content Standards—content or material that should be taught

Performance Standards—level of performance or mastery of content

System Performance Standards—measures indicating how well a school system is doing its job in educating all students

School Delivery Standards—a school's instructional effectiveness

Tactic: Set Performance Standards and Success Rates

Effective instructors decide, before instruction begins, what the acceptable level of mastery is for demonstrating successful performance. These levels of proficiency will vary according to the different phases of learning (acquisition, mastery, automaticity). Decisions about levels of proficiency may depend on the importance of the skill(s) across settings, relation to other skill development, and position of skill in a hierarchy of development. Make judgments about the level of proficiency desired based on the importance of the knowledge compared to late acquisition of a skill or concept. For example, 100% accuracy is desired of a student learning to cross a street, while 80% accuracy may be sufficient for naming the capitals of the 50 states.

Remember:

- In order for students to retain a skill they must not only attain fluency but also be provided with lots of opportunities to practice. So consider the cost in time spent instructing and providing practice now versus reteaching and backtracking later when the skill is once again called upon.

- Instruction is sequential and the learning of complex behaviors is often dependent upon the successful mastery of prerequisite skills. Decide whether the skills you are teaching are basic to mastery of later content. Require higher

planning

levels of proficiency for skills needed for subsequent content.

Tactic: Conduct Environmentally Specific Inventories

An ecological inventory is an appraisal of the kinds of skills a group or individual student needs to be successful in a specific environment. These environments can be vocational or instructional in nature. The information gained from conducting such an inventory facilitates decision making in both identifying necessary skills and setting standards or rates of success for performance as a result of instruction. Effective teachers prioritize and set higher levels of mastery for those activities or objectives identified to be critical to student survival or success in the specific environment.

Tactic: Prioritize Activities and Performance Standards

Instructional decisions about activities and performance standards are based on the prioritized importance of content and skills to immediate learning environments. Effective teachers plan instruction so that students will be successful at least 80% of the time, but establishing this level of accuracy for every skill is not appropriate. Students need to experience success to maintain interest. If instruction contains too much information or demands different types of knowledge from a student, frustration results. For some students it will be necessary to create activities

that provide opportunities for errorless learning. That is, structuring a task so that only the correct answer will be produced. Other students will work best if immediate corrective feedback is provided. Both of these approaches are effective.

For errorless learning tasks, depending on the task, teachers can provide students with study guides or methods that when used lead them to the only correct answer. Immediate corrective feedback can be given through cross-aged tutors, cooperative learning structures, small group instruction, and guided practice as well as making answer keys available upon task completion. Audio and video tapes can also help students understand the procedure to use to arrive at the correct answer.

Choose Instructional Methods and Materials

Once the instructional standards, goals, and objectives are specified, instructional methods and materials must be planned. The selection of these materials should align with the goals and objectives written for the instructional content to be learned. The task of selecting methods and materials can be complicated. There are many variables to consider including the needs and learning histories of the students, budgetary constraints, school or district philosophy, or past practice.

planning

Tactic: Adjust Methods and Materials as Needed

Often specific students' needs are not known ahead of time and educated guesses on instructional methods and materials are made. Regardless, knowing whether the materials or methods are appropriate for students will be revealed in the data you collect on the progress students make toward accomplishing objectives. In making decisions about the effectiveness of selected materials it is necessary to engage in direct and frequent measurement of the progress students are making. Use this information to help make necessary adjustments in materials and methods.

If data indicate that some students are not making progress there are a number of things you can do:

- Interview the student to clarify the problem.

- Monitor and modify assignments given directly from the textbooks.

- Adapt readings and provide study or homework guides to aid in student learning and assignment completion.

- Use cooperative learning strategies and tutoring paradigms.

- Collaborate with a colleague for feedback and additional ideas and strategies.

- Rewrite or substitute other materials for those that give students most difficulty.

Tactic: Create a Methods and Materials Diary

Over time and many students, teachers develop alternative ways to teach the same fact, concept, or strategy evolve. If you take the time to develop alternative methods and materials, take the time to log them into a digest that can be used as a reference or idea starter when faced with the same or similar challenge at a later point in time. Collaborate with other teachers and record ideas on how they teach the identified skill or task. Observe how others teach the skill and adapt their method to meet your style of instruction.

Tactic: Beware of Learning Styles

When students do not respond to instruction in the same or similar ways, it is easy to blame the influence of a student's unique learning style. Some educators claim that instruction can be adapted to account for the influence of individual learning styles.

Learning styles instruction is not to be confused with teaching students different objectives at different skill levels or assuming some instructional approaches are more effective than others. The latter is effective instruction based on the monitoring of student learning as a result of direct and frequent evaluation of progress.

The learning styles approach to instruction is based on the premise that, as a result of a summative test or questionnaire, predictive statements can be made about how a student will perform in future instruction or how current instructional methods can be tai-

planning

lored to accommodate a student's identified learning style. In the past, educators have struggled with efforts to evaluate students with tests that attempt to predict which students will do best in which materials or methods of instruction.

The reality is that there is an absence of validation. There is little to no empirical support for this method of instruction. Instead of selecting an empirically proven method of instruction and placing the student(s) in it and seeing how they do (in a matter of days), the learning styles approach to instruction strives to select a method that matches or interacts with the preferred learning modality of a student (which by the way can vary by content, time of day, and moon phase). The ultimate goal of effective instruction is measuring instructional performance, student behavior, and achievement on learning tasks—not measuring and identifying abilities or styles of learning to blame for lack of achievement.

Establish Grouping Structures

Much is known about how students learn and what schooling practices foster growth and learning. No two students arrive at school with identical dispositions to learn. As students commence the essential task of learning, it is clear that many already have acquired many of the prerequisite skills, and others have not. Some make rapid gains while others require more time before progress is noted. With this in mind, effective teachers groups students for instruction and take into account student characteristics, task demands (types of knowledge—factual, conceptual, strategic), proficiency levels (accuracy, mastery, automaticity), and the content of instruction. Often teachers use different grouping arrangements for different types or domains of instruction (e.g., academic, social).

There is considerable research and debate on tracking and ability grouping. While rigid ability grouping may have its place, regrouping simply for teaching specific skills can add instructional variety and facilitate student motivation and learning. A learning environment that is both challenging and nurturing is the most critical ingredient for success for all students. Effective teachers use different instructional techniques based on the specific objective or skill and group taught. Instructional groups must be assessed frequently so that students no longer needing such instruction (including enrichment or remediation) are assigned to different groups working on different or related tasks. Teachers can choose from a variety of different instructional grouping structures that are not rigid but provide fluid movement of students from activity to activity based on monitored progress toward a specific learner competency. After all, it is not about what group a student is in, but what instruction occurs and what the student does that counts in the learning continuum.

planning

Tactic: Create Random Groups

There are a number of ways effective teachers can create random groups. Here are a few favorites:

Deck Groups

(form groups of four)

1 Using a deck of playing cards, sort them by suit and number (four jacks, four threes, four kings, four sixes, etc.). Then select one card for each student in the class from each of the sorted stacks. (e.g., 26 students = 26 cards).

2 Shuffle the cards and pass one out to each student.

note: If your class has an uneven number of students or does not divide evenly into teams of four, adapt the procedure to create teams of five or three. Predetermine what extra cards will go with what suit or number. For example, in a class of 29 students you could predetermine that the 8 of diamonds will join the kings, and the 4 of hearts will join the threes. It is important that the teacher know which cards are extra before handing out the cards to the students.

3 Direct students to find their team by joining those who have the same number or face card in any suit. For example, all of the twos form one group, all the kings form another.

It's Snowing!

(form groups of two)

This activity recreates an indoor snowball war. Also called Nameballs, this grouping procedure is as follows:

1 Divide your class into two even groups. Designate one half Group 1 and the other Group 2.

2 Hand out a piece of paper to each student in Group 1. Tell these students to write their names on the individual pieces of paper and then make a snowball out of it (crumple it up). Some teachers use colored paper to create colored snowball wars.

3 While Group 1 is writing, tell Group 2 to move to the other side of the room.

4 Set a timer or designate a time of 30-60 seconds for the snowball war. Then give the direction: "When I say 'Begin,' Group 1 will throw their snowballs and members of Group 2 will pick them up and throw them back. Pick up any snowballs that fall near you and throw them back. Continue until I say 'Stop.'"

5 After 60 seconds (or less if you wish) has lapsed say "Stop." Tell all Group 1 members to throw all snowballs on their side of the floor over to Group 2's side. All snowballs should be on the Group 2 side.

planning

6 Each member of Group 2 is instructed to pick up one snowball and open it up. The name that appears on the paper is that Group 2 member's partner for the upcoming instructional activity.

note: If you have an odd number of students in class, modify the procedure by instructing the "odd" student in Group 1 to take two pieces of paper and write his/her name once on each. After the 60 seconds is up two members of Group 2 will have the same name and thus form a threesome. Another alternative is to have a "Wild Ball" snowball for each of the extra students. Write "Wild Ball" on the number of pieces of paper that correspond with the number of extra students. Crumple them up and throw them into the mix of snowballs. The Group 2 students who pick up these "Wild Balls" are directed by the teacher to the extra student who will be their partner.

Puzzle Time

(form groups of two)

Here is an easy tactic that can be reused with classes that have an even number of students. All you need is index cards.

1 Count out enough index cards for one half of your class.

2 Cut each index card in half, varying the edges and likening them to a two-piece puzzle (see Figure 10).

3 Put all the pieces into a container. Have each students pick one piece out of the container.

4 Have the students quickly and quietly find their partners by finding the matching puzzle piece. You may want to set some parameters for noise (e.g., use a "silent find" procedure—find your partner quickly, no talking).

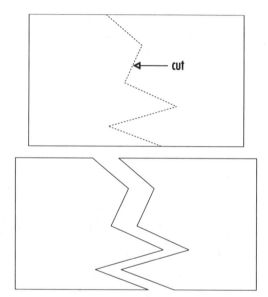

Figure 10

note: If you have an odd number of students in your class, cut one of the index cards into three pieces to form a threesome. For groups of four count out enough cards for one-quarter of your class. Cut each index card into four pieces.

planning

Color Me Cooperative

(form groups of two, three, or four)

For this procedure you will need a variety of colored paper. The number of colors will depend on the number of students per group. For example, in a class of 28 students, for groups of:

- Two—You will need 14 colors of paper. Two pieces of each color for a total of 28 pieces.

- Three—For groups of three in a class of 28, you will need to make the following adaptation:

  You will need nine colors of paper. Nine pieces of each color for a total of 27. For the extra person, you choose one extra piece of colored paper. That color will have a foursome instead of a threesome.

- Four—You will need seven colors of paper. Four pieces of each color for a total of 28 pieces.

Place pieces of paper into a container. Then, have each student randomly select a piece of paper from the container. Once all students have pulled their paper, direct them to quickly and quietly find other students with the same color.

Line Up!

(variable group sizes)

Here is a fun way to group students for instructional purposes. The teacher tells the class to "line up" in order of:

- Height

- Birthday—first by month, then by day (For example: All students born in June group together, then line up by date [1, 7, 13, 26]. June then lines up between May and July birthdays.)

- Alphabetical order of first or last name or middle initial

Once the class is in line, the teacher can have the students count off (1-2-3 or 1-2-3-4) or form any size group.

Many problem-solving and social skills are tapped in this grouping activity. Both students and adults enjoy this strategy of grouping.

Source: Kagan, S. (1994).
Adapted from: Workshop materials, Sacca & Elliott (1994b).

Tactic: Create Formal Groups

Formal groups are those that are teacher designed. They are created to allow for controlled membership in both academic and social domains. There are many ways to create these groups. Once again, it is imperative that these groups remain fluid. Effective teachers continually monitor students' progress and

planning

allow for constant movement from group to group based on individual student progress. Often teachers find pairing students with complementary skills an effective way to assign students to groups for research and writing projects. For example, by creating rank-ordered groups for each content area (e.g., writing, art skills, etc.) a student with strong writing skills can be paired with another who is artistic to create a balanced team. As always, work load and responsibility must be monitored to avoid task overload on one student. Other teachers have found this method helpful when grouping or pairing students with solid comprehension skills with peers who are proficient at decoding but less so at understanding what they read. For example, grouping all Es together results in a group of high, middle, and low students who help each other with the assigned task.

Figures 11 through 14 describe several methods of grouping.

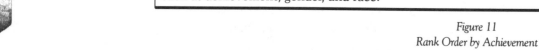

variation 1

The teacher creates a rank-ordered list of three ability groups of students according to High, Middle, Low. Letters are arbitrarily assigned within each group. For example:

High Students			Middle Students			Low Students		
1	Bob	A	7	Megg	F	13	Herb	A
2	Rob	B	8	Matt	E	14	James	B
3	Stu	C	9	Swatdee	D	15	Howie	C
4	Rex	D	10	Bart	C	16	Myata	D
5	Kate	E	11	Melea	B	17	Caleb	E
6	Ned	F	12	Jane	A	18	Garth	F

Once created the teacher may choose, for example, to group As and Bs together for science instruction, Cs and Fs for social studies, and 1-6 for reading, or all As for writing, all Bs for a social studies project, etc. This assures that each group will have a mix of high, middle, and low students. So while these groups are initially rank ordered by achievement, this procedure allows the teacher to create any number of grouping variations based on the letters or numbers chosen, and by academic area. Be sure to check that the groups are balanced for variables such as achievement, gender, and race.

Figure 11
Rank Order by Achievement

planning

variation 2

The teacher creates a rank-ordered list of students according to a specific skill area. Then the teacher takes the first and last student as one twosome, the second and second last student as another twosome, and so one. These twosomes can then be combined into groups of four students.

Achievement	1st Group	2nd Group
1	1 & 16	1,16,8,9
2	2 & 15	2,15,7,10
3	3 & 14	3,14,6,11
4	4 & 13	4,13,5,12
5	5 & 12	
6	6 & 11	
7	7 & 10	
8	8 & 9	
9		
10		
11		
12		
13		
14		
15		
16		

Figure 12
Rank Order by Achievement

variation 3

Create a rank-ordered list of students according to a specific skill area. Use the following achievement compositions to create groups of three or four.

- High Achiever, High Achiever, Middle Achiever
- Middle Achiever, Middle Achiever, Low Achiever
- Middle Achiever, Low Achiever, Low Achiever
- High Achiever, Middle Achiever, Middle Achiever, Low Achiever
- High Achiever, High Achiever, Middle Achiever, Middle Achiever
- High Achiever, High Achiever, Low Achiever, Low Achiever

Figure 13
*Mixed Ability Groups**

*Need to be teacher generated. Be sure to monitor groups for sharing of work load among all students regardless of ability.

planning

variation 4

Create a rank-ordered list of students for each content area of instruction requiring small group instruction, practice, or projects. Within each section of the clock write the names of students of similar abilities. Use the grouping configurations in Variations 3 and 4 to guide your decisions. Consider area of instruction, student prior knowledge, type of knowledge being instructed, and proficiency levels of the students. Be sure to balance groups for gender and race.

Using the clocked groups at right, for example, you may call students to a group activity by stating the number or time of the group and/or content area. For example, "It is time for reading, I would like one o'clock, four o'clock, and eight o'clock groups with me at the reading table." Or, "Let's practice this experiment in the following science clock groups: six, seven, eleven, twelve, and one." There are numerous uses of clock groups. They can be formed by:

- Content
- Skill level
- Content and skill
- Type of knowledge: facts, concepts, strategies
- Proficiency level: Acquisition, Fluency, Mastery
- Practice groups: large, medium, or small

Using this formal grouping structure allows students to partake in instructional activities without labeling the groups high, medium, or low. Students can be grouped without knowledge of distinct levels of ability.

Figure 14
Rank Order by Ability

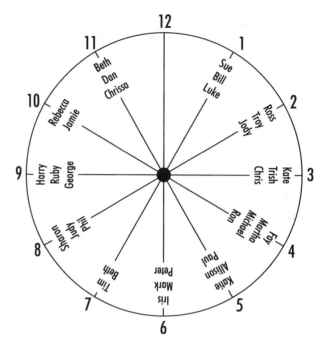

Reading Clock Groups 1,4,8

Sue	Michael
Bill	Ron
Luke	Sharon
Fay	Judy
Martha	Phil

planning

note: For all of the variations above, consideration must be given to the type of task or knowledge demand and level of proficiency of each student member for the instructional activity the students are being grouped for. Some activities require skills or prior knowledge that some groups members may not yet have learned. As always direct and frequent measurement of student skill and learning will facilitate student success.

Pace Instruction Appropriately

Instructional pace is considered as the rate at which students are expected to meet instructional objectives. Optimal pacing is evidenced when the amount of content is maximized without frustrating the learner. An efficient pace keeps the student actively involved, with little time spent waiting for the teacher to locate materials or for another student to respond. There are a number of considerations effective teachers consider when establishing instructional pace.

Tactic: Use Active Decision Making

Effective teachers take into account the amount of instruction and content they want to accomplish within a year of curriculum, unit of instruction, and lesson. They consider the skill and proficiency levels of students and the rate at which individual students progress. It is one thing to plan content coverage; it is another when considering ability and frustration levels of students. Effective teachers monitor, on a daily basis, how their students are doing in each lesson presented. By checking often teachers gain information about student mastery of content. Moving to new content is again based on the needed level of proficiency and needed skill development in the larger hierarchy of concept or skill acquisition. If the skill is needed as a prerequisite to a later skill it is important that students demonstrate higher levels of proficiency before moving to new content.

- Check often for understanding. Ask students to tell or show you what they are doing. Instructional pace should be altered in areas where students are having difficulty.

- Provide opportunities to practice. It is not uncommon for students to "get" a fact, concept, or strategy, but their fluency may be weak. Consider using cooperative learning structures to provide reinforcement and additional opportunities to become fluent in the skill.

- Monitor for boredom and frustration. The antecedent to many classroom behaviors can be linked to students' boredom or frustration with classroom routines or assignments. Effective teachers watch for nonverbal cues to help indicate whether the instructional pace is too fast or slow. Both boredom and frustration are indications that the instructional pace is inappropriate.

- Consider normative peer comparisons. Effective teachers set progress expectations based on what they know about a group or individual student. Often the performance of students is compared to what the average (or typical age or grade) student's rate of progress is. By frequently monitoring students, teachers can chart progress and adjust instructional pace for those advancing or lagging in their learning rate.

- Consider curriculum-based probes. By using curriculum-based evaluation, effective teachers monitor on a daily or weekly basis how well stu-

planning

dents are doing in content areas. These probes are developed directly from the day to day curriculum and are administered within one to five minutes. The information gained relates directly to where students are having difficulty or have mastered material.

Tactic: Regulate Assignments to Increase Performance

By carefully selecting items or tasks, teachers can control the level of difficulty of any assignment. Independent practice assignments in which students demonstrate high (i.e., 80-90% correct) levels of proficiency are better than practice in "harder" work with lower levels of accuracy. Having a student learn something correctly and perform a task proficiently at an easier level is better than having a student complete a harder assignment incorrectly. In the latter case unlearning may need to take place. That is, the student will need to unlearn the incorrect procedures used to incorrectly complete the "harder" assignment.

Because most students perform skills at different levels, effective teachers prepare varied opportunities for practice in their assignments. For example, some students may be assigned the questions at the end of a chapter, while others create ones that students should know after reading the chapter itself. Another group of students, using study guides, is directed to the page on which the chapter questions can be found.

Tactic: Keep a Brisk Pace

When developing lessons, plan to use a brisk pace. This includes the presentation, response, and corrective and supportive feedback phases. Generate an ample number of instructional examples to allow for this. Present facts, concepts, or strategies in a variety of ways. Avoid extended time with individual students during lessons. If clarification cannot be reached with a reasonable number of examples or explanation, make a note of it and tell the student that you will follow up with them immediately after the presentation. Corrective or supportive feedback should be the point. Avoid use of elaborate explanations and "bird-walks" (engaging in off-task topics). Students are often quite skilled at introducing extraneous topics to delay or avoid lesson content. When this happens acknowledge interest and simply state that you would like to discuss it further or at length at another time (perhaps after school) and return to the lesson or task at hand.

Tactic: Vary Practice Formats But Not Skills

It is often necessary to provide students lots of opportunities to practice a skill to mastery. One way to provide extended practice without risking boredom is to maintain the same skill areas but vary the format of presentation and practice. This technique is critical to all students, especially at the acquisition stage of skill development. For example, for young children learning to read the names of the month, first present the names on flash cards written in different colors. Next write the words on the chalkboard and have

planning

students read them. Another format could include a game activity format in which several cards are placed in a shoe box or container along with a joker card. The cards are drawn from the box one at a time and if read correctly remain out of the box. Students try to remove all of the cards from the box before the joker card is drawn. Each of these activities requires students to practice the same skill but in different formats. For older students, provide instruction and practice in contexts that have personal meaning to them. For example, the content of practice activities could include fantasy figures, sport figures, practice activities students generate, or daily living activities in which students are involved. Planning for these format variations allow the lesson or skill introduction to continue at a brisk pace with a high level of interest.

Monitor Performance and Replan Instruction

Effective teachers keep an accurate record of students' progress and compare progress of individual students to that of others in their class or grade. They use these data to decide the extent to which instruction is working, and whether or not it makes good sense to change what is being done. Too often, educators change something that is working or is effective because they see little noticeable progress. Others continue with ineffective techniques. Why? Because there is a lack of student performance evaluation.

Therefore, without any performance data, teachers leave instructional planning and decision making to chance, often resulting in inappropriate instructional decisions. It is imperative that direct and frequent performance evaluation occurs. While it can be said that effective teachers are always monitoring student performance, it is critical to use data on performance to plan subsequent instruction.

Tactic: Use Data to Plan Subsequent Instruction

The goal is to maximize instructional effectiveness and efficiency by frequently monitoring and evaluating student performance. Interpreting data and making instructional decisions can be enhanced by using visual aids or procedures. One useful method is the minimum 'celeration line. Basically, this method allows you to connect initial information collected at baseline or preteaching skill level to data points of desired proficiency rates and a time goal. The use of this method allows you to describe the rate of progress or minimum growth required to meet an instructional goal within a certain time frame. Constructing a minimum 'celeration line is easy:

1 Gather three to five days of baseline data to determine current levels of student functioning.

2 Draw a mark or star (often referred to as an aim star) at the desired level of proficiency and date at which achievement is expected (see Figure 15). Aim stars are usually set by using information from instructional objectives, using the

planning

Alberto's baseline vocabulary test scores:

Week 1   40%
Week 2   60%
Week 3   50%

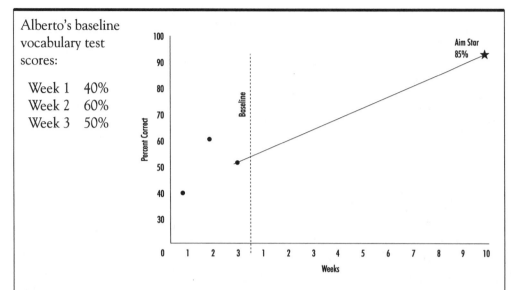

Alberto's teacher is concerned about Alberto's vocabulary scores on the weekly tests. The teacher writes the following objective: Alberto will obtain 85% on his weekly vocabulary by week 10.

After taking 3 data points for baseline, the teacher plots them on the graph above and places a star at week 10, 85%. He then takes the median (mid) date/week test and mid score and draws the 'celeration line to the star. The result is a graphic illustration of minimum progress Alberto needs to reach in order to meet the objective and the Aim Star.

Figure 15
Constructing a Minimum 'Celeration Line

planning

criterion rate and date at which the objective should be achieved.

3 Locate the start mark by finding the intersection of the middle (median) date and middle (median) rate of the collected baseline data points.

4 Draw the minimum 'celeration line by connecting the start mark and the aim star with a direct and straight line (aim line).

As a general rule, if students' performance data points fall below the aim line for three consecutive days, a change in instruction should be made.

Tactic: Use Data Patterns to Decide Next Steps

By consistently collecting data on an aim line, effective teachers can visually see when instructional decisions need to be made. Using data patterns, teachers can decide if they need to "slice back," "step back," try a different instructional procedure, or move on to a new learning phase or new skill. After baseline is gathered, use progress data to make instructional decisions.

- "Slice back" means to move back and teach an easier version or subcomponent of the same skill. The visual display of these data is indicated by students' data points that show that they are performing some but not all of the tasks, yet are not making any progress. (See Figure 16.)

- "Step back" means to back up and teach a prerequisite to the larger skill at hand. It differs from a slice back in that the student's performance data shows that he/she is not performing any part of the task correctly. Visual data clearly indicates that the task is simply too difficult and an easier skill must be learned first. (See Figure 17.)

Julianna is receiving between 30-40% on her daily one-minute timed probes of 0-9 multiplication facts. She is not improving her performance. Although Julianna is proficient at her facts, she is not fluent. This is evidenced by the timed probes. The decision to slice back to 0-4 multiplication facts per one-minute probe will allow Julianna to concentrate on fluency of fewer math facts.

Objective: Julianna will score 80% on her one-minute timed probes for math facts 0-9 by Oct. 26.

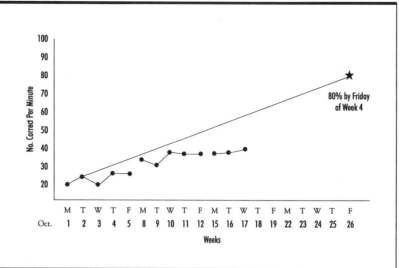

Figure 16
Slice Back

Juanita is learning to read CVC words (e.g., cat, tat, dog) by sounding out the sounds within each word. It is apparent that Juanita is unable to perform this task of reading. She is unable to perform the letter-sound correspondence. The decision is to step back and teach the prerequisite skill of letter sounds.

Objective: Juanita will correctly read 10 of 10 CVC words by Friday, Oct 19.

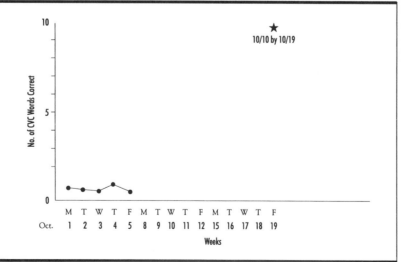

Figure 17
Step Back

planning

Peter is in the acquisition phase of learning Spanish vocabulary words for colors and shapes. While the learning task is appropriate for Peter, he needs more instruction, modeling, and practice. Peter's pattern of a high rate of errors, but with some corrects, indicates that he needs more practice on those words that are troublesome to learn.

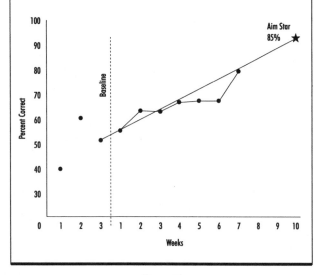

Figure 18
Different Instructional Procedures

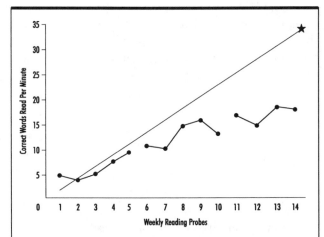

Fay is reading from her 7th grade social studies book. She has shown steady increase in her accuracy of reading, however, she is not increasing her rate. Her reading rate and accuracy appeared to plateau at 15 cwpm. This pattern suggests that Fay is bored or unmotivated to continue rate or fluency of performance. The decision is to move to a fluency-building phase of instruction and provide incentive for improvement.

Figure 19
Moving to a New Learning Phase

planning

- Different instructional procedures are used when the teacher is sure that the task is appropriate, but the student needs more instructional help, prompts, or practice. The data display is usually characterized by a high number of errors but some corrects. While this pattern may look very similar to slice back, the difference is that the

problem may not be sliceable (e.g., just needs more opportunities to practice). (See Figure 18.)

- Moving to a new learning phase is recommended when a student exhibits a high number of correct responses, but the rate is slow. The student may be accurate, but needs to build fluency. (See Figure 19.)

■ Moving to a new skill is done when the student has met both the accuracy and fluency levels of expected performance (see Figure 20).

Adapted from: Wolrey, Bailey, & Sugai (1988).

Marilyn has shown continued progress in the completion of her study guides for Unit 10 in her science book. She is ready to move on to the next unit and the corresponding study guides.

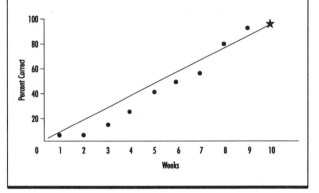

Figure 20
Moving to a New Skill

planning

principle

Communicate Realistic Expectations

Effective teachers set realistic expectations for students and communicate those expectations to them. When teachers do not expect enough from their students, they shortchange them. When expectations are realistically high, students succeed; when they are unrealistically low, students fail. Effective teachers teach students the goals, objectives, and standards that are driving their instruction. They also teach them to be active, involved learners because those who do not get actively involved cannot be expected to do well on measures of mastery. In communicating realistic expectations, effective teachers also teach students to understand the consequences of success and failure.

Component	Principle	Strategy	Page
Planning Instruction	**Communicate Realistic Expectations**	Teach Goals, Objectives, and Standards	54
		Teach Students to Be Active, Involved Learners . .	54
		Teach Students Consequences of Performance . . .	56

planning

strategy

Teach Goals, Objectives, and Standards

Effective teachers communicate clearly to students what they are expected to do and to what level of proficiency. Students need to know what is to be done, under what conditions, and at what level of performance or standard. This information should be shared at the start of every lesson, unit of instruction, or any other learning activity. This practice not only keeps students abreast, but aids in monitoring teacher instructional behavior as well.

In effective learning environments, teachers engage in active teaching and monitoring of student performance to a predetermined goal. Students are actively engaged in completing relevant academic tasks successfully. These tasks are those that refer to a set of goal-directed activities toward a specific objective and standard.

Tactic: Visually Display Goals, Objectives, and Standards

Write your instructional goals on the board or overhead at the start of each day, lesson, and/or unit. This is a fine way to give students a glance at what they can be expected to produce and to what level of performance. Review the progress toward achieving the goals periodically during the day, lesson, and/or unit.

Often teachers have students develop goal notebooks for content areas or behavior. Students can develop personal goal notebooks in which they, together with the teacher, identify areas and write personal goal statements. These can be academic or behavioral in nature. It is important that these goal notebooks specify what the students will do, under what conditions, and to what level of proficiency. As the goals are achieved they can be signed off by initialing them. It is important to evaluate progress daily and weekly. Have students, teachers, and parents comment on progress. Encourage all parties to evaluate progress in terms of "best." What was the "best" day? Have students tell why. For those days that weren't "bests," ask students to identify what they need to do to improve.

strategy

Teach Students to Be Active, Involved Learners

Research has shown that students who are actively engaged in instruction profit more than those who are not. Effective teachers have a stockpile of techniques they use to get students actively engaged in the instructional process. Effective teachers believe that instruction can alter the rate at which all students progress through the curriculum. In planning instruction and proactively managing students' active involvement in lessons, effective teachers make sure they vary the way they ask questions to students. They consider the types of knowledge types they are

planning

working with (fact, concept, strategy) and the desired student behavior. Effective teachers look for ways to increase opportunities to learn. Research has shown that providing students with opportunities to learn is not only directly related to student achievement, but is impacted by four instructional variables:

1 Time allocated to instructional activities

2 Classroom management

3 Consistent success and academic learning time

4 Active teaching

All of these are alterable variables that directly influence what and how a teacher plans for instruction.

Tactic: Vary Question Format

Teacher actions can be divided into four distinct categories: delivering information, asking questions, responding to student efforts, and using learning activities (Howell, Fox, & Morehead, 1993). Effective teachers relate these behaviors to the types of knowledge demanded of the student—factual, conceptual, strategic.

A teacher delivering **factual** knowledge about the solar system would show the planets and give the names, keeping the presentation short and precise. The same teacher would encourage rapid responses to questions. For example, "This is a picture of Saturn. Class, what planet is this a picture of?"

While delivering information on **concepts**, the teacher would utilize lots of examples and nonexamples of the concept. Questions would elicit student examples of things that are always, never, or sometimes attributes of the concept.

When delivering **strategic** knowledge, the teacher makes direct connections with students' prior knowledge. Here teachers show how to solve problems or arrive at answers in a step-by-step manner.

Tactic: Call on Students Randomly

Get into the practice of varying who you call on and how you call on them for responses. Calling on students at random using different formats keeps students alert and engaged. It is difficult for students to anticipate who teachers will call on when there is no routine. For example, call on one student to answer a question. Then have that student choose another student to answer the next question, and so on. Some teachers use a hat routine to provide variety to such activities as summarizing main points of a story. For example, all classmates' names are on slips of paper and in hat. After a discussion or reading, have students summarize the main points by randomly picking the students' names from the hat. This can also be used for summarizing directions. Each student whose name is drawn must summarize, in sequence, what is to be done first, second, and so on. Vary the routine and keep students alert. This also serves as a monitor and check of students who truly have an un-

planning

derstanding of what is expected of them, and/or who were not attending.

Tactic: Use Peer-Mediated Learning Procedures

Many teachers find that students not only enjoy but respond better to peer-mediated learning activities than teacher-directed activities. Dyads, triads, or groups of students can be teamed to complete assignments and practice opportunities. (See Delivering: Provide Relevant Practice.)

- Cross-aged tutors (older students working with younger students on academic skills and/or behavior) have been found to be very effective with younger students.

- Teaching stations are another creative way to provide students with constructive movement about the room. The teacher may assign groups of students to stations for a specific period of time and then have them rotate to the next.

- Students who have demonstrated mastery of a skill may design and develop learning activities for other students. These activities can range from creative puzzles or worksheets to bulletin boards. There is no limit to what students will come up with to "help" their peers learn. Try it!

planning

strategy

Teach Students Consequences of Performance

Effective teachers set clear and precise expectations and consequences for both appropriate and inappropriate classroom behavior. So often teachers leave well enough alone and do not reinforce students for the appropriate behaviors they exhibit. It has been shown that in some cases 85% of the time a student does exactly what he/she is told, this appropriate behavior is not recognized. Students perform better when they know what is expected and the contingencies or consequences for their behavior. Some teachers have students list attributes that lead to success. This could be successful completion of an assignment, securing a job, initiating a discussion, or any other situation that is relevant to the students. Here it is important that teachers emphasize that effort and skill, not luck, is what counts. Engage students in discussion and/or role play to provide opportunities for them to see the correlation between effort and accomplishment.

Tactic: Use Community Members to Value Achievement

An effective method of showing students what effort versus luck is all about is inviting guest speakers to join your class. There are many community members who serve as excellent models for perseverance under many different conditions. It also provides students with firsthand opportunities to ask questions and process thoughts/concerns they may have. Volunteer agencies also serve as an excellent resource.

Some teachers have students read biographies of individuals who have overcome diversity and have gone on to be successful professionals in different careers. Encourage students to discuss any parallels they see between their lives and those of classroom guests or biographical figures. Some students will feel more at ease keeping a log or diary on these similarities.

Tactic: Teach Students to Be Accountable

Students profit more from instruction when they use classroom time effectively. Effective teachers allocate sufficient time to instruction and establish clear rules and procedures for how students are to spend their time in class. Teach students ways to be accountable for their behavior. Have students keep records of assignments due and those that are completed. Teach them to proactively plan what they need to do to structure their day or time to facilitate task completion. Often it is assumed that students have the prior knowledge to set up personal schedules or daily routines to allow them to complete all of the demands of life in general, let alone demands of school. These skills need to be taught just like science or social studies curricula.

Tactic: Consider Contingency Contracting

Contingency contracting is a very effective way of communicating realistic expectations and conse-

quences of student performance, within limits, for academics and behavior. There are a number of things to consider when entering into a contract with a student. It is important to specify what the student will do, under what conditions, and to what level of performance or standard. Often teachers and students (and parents) together create the menu of consequences for successful and unsuccessful completion of stipulated tasks. The ultimate goal of using a contingency contract is to teach students self-management skills and to have them assume responsibility for what is expected. Here are some components that must be present for a student contract to be successful:

- **Agreement**—It is important that all parties involved (e.g., teacher, student, parent, administrator, counselor, etc.) agree on the target behavior and the incentives and consequences for it. That is, one person (i.e., the teacher) cannot dictate what behavior(s) he/she feels the student needs to work on without some input from others. After all, the student's behavior of tapping a pencil continually may be driving the teacher crazy, but does it warrant a contract or perhaps a less intrusive intervention? The student must have say in the negotiating of the behavior and what incentives and consequences will be delivered.

- **If, Then, or When Statements**—It is important that the contingencies for both the incentive or rewards as well as the consequence be stated in if, then statements. If (behavior), then (reward or consequence). For example, "If I finish all my work

planning

on time, then ..." or, "When I arrive on time to class, at least three times per week, then I earn ..."

- **Incentives**—Incentives are the key to an effective contract. If the reward or incentive is highly desirable to the student, then he/she is more likely to buy into the procedures or terms of the contract. Here negotiation should include ways to earn bonus rewards as well as penalties.

- **Target Behavior**—Here the target behavior in need of change is discussed and put into observable and measurable behavior. By doing this it is easier to keep track of the target behavior because you can both see it and count it. It is a good idea to include criteria or standards and timelines of the behavior to be performed. For example, if homework is the target behavior it must be completely finished by the start of every class.

- **Goal for It!**—Encourage students to set goals for themselves. These can serve as benchmarks to the final goal of the contract. Set dates for these and include bonus rewards if the student meets the goal ahead of schedule. In the same manner, penalties for lagging behind benchmark goal dates can also be implemented.

Be careful not to assign penalty points simply because students are behind schedule. Take all variables into consideration.

- **Publicly Post Efforts**—Depending on the students and the behavior, it is best practice to publicly post efforts toward the final goal. If the contract is for an individual student, then classmates can cheer each other on. However, if the behavior is a sensitive one (e.g., wetting, personal touching, etc.), a different kind of public posting may be more appropriate. For example, one student had a contract to reduce the number of time during the day he touched himself. His contract was posted in his counselor's office. This proved effective for this student as his counselor was part of the contract and her office was a safe environment for posting.

Important Considerations:

- Remember, students are all different and will need different individualized contracts (unless you are using a group contingency). Do not make a carbon copy contract and simply fill in students' names. The time put into creating an individual contract, using the general steps above, will be worthwhile.

- Consider the capabilities of the student and the tolerance for delay of incentives or rewards. Avoid long periods of time in which the student must demonstrate target behaviors. Reinforce frequently, at least initially. For example, Larry never does his homework. The goal is to have Larry complete at least two assignments per week for two weeks, then three per week, and so

planning

on. Upon handing in his assignment, Larry is immediately reinforced with a discount coupon to a local fast food restaurant. This immediate feedback, if highly motivating, may have an effect on Larry's homework completion. He will hand in more assignments per week than contracted for. This is where a bonus clause would kick in. If Larry chooses to hand in more than two assignments for the first two weeks of his contract, he will continue to earn coupons from his favorite fast food restaurant. However, if Larry was not eligible for any incentive until he handed in five out of five assignments within a two-week period, his behavior may remain unchanged. Too long of a wait period for incentives and too high a standard discourages students before they start.

- Make sure goal behaviors and contract demands are within reach and doable by the students. Often during the negotiation stage, students promise more than they are capable of doing (even more than Superman®!). It is important to point out that the goal of the contract is positive practice, improvement, and reward in the target areas. Help students moderate their proposed efforts.

- Build in penalty clauses. If, for example, Larry does not hand in any assignments for the two-week period, he will have to eat lunch in the "time out" room. This is assuming that to miss lunch and the opportunity to socialize and be cool with his friends is as uninticing as eating a plate full of cold peas! Build in penalties clauses and make sure students understand and buy into the concept.

- Be sure the student understands and takes ownership of the contract and the terms therein. Let them know that timeliness, standards, penalties and bonus rewards are all negotiable, but the contract itself is not. Students need to know that their behavior needs improvement, and since they have not been able to monitor and adjust their behavior to this point, a contract needs to be implemented. Of course, depending on how you deliver this information to the students, they may feel the need to show you otherwise and sabotage the entire effort. Be diplomatic and show genuine concern when delivering this information.

- Make sure all parties included in the contract are present, and sign and date the written documents.

- Be ready to counter the argument that "Contracts are just crutches for students. If they would just do the work, contracts would not be needed." Contracts are not a crutch and should be designed to be faded out slowly. The student has obviously shown that he/she is incapable of "just doing the work," therefore, a contract is a good next step. A contract can provide the motivation for a failing student to work harder toward a goal, thereby becoming successful.

planning

managing

If effective teaching just involved making decisions about what to teach, how to teach it, and how to make students believe that learning is important, job satisfaction ratings for teachers would probably be much higher than they typically are reported to be. Every teacher knows that classroom disruptions are among the greatest deterrents to the best laid plans for effective instruction. Discipline is consistently identified as a concern on public and professional opinions polls about education. Few of us are comfortable in situations that are unstructured and chaotic; this is particularly true for classrooms. Most students need and function better in orderly environments. This is why managing is a key component of effective teaching.

Effective instruction requires managing the complex mix of instructional tasks and student behaviors that are part of every classroom interaction. This means making decisions that control and support the orderly flow of instruction. To do this, effective teachers make decisions about classroom rules and procedures as well as how to handle disruptions, how to organize classroom time and space to be most productive, and how to keep classrooms warm, positive, and accepting places for students with different learning styles and performances. As illustrated in Figure 21, there are three principles of effective managing:

1 Prepare for instruction

2 Use time productively

3 Establish positive classroom environment

Component	Principle	Strategy
Managing Instruction	Prepare for Instruction	Set Classroom Rules Communicate and Teach Classroom Rules Communicate Consequences of Behavior Handle Disruptions Efficiently Teach Students to Manage Their Own Behavior
	Use Time Productively	Establish Routines and Procedures Organize Physical Space Allocate Sufficient Time to Academic Activities
	Establish Positive Classroom Environment	Make the Classroom a Pleasant, Friendly Place Accept Individual Differences Establish Supportive, Cooperative Learning Environments Create a Nonthreatening Learning Environment

Figure 21
Three Principles of Effective Managing

Each of these principles implies a set of strategies that teachers use when managing.

Prepare for instruction means making decisions about what to permit, tolerate, and control in the classroom. In doing this, effective teachers establish classroom rules and communicate them early in the school year. They teach students the consequences of following and not following their rules, and they handle rule infractions and other classroom disruptions as quickly as possible after they occur. An overriding concern for many effective teachers when preparing for instruction is deciding ways for students to manage their own behaviors. The goal of preparing for instruction is to try to anticipate, avoid, and address problems that might disrupt the orderly flow of instruction.

Use time productively means making decisions that maximize the amounts of time students spend actively engaged in learning and minimize the time spent on activities not related to learning. This means establishing routines and procedures, organizing physical space, giving clear directions, setting transitions between work sessions, allocating time to academic activities, and maintaining an academic focus. The goal of using time productively is to get the most out the time teachers spend teaching and students spend learning.

Establish positive classroom environment means making decisions about ways to motivate students, interact positively, and create supportive, cooperative classrooms. Students like school more when their classrooms are pleasant, friendly places. Students like school more when teachers are accepting and caring. An overriding goal in classrooms of effective teachers is positive interaction that fosters active student responding. The goal of establishing a positive classroom environment is to make the classroom a place that students like and where they enjoy learning.

These three managing principles are addressed in this chapter. An overview for each principle is provided, illustrating relationships to effective managing and describing specific strategies that effective teachers use. The main content of the unit is a set of tactics that illustrate specific ways to actively address each principle and strategy when providing effective instruction.

principle

Prepare for Instruction

A fundamental part of instructional management is preparing to teach. Most people learn better in orderly environments where consequences of success and failure are known. Most students need structure to be successful in school. They like to participate in establishing classroom rules, and they need to have the rules reviewed periodically during the school year.

Effective teachers establish reasonable classroom rules and communicate them clearly to their students. The students understand what the consequences of good and unacceptable behavior will be. When disruptions occur, the prepared teacher knows how to handle them efficiently. The goal is for students to be able to manage their own behavior.

Component	Principle	Strategy	Page
Managing Instruction	**Prepare for Instruction**	Set Classroom Rules	66
		Communicate and Teach Classroom Rules . . .	68
		Communicate Consequences of Behavior	71
		Handle Disruptions Efficiently	77
		Teach Students to Manage Their Own Behavior .	82

Set Classroom Rules

A rule is a statement of standards for behavior. In fact, some teachers don't use the word "rule." Instead, they list classroom expectations. For some students the simple utterance of the word "rule" incites a challenge of authority. Here, "rule" and "classroom expectations" are used interchangeably.

Classroom rules help both teachers and students set limits and identify expected, appropriate, and unwanted behaviors. Classroom rules are a very important part of the overall management of the learning environment. To be truly effective, rules must be taught like any other content area. Classroom expectations are not to be merely posted in a classroom. They need to serve as an active framework for guiding both students' and teachers' behavior throughout the year. However, it is important to recognize that rules alone do not provide enough structure to keep students out of trouble. Students need to be "caught being good." Reinforcement and recognition for positive and appropriate behavior is vital to modeling and demonstrating desirable classroom and age-appropriate behaviors.

Tactic: Have Rules for Rules

Effective teachers set rules, enforcing, and reinforcing them constantly and consistently. All students need to know what the class expectations are and be able to cite them as well as examples and nonexamples of them. There are four basic rules for setting rules:

1 Limit the number of rules to 5-7.

2 Write or state the rules positively. Avoid "don'ts" and other language that emphasizes what is not allowed.

3 Avoid the use of question formats. As the saying goes be careful what you ask for … students may answer you! For example, "Are you prepared?" Student response: "Yes I am, but unfortunately I left my books at home!"

4 Rules should be measurable. Not only should everyone know exactly what each rule looks like (observable), they should be able to count them every time one occurs and recognize them. For example, "Thanks, John, for following rule number three." Or, "Someone isn't following rule number four."

Example of Rules

1. Raise your hand to speak and wait for permission to speak.

2. Be in your assigned seat when the bell rings.

3. Put all work materials away before leaving class.

4. Use an "inside voice" when working in cooperative groups.

At the risk of overemphasizing, it is important to understand this point: Rules must be observable and measurable, and students must know what each looks like in order to spot it, monitor it, and correct it if necessary.

Adapted from: Rhode, G., Jenson, W., & Reavis, K. (1993).

Tactic: Create Classroom Rules

There are many theories about whether or not students should participate in creating rules and expectations for the classroom. Sometimes students can be their own worst enemy. It is not uncommon for them to set high expectations and harsh consequences for rule infractions. "If you are late you must eat lunch in the boiler room for the rest of the year!" Identify what areas you feel need to be included in rule setting for your classroom. Identify the limits and what kinds of rules should be in effect. For example, you may consider including something about the following broad areas:

- Arriving on time
- Having appropriate or required materials
- Self-monitoring behavior during a lesson or while in class
- Completing assignments

Based on these four areas, generate some rules or minimal expectations. For example: Be in your assigned seat when the bell rings; Have needed books, pens, notebooks, and assignments organized at the start of class. Armed with these basics, you are ready to meet with the students to collaboratively set the classroom rules. Tell students the four areas and share your minimal expectations. Students can then help with the actual writing of the rules. This method is recommended regardless of the age of the students. The bottom line is that both the areas and the minimal expectations have been predetermined by the teacher. After all, you are the one ultimately accountable for your students' learning and behavior.

There may be cases where a middle or secondary school teacher may see eight or nine periods of students daily. Most of these students will be capable of following the set rules. But for those more difficult classes, additional or different rules may be needed. Teachers don't need many different sets of rules, but be aware of those individual classes that may need more structure.

Adapted from: *The Tough Kid Video Series* (1995).

Tactic: Have a Safety-Valve Rule

Consider a blanket rule or "safety valve rule" in your classroom rule list. It is inevitable that classroom situations will arise that are not specifically covered by any of the rules. Situations or behaviors may escalate where none of the classroom rules fit the situation. During these times you use the "safety-valve rule"— "Do what your teacher tells you, immediately!" Effective teachers know that this rule is reserved for only those times when it is imperative that a student respond to a request immediately, perhaps when physical harm may befall the teacher or another student. But beware—overuse of this rule will result in little or no response to it from the students. Students learn very quickly, "Oh brother, here he goes again. He can't control the class so he uses that rule that no one listens to anyway."

Adapted from: Rhode, G., Jenson, W., & Reavis, K. (1993).

Communicate and Teach Classroom Rules

Effective teachers know it is not enough simply to set and post classroom rules and expectations. They must be communicated and taught. The rules should be posted in a highly visible place and reviewed daily, at least initially, then again after long weekends, holidays, or—just because. Keeping the rules to no more than seven allows the students to commit them to memory. In doing so a teacher can simply say, "Sarita, rule number three." Sarita will know what the rule is and self-regulate her behavior—if the rules have been taught and communicated.

Tactic: Teach the Rules

Be assured it is not enough to simply post classroom rules. Students must be able to cite examples and nonexamples of set expectations or rules. Like any content area, classroom expectations and rules must be communicated and taught. Have fun with this.

Create cooperative group activities and even role play situations that are likely to occur in the classroom. Use mimes to act out an example or nonexample of rule-following behavior. Students can draw paper strips from a hat and act out, individually or as a group of students, the rule or examples. Make sure students can not only identify examples and nonexamples of the rules, but also consequences that accompany rule infractions and inappropriate behaviors.

Tactic: Post Rules Constantly

Once you have established the classroom expectations or rules, post them for all to see. Rules stay up all year, but you may move them around the room and change the format. To keep students attuned to class expectations, some teachers will, for example, put them on different colored paper, have a student write them, and so on. One teacher had an art student write the expectations in calligraphy. These little tactics help maintain the presence of the rules and their importance.

In tandem with this tactic is the frequent review of the rules. Frequent reviews are essential and necessary, especially at the beginning of the year, after long vacations/weekends, after a classroom or school incident, or when rule infractions seem to be on the rise. The ceremonial moving of the rules to different spots in the classroom offers a fine opportunity to review the rules.

Tactic: Raise the Flag

There are many ways effective teachers signal rule infractions, but less-intrusive tactics should be tried
first. Effective teachers are constantly scanning the
room, observing students' behavior. In doing so,
many behaviors can be proactively managed before
they worsen, cause disruption, or prevent students
from active participation in a lesson. "Raise the Flag"
is a tactic that helps teachers monitor rule compliance. Here's how it works:

1 Make a mini flagpole out of a pencil or ruler
and a piece of construction paper. To make the
flag, cut a proportional piece of the paper and
fold it in half. Wrap the paper around the flagpole. Staple the flag (paper) close to the flagpole.
Be sure to leave enough slack to allow you to
freely move the flag up and down the pole.
Ground the flagpole in some clay or other material that will steady it (see Figure 22).

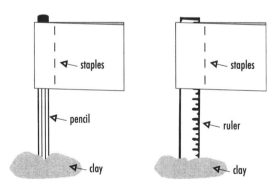

Figure 22

2 Place your mini flagpole on your desk in clear
view of all students.

3 Explain the procedure as follows (or wait for
them to ask—don't worry they will!):

> *Today we are going to use this flagpole
> to help monitor our classroom behavior.
> We will keep to our usual lesson format.
> When everyone is with me and we are
> working together as we should, the flag
> will remain at the base of the pole. How-
> ever, when I observe someone in here
> that is not doing what they ought to be,
> I will hoist the flag, sending out an alert.
> The alert simply means you need to
> check your behavior—are you doing
> what you should be doing? I may say
> "Someone in here is not following rule
> number three," or, "Someone in row
> two is not with us."*

> *Once I see that everyone is back on
> task, I will lower the flag and say,
> "Great, we are all back on task."*

After students have the tactic down, you can simply
walk over and lower or raise the flag while continuing
instruction. There is no disruption of the lesson, and
students immediately regulate their behaviors and
often prompt students who need it.

Tactic: Choose Battles Wisely

Too much teacher attention can reinforce inappropriate behavior for some students. When this is the case, planned ignoring is an effective tactic to consider. Planned ignoring is simply choosing ahead of time what student behaviors you will ignore. This can be for an individual student or class. When these behaviors occur, effective teachers ignore them and look for the slightest increase or demonstration of improvement to praise from the target student or others around that student. By not giving attention to the inappropriate behavior and focusing on giving attention when appropriate behaviors are performed, you will teach attention-hungry students what behaviors will indeed receive teacher attention. It may be necessary to tell your students at the beginning of the year that you are very aware of what goes on in your classroom—in fact, you have eyes in the back of your head! Tell them that there may be times when, for good reason, you choose to ignore inappropriate behavior. (Because after all, you are the master of time, space, and dimension in your classroom.) Tell your students that during those times, they are to continue to work and ignore the behavior also.

caution: Just the mere use of planned ignoring can create a challenge for the student to continue the inappropriate behavior to the degree you must intervene. In these cases discontinue the use of planned ignoring. It has become a coercive game created by the student (the "say uncle" ploy).

Tactic: Model Appropriate Behavior All the Time

Teachers are role models for students 100% of the time. Therefore, it is important to remember to model those same behaviors you expect from your students. For example, you can't monitor and model on-time class behavior if you aren't in your classroom when you expect the students to be there— at the bell. It is important to model other classroom behaviors as well. For example, if you give the students a silent reading assignment, it is important that you engage in one also. Sometimes this is a difficult concept for teachers to accept. Some feel that their position of authority allows them to do what needs to be done, when it need to be done (e.g., grading papers during silent reading). However, "what is good for the goose is good for the gander." Students are very observant and will often seize the opportunity to model your behavior, which can often lead to possible confrontation. For example, "Why should I read silently, you're not!" Be a good role model, 100% of the time!

Tactic: Deliver Specific Praise

When delivering reinforcement to groups or individual students it is important to use specific names and cite the behavior(s) you are reinforcing. Using this tactic teaches students what behaviors are appropriate and what will gain your attention. For example, "Jim, Bob, and Marti, thanks for working cooperatively and quietly. I appreciate that." Or, "Judy, Trish, and Rick, thanks for following rule number one—Work Cooperatively and Quietly." In both examples, students are recognized for their work habits and appropriate behavior. The reinforcement has been stated in a specific and positive way in order to recognize each student's effort and behavior.

Tactic: Use Schedules of Reinforcement

Research has shown that schedules of reinforcement are effective in increasing, decreasing, and/or maintaining behaviors. When initially introducing a new skill, rule, or desired behavior it is important to deliver specific reinforcement to students immediately following the attempt or performance of the desired behavior. This could simply be, "Kathleen, great job on that algebra problem." Once the desired skill or behavior has been acquired or established, gradually reduce the amount and number of times you deliver recognition to the student to a schedule of variable reinforcement. Variable schedules of reinforcement are the most powerful in maintaining and/or increasing or decreasing a target behavior. A schedule of variable reinforcement means that reinforcement is specifically given to students at times that are unpredictable. Reinforcement can occur after the passage of, for example, a few minutes or the number of times the behavior occurs (e.g., The second time Ron raises his hand he is reinforced; the next reinforcing statement is delivered after four hand raises). In either case there is no set pattern. Students continue to work and maintain high levels of appropriate behavior because they are unaware of when or what kinds of behavior will elicit specific praise or incentives from the teacher. For example, observe people playing slot machines, or listen to stories about them. This is a clas-

sic example of variable reinforcement. One never knows when the jackpot will come. It could be this quarter or the next or the next. The suspense of that wonderment keeps folks playing, waiting to hear the thunder of money pouring out of the machine.

Communicate Consequences of Behavior

It is not the magnitude of the consequence, but the consistent delivery of it, that impacts behavior. What happens after a student behaves appropriately or inappropriately has a direct impact on future behavior. The consistent presentation and delivery of a consequence for inappropriate behaviors increases the likelihood that the target behavior will not continue. These consequences must be undesirable to the student. If they are not, they serve little purpose, as when a child is grounded to his/her room where there is a phone, TV and VCR, radio, or other entertainment. Effective teachers set incentives and contingencies for both appropriate and inappropriate behaviors, respectively. Too often students are not reinforced for rule compliance, even after they do exactly what they are told. In fact, research shows that 85% of the time students complied to requests, they were not reinforced. Be consistent and deliver incentives and consequences for appropriate and inappropriate behaviors.

Tactic: Establish Hierarchy of Incentives and Consequences

A good discipline plan incorporates a hierarchy of consequences for appropriate and inappropriate behavior. This tactic establishes a stepwise list of consequences. Student participation is always an option, but should be monitored for appropriateness, making sure the punishment (or reward) fits the behavior. For example, consequential hierarchies could go like this:

- **Level One:** Verbal reminder
- **Level Two:** Five minute time out
- **Level Three:** Ten minute time out
- **Level Four:** Phone call to parent
- **Level Five:** Visit to the office

For positive hierarchies:

- **Level One:** Sit anywhere in the room
- **Level Two:** Five minutes of free time at the end of the lesson
- **Level Three:** Two-Minute Head Start—allowed to leave two minutes early, with a signed pass, for the next class
- **Level Four:** Lunch in the classroom with the teacher and/or guest of choice
- **Level Five:** Phone call home praising the student's efforts

Level Five could also be treated like a Free Space on a game board. Allow the student to pick an incentive; if a student has made it to Level Five, he/she has earned it! Consider offering a menu of Free Space incentives, including, for example, a free homework pass to be cashed in on any homework assignment of the student's choice.

The hierarchy of incentives can be tied to points needed to earn in order to obtain the level. For example, Level One requires at least 10 points to earn that privilege, Level Two requires 20 points, and so on. The points represent a system you have established in your classroom. For example, you may give two points for every on-time and completed homework assignment. Or, after five assignments, students will have had the opportunity to obtain the Level One privileges. Student behavior can also cause a loss of specific points. For example, Level One students could automatically lose eight points for violating a class rule. The point increases and decreases must be proportional to the hierarchies. For example, if a student only loses three points at Level One, it's no big deal, especially if 50 points can be earned in a day. However, a loss of 15 points puts more of a dent in the point bank. This tactic can be used with an individual, small group, or whole class of students.

Tactic: Provide Complete Consequences

It is important to develop a classroom discipline plan that includes both positive and negative consequences for rules. Planning for both ensures that both appropriate and inappropriate behaviors will be recognized and dealt with in an appropriate manner. By the simple nature of this tactic, students often self-monitor their behavior(s). Students may participate in formulating the consequences for both types of behaviors. However, it is important for you to have in mind what reasonable consequences are for both appropriate and inappropriate behaviors. Students can be overly generous or punitive. As in setting classroom rules, you will need to guide student participation and facilitate the development of reasonable consequences and behaviors. Here's how:

1 Together with your students identify desired behaviors—the "dos." Ask students, "What are the behaviors we want in our classroom that will make it a place to learn and feel safe? What does the ideal classroom look like?" Students will tell you what they would ultimately like to see or have as a part of their class community.

2 After these behaviors have been identified, generate a list of incentives to recognize these efforts.

3 Then do the same for "don'ts." These can be the opposites of "dos" or incorporate other behaviors. Ask students to list behaviors that are unwanted or intolerable.

4 Generate a list of consequences for each "don't."

5 You may have pages of items for "dos," incentives, "don'ts," and consequences. Together with the students prioritize all lists. Be sure your own items are on the lists.

6 Write the top three items on the respective sides of a "What If We Do? What If We Don't?" chart.

7 For "What If We Do?" list the "do" and underneath list the incentive.

8 For "What If We Don't?" list the "don'ts" and underneath list the consequences.

9 Write your "do" and "don't" statements to include a criteria, almost as an objective. For example, "We will all be on time for class for at least five consecutive days." By setting this criteria students know what they need to work toward and achieve to earn the incentive. Likewise for the "don'ts": "Name calling will not be tolerated or permitted at any time."

10 Finally, at the bottom of the chart provide three summary statements that capture the "do" statements. For example:

- We are working toward a cooperative environment.

- We are working toward a safe and open class community.

- We believe we are all special in our own unique way.

- We are working toward a productive learning environment.

It is important that all students understand what each statement means. Each student should be able to articulate or demonstrate what each one means.

caution: Some students may not buy into the chart and set out to sabotage the class goals. These students have their own "What If I Do? What If I Don't?" chart or use an alternate tactic. They are not participants in the class chart and therefore cannot sabotage group efforts. Be careful not to keep these students in their own group forever. Find ways to work the student back into the group process.

Variation 1
"What If We Do? What If We Don't?"

The steps above remain the same. The variation is in the delivery of the "dos" and "don'ts" incentives and consequences. With the "dos" and "don'ts" established, you may find that different students require different types of incentives and consequences. For these students feel free to tailor incentives and consequences. Be sure to get student input. What you may feel is incentive, the student may not.

Variation 2
"What If I Do? What If I Don't?"

Follow the same steps above with an individual student or small group of students.

Finally, you may find this chart useful in backing up the rules you have set prior to using this tactic. In fact, you may want to purposefully guide students to create a chart that reinforces the classroom rules.

Once completed, the chart is clearly posted near the classroom rules. Students now have two visual cues of class expectations and know what to expect if they "do" or if they "don't."

Adapted from: Rhode, G., Jenson, W., & Reavis, K. (1993).

Tactic: Wheel of Reinforcers

This is a fun tactic that can be used with an individual, a whole class, or a group of students. In any case, a menu of reinforcers of 5-10 items are identified and placed on a spinner. However, the spinner sections are not uniform. The sections vary in sizes from a line to a third of the circle. Anything goes.

Procedure:

1 Together with students generate a menu of incentives.

2 Have students, by consensus, prioritize them from most to least desirable.

3 Starting with the item deemed most desirable, write one in each section of the spinner, starting with the narrowest section and progressing to the widest (e.g., The most desired incentive is placed in the narrowest section. See Figure 23.).

4 When students have earned the opportunity to be recognized for appropriate behaviors, select a student to spin the spinner.

5 Selecting students to spin can be done at random (e.g., pulled from a hat) by class vote, or by teacher choice. The chosen student spins the spinner. Where the needle lands is the incentive of the moment.

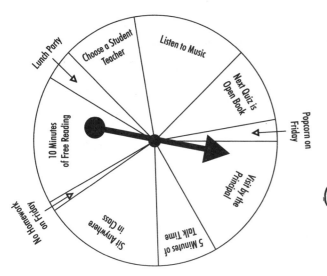

Figure 23

Remember, all reinforcers reach a point of satiation. That is, they no longer are novel or motivating to the students. Effort and excitement begins to wane signaling a time for change. Keep a watchful eye out and be ready to replace old incentives with new ones.

The key to the success of the spinner is the desirability of the incentives. Be sure students identify them, while you moderate the reality of use. For example, one student wrote $100 for his top priority, another wrote sleep

in late every day. You know the routine—negotiate and help students identify classroom-based incentives or those that parents/guardians can deliver.

Variation

A quick way to plan for the ever-changing reinforcement menu is to create a color-coded or patterned spinner. The sections in the spinner are still varied, however, the menu of items is placed on a color-coded list or patterned list that corresponds with the spinner sections. Laminate the spinners. When the incentives need to be altered, simply wipe off the menu and sections and fill with new ones. This tactic is effective and motivating for all age groups, including adults!

Tactic: Wheel of Aversives

This tactic is the same as above except instead of a menu of reinforcers, students develop a list of consequences for rule infractions. The consequences are prioritized as above and placed in the spinner sections. Not all students will willingly prioritize consequences. You must have a feeling for what consequences will have the greatest impact on behavior. For this tactic, the consequence having the greatest impact goes in the widest section and the lesser consequence in the narrower sections. This tends to be a more negative than positive approach to addressing behavior. And, you do not want to use this with chronic behavior problems. This tactic is intended to keep students aware of their behavior and consequences attached to them. Nonetheless, it has been used successfully where consequences for inappropriate behavior are common and the cause of lost instruction time. It is useful where rule infractions and the delivery of consequences often spark coercive arguments. In these situations, using the spinner takes the delivery of a negative consequence away from the teacher and places it with the spinner. Again, this tactic can be used for an individual, whole class, or a group of students.

Tactic: You Get What You Flip

This tactic is easy and effortless to use. Simply take ten index cards and number them 1-10. Write the numbers largely in the middle of the card. Make two or three hole punches across the top of the cards. Insert loose ring binders into each hole. Display the card flip chart where all can see it and where it is easily accessible during the teaching of a lesson. Start with the number 10 showing (see Figure 24). This connotes how many minutes the students have as "visit time" at the end of the class. At any time during the lesson when a student engages in a behavior that is distracting to others, himself or herself, etc., walk to the cards and flip to card 9. This signals to the students that someone is not on task (if it hasn't been announced) and shows them the total number of minutes left. Similarly, minutes may be earned back at any time during the lesson. Tell students that self-correcting and monitoring behavior count. You can also add additional minute cards to the deck. Card 11 could be bright fuchsia and mean the student's behavior and effort have been so wonderful and exemplary that they have earned a bonus minute. Be sure to

use specific praise and feedback statements to students for their behavior and as the basis for flipping the card.

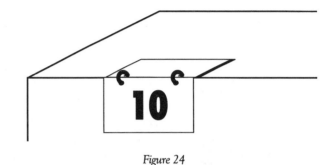

Figure 24

Tactics: Use Parents as Partners

Effective teachers keep parents informed of classroom procedures and expectations. Research has repeatedly shown that student achievement is strongly correlated with home support. That is, the more parents/guardians are involved in their students' learning, the better the overall schooling experience. Effective teachers make every attempt to involve parents/guardians as partners in their child's schooling. Starting with classroom expectations, parents/guardians should be informed about the rules and consequences for both appropriate and inappropriate behavior. There are many ways to do this. A home note system is one that has proven successful in the past. With home notes, teachers target specific behaviors, periodically assess progress toward them, and send notes home for signatures reflecting parents' recognition of improvements in school behavior.

Tactic: Use Positive Practice Overcorrection

Here is a tactic that demonstrates that the proof is in the practice. Upon breaking a rule or performing an inappropriate behavior, the student is provided an opportunity to either correct or practice the misbehavior many, many times. So many times, in fact, that the likelihood of the student engaging in the misbehavior again will probably not occur for a while. One teacher used this behavior for an elementary student who insisted on sliding down a banister. The student, under supervision by the teacher, performed the behavior numerous times. Eventually the student asked if he could stop. Needless to say, he did not slide down the banister (at least in the presence of an adult) for a long time. Another teacher used this with some high school students who defaced a wall of the hall. In this case, the students were given soap and buckets of water and were required to wash the graffitied wall and the rest of the walls in the corridor. Positive practice overcorrection is most effective with behaviors, or results of the behaviors, that can be practiced or restored to their original or correct format. For example, one parent used this positive practice overcorrection with a child who insisted on slamming her bedroom door every time she tantrumed. The parent, after modeling the appropriate door-closing behavior, supervised the daughter while she opened and closed the door 100 times. The door slamming behavior ceased.

caution: Be very sure that you don't overdo overcorrection. Be sensible and safe. Check it out with a colleague if you are unsure of how much is enough.

strategy

Handle Disruptions Efficiently

There are many reasons for classroom disruptions. Some behavior disruptions are correlated with boredom or things that are said to students. Both of these are antecedents to behaviors that can be avoided. Both boredom and what you say to students are alterable. Effective teachers reduce disruptive behaviors by keeping students actively engaged in highly motivating lessons and by their method of communication and relations with students. When classroom behaviors do erupt, effective teachers deal swiftly and efficiently to defuse and restabilize the situation. Tactics for defusing can be as unobtrusive as a raised eyebrow, closing the space between you and the student, a hand on a shoulder, and/or direct verbal commands or requests. Know your students and know what works best for them.

Tactic: Keep It Short and Simple (KISS)

Ororverbalizing about a disruptive situation, mild or severe, tends to call attention to the problem and as a result may reinforce the behavior. This is contrary to the desired outcome—eliminating it altogether. Verbalizations during an act of disruptive behavior should serve a purpose, namely to diffuse the situation by offering alternative solutions or consequences. For example, "Rose, you can do the assignment now, during lunch, or after school." You've given Rose alternatives and the power to decide her consequences. Avoid issuing ultimatums to a student. Doing this places you at the center of a potential power struggle in which you will inevitably lose. The majority of time that a student engages an adult in a coercive debate, the student wins. Sometimes when emotions are running high, things are said that cannot be followed through on by those who say them. "Brian if you don't stop it now, I will see that you are banned from every pep rally for the rest of your school days." Some teachers feel it is necessary to process or explore the underlying reasons that triggered the misbehavior. Often this is better left to a counselor or done after a consequence has been delivered. Attempting to "moralize" or have the student identify the "whys" of his/her behavior is in and of itself an ineffective consequence for misbehavior.

Tactic: Use a Warning System

Once rules and contingencies for appropriate and inappropriate behavior have been developed and taught, effective teachers develop a warning system to use should behaviors escalate (which can happen at any given time). For these times it is important to develop and communicate a verbal warning system for students whose behaviors become disruptive. As always, requests are to be delivered firmly and efficiently. A direct request using the student's name is important. For example, "Jim, please stop whining." Wait at least ten seconds to see if Jim complies. If Jim continues to whine and disrupt classroom procedures, a second statement should be delivered such as, "Jim, you have one warning, please stop whining now." This request is succinct and direct. Jim knows that

the next time he is spoken to a preplanned consequence will be delivered. And, of course, these consequences have been communicated to the students, and they know what to expect. As with all reinforcement procedures, the consequence to be delivered must be aversive enough to the student that he/she will stop the disruptive behavior and reengage in the learning process. However, if the consequence is not sufficiently aversive to the student, it is quite likely that the warning procedure will not work. Other teachers have used "three checks and you're out." When disruptive behavior is displayed the teacher writes the student's name on the board (strike 1). If the student needs another reminder, a check is placed by his/her name. If a second check is placed after the student's name, he/she is officially "out." The "out" will need to be preplanned. It can range from removal from a class activity, to a time out from class. The "out" can be individually tailored or designed for a class or group of students.

Tactic: Defer Disruptive Behaviors Proactively

Minor disruptive behaviors often can be effectively deferred if "caught" early enough. Unobtrusive techniques such as eye contact, proximity control (closing the space between you and the student), or signals such as a head nod, hand gesture, or pointing can be used. In using any of the above techniques, you must decide whether the attention will reinforce a student's behavior rather than eliminate it. Each student may respond differently. Effective teachers assess which techniques are most effective with each student and use them accordingly. The goal is to defer or stop a potential chain of events or behaviors from starting. Effective teachers speak individually with students to develop personal signals. Take David for example. David was a student who would start a chain of noncompliance with relatively mild behaviors such as ignoring a request. When a request was restated, David would shuffle books and papers, drop his pen, or put his head down on his desk. When given a warning statement with the request repeated, David would launch into arguing behavior and accuse the teacher of singling him out and "picking on him." At that point, David was beyond "the point of no return." Reeling David back in was a difficult and arduous task. Meanwhile, other students lost instructional time and David was given center stage. During his fits of anger David would blame his behavior on his parents and family situation and the cool heartedness of the teacher. "Why is everyone trying to run my life?" he would complain. David was a perfect candidate for this tactic. During a private conference, David and his teacher established some limits and interventions to allow him the opportunity to make choices to "control" his behavior. They agreed on a system where David was responsible for telling the teacher when he was "having a bad day." They developed a personal signal that David could use to give the teacher a sign he was about "to loose it" and needed to "take five." Taking five meant David could go get a drink of water or grab a hall pass, clear his head, and return to class. He was solely responsible for his behavior, and therefore no excuses for disruptive behavior were acceptable. This signal system

worked both ways. When the teacher observed David becoming agitated, she would give David "the signal," and he would check his behavior and decide if he needed to "take five." Proactively planning to defer disruptive behaviors takes time and thought. Students will assist you in developing a system that will work for them. Ask them.

Tactic: Help Students Be Successful

Regardless of rules, warning systems, and proactive management, confrontations will occasionally occur. Most often confrontations can be avoided by offering choices, not ultimatums. If a student does not respond to a rule check or a warning system and you deliver a preplanned consequence, the student may refuse to accept it or respond to it. For example, if a student refuses to move his/her seat, the following choices can be offered:

> *Bob, you have chosen not to move your seat as directly requested. Here are your choices:*
>
> *One, you can stop talking, finish your assignment, and earn five minutes of free time at the end of class, or*
>
> *Two, you can finish your assignment when you feel like it and spend 20 minutes of lunch with me, or*

Three, you can continue to talk as we walk to the office to call your parent/guardian and discuss another option with them. (Make certain the parents are accessible and there is a phone on the premises.)

Choices are delivered in a calm, matter-of-fact tone. A wait period of 10-15 seconds is used after the final choice is given. During this time you should continue working with other students who are engaged in positive behavior and ignore the student while he/she is making a choice. The looming confrontation is avoided, and other students remain engaged in the learning process. If after 10-15 seconds the student has not reengaged in the requested behavior, ask for his/her decision. Follow up as per the student's choice. The simple act of giving students choices defers many power struggles and negative reactions students may have to a request from an "authority figure."

Tactic: Teach Students to Self-Monitor Disruptions

Disruptions can be managed effectively by teaching students to monitor their occurrence. The mere act of counting a behavior reduces the frequency of their occurrence. There are many ways to teach student to self-monitor their behavior.

1 Define/describe the target behavior in observable and measurable terms with the student.

Make certain you and the student can see it and count it.

2 Write the behavior across the top of an index card and tape it on the student's desk or folder. The student should make a tally mark on the card each time the inappropriate behavior occurs.

3 Be sure the student knows exactly what behavior you are monitoring and counting. Make sure the student can accurately perform the behavior. Model the appropriate behavior.

4 It is not uncommon for the student to be unaware of how often the target behavior actually occurs. Therefore, initially, both you and the student should tally the number of times the inappropriate behavior occurs.

5 At the end of a designated period of time, compare your tallies or total number of counted behaviors. Note discrepancies and observations.

6 The goal is to fade out your own counting and rely solely on the student's count.

7 Keep track of the tallies. Teach students to set goals for reducing inappropriate behavior or increasing appropriate behavior.

8 Consider incentives that may be needed to motivate the student toward goal attainment. Do not leave well enough alone. Recognize and reinforce small successful approximations of behavior toward the goal.

9 Teach students how to draw their own personal aim lines. (See Planning: How to Teach; Use Data to Plan Subsequent Instruction.)

note: Self-monitoring procedures can be done individually or as a group. A group procedure indicates that the class is monitoring the occurence of a behavior (e.g., number of talk-outs, or number of homework assignments handed in).

Tactic: Use Planned Ignoring

Sometimes it is effective to publicly ignore minor disruptions rather than attend to them. Often effective teachers use planned ignoring to avoid reinforcing or giving attention to a student. For example, sometimes students will swear under their breath and it is audible to the teacher. Depending on the classroom rules and teacher tolerance, ignoring this behavior may be sufficient enough to keep it from reoccurring, especially if the student is doing it for effect. Sometimes students "slip," and they mutter things under their breath. In these cases a mere "look 'em in the eyes" lets them know you heard and do not want to hear it again. Sometimes these students have their hand over their mouth before you even respond, as though to keep anything else from falling out of their mouth. In these cases planned ignoring is most effective. Yet other times a student may slam a book closed in anger. You can choose to ignore the behavior and continue teaching, reinforcing other students

along the way, without missing a beat. It is best to use this tactic for those behaviors that are not likely to escalate if ignored. Deciding when to ignore some behaviors allows the flow of instruction to continue. Know which behaviors can be ignored without threat of escalation. You know your tolerance level and which behaviors you can comfortably ignore and those you cannot.

Tactic: Teach Students to Use Planned Ignoring

Often students engage in behaviors that annoy other classmates. In these cases it is extremely helpful to teach students about situations that warrant the use of planned ignoring. These may be situations that occur in the lunchroom, hallway, or classroom. If the need for planned ignoring is directed at a particular individual or group, the reason for using and practicing the technique is best done in the absence of those individuals. Effective teachers point out the benefits of using the tactic, both for individuals and classes of students. It is important that the teacher frame the technique as a positive one to help both the ignorer and the ignoree. For example, "We need to help Michael refrain from saying, 'I hate my mother. I'm going to stab her in the head.' We can help him by ignoring these outbursts and keep working. We can also help him by telling him 'nice job' after he gives an answer without an outburst." (Avoid overdoing it! Michael is a bright kid and he'll figure out something is going on.) In this way, students are taught a skill they can generalize to other settings, are able to continue assignments, and can assist Michael and themselves get to a desired goal—learning.

Teach Students to Manage Their Own Behavior

One of the many goals of educating students is to teach them how to self-manage their behavior. Teaching them to be the agent of change or control of their own behavior is a tool that will be useful throughout their lives. Instruction in this area is made particularly easy when students are motivated to change and when keeping track and managing their behavior is reinforced by the social environment. Once acquired, self-management skills can be taught under a variety of conditions and situations, thereby increasing the chance of their use in generalized settings. When students gain control of their behavior and maintain an awareness of what triggers it, they are more likely to use this knowledge across settings, time, and activities. Self-management strategies are very powerful techniques that can be applied across age groups for both academic and nonacademic behaviors.

Tactic: Play the Good Behavior Game

This tactic can be adapted to meet any participatory need in the classroom. Some teachers choose not to refer to this tactic as a game because it connotes a task that is for fun instead of for real. It is actually both. However, the word "game" means different things to different people. You decide the best way it will work for you. Here's how:

1 Divide class into two teams—be sure they are balanced for skill and ability. Do not put all the behavior management problems on one team and/or the more skillful students on the other.

2 Identify one or two target behaviors to work on.

3 Decide on the criteria or the behavior you expect the students to display in the classroom. Post it and discuss it with the class so that all students understand what is expected of them and what they need to do to gain or loose points in the game.

4 As a class, students vote on a menu of reinforcers they wish to earn for their "good behavior" (target behavior[s] displayed). This menu can be set for the week, day, or any other combination that suits your situation. When the students meet the set criteria, a preplanned incentive is delivered. Keep in mind that the teacher can either pick one reward from the menu, pick a student's name out of a hat to choose the class reward, or put all items on the reward menu in a hat and pick one. Remember, not all students or classes need a tangible reward. Just "winning the game" is often satisfaction enough. Some teachers post the team color or name on the "top of the mountain." The goal is to conquer the mountain through good behavior. This visual motivates students to work toward getting their team to the top of the mountain. Other teachers have winning team names announced over the Public Announcement (PA) System. The options are endless.

5 At the end of the designated time (either a class period or a day), points for each team are tallied. If you are doing this class by class, the team with the most points "wins." Or if you are doing this by a weekly tally, the points are written in a weekly tally sheet.

Variation 1

For academic accountability use the following procedure:

1 In private, randomly select the names of two students whose classwork or homework will be graded.

important: You need to make sure the students have the skills and prior knowledge to actually complete the work. And, you need to collect all students' work to avoid potential scapegoating of the selected students. For example, if Bob and Jim are publicly selected and neither have the skill to do the work, nor do they have their work completed, then the chance of peer scapegoating and badgering is very high. In essence, Bob and Jim have taken away the class' opportunity to gain points.

2 Set a criteria of acceptable performance (CAP) for the assignment, perhaps 80%.

3 After selecting the target students, separately correct their work and average their performance. Compare it against the criteria.

4 If their collective performance matches or exceeds the CAP (80%), deliver points or reinforcement to the entire class. Never tell the class whose work was graded, unless, of course, there is a grand opportunity to let students shine. But if you do it once students will ask mercilessly, "Whose work was it this time, 'Teach'?"

Variation 2

For this option, two students from each side are chosen. And, if both sets of students meet CAP, their performance earns their team points.

Using this tactic results in an increase in the completion rate of class and homework assignments, and the rate is maintained at high levels due to the random selection of students.

Things to consider in using this tactic:

- **How do I set the CAP for both behavior and academic work?** Make sure all students have the skill and prior knowledge to complete the tasks you assign. For example, can the students sit in their seats for 45 minutes? Are all students capable of raising their hand before speaking? Do all students have the prior knowledge and skill to write an essay on the events leading to the outbreak of the Civil War? Only you know what your students are capable of doing. Do not set students up for unintended failure or peer pressure. Evaluate and plan this tactic thoroughly and the benefits will abound.

- **What schedule of reinforcement should I use?** Consider how often you will award team points. By class? By day? By week? What will you do with the points?

- **What's the focus, and will it change?** Consider when you will alter the target behavior. By day? By week? By month? When specified progress is made? Use student progress data to make these decisions.

Tactic: Check by Chimes

This technique is used often and successfully with all ages and types of target behaviors. Using a tape recorder, record at random intervals chimes or beeps. Have students chart or mark whether they were engaged in learning when they hear the tone. A simple yes/no checklist works well. Some teachers prefer to use a kitchen timer set at random time intervals. Each time it rings, students chart their behavior. Teaching students to quietly ask themselves, "Am I doing what I am supposed to be doing?" is an effective way to frame the idea of self-monitoring engaged learning.

Tactic: Use Nag Tapes

A variation of Check by Chimes is using Nag Tapes. This tactic can be more personalized to students and less obtrusive to others in the classroom. Using a personal headset, students listen to a prepared tape of tones or talk. Here a significant others' voice (teacher, principal, parent, guardian, friend) delivers gentle reminders to stay on task (e.g., "Are you working? Check yourself—if you are working, nice job. If you are not, get back to your task."). For some students hearing a parent's voice is not only soothing but reinforcing. For others someone else's voice works better. It is a nice idea to ask the student to suggest who he/she would like to be the voice on the tape. Some students have elected to be their own checker. Older students have used voice impersonations to motivate their checking. The sky is the limit. Fondly called Nag Tapes, they truly are a winning tactic for students.

Tactic: Use Buddy Systems

Students can be taught to use a "buddy system" to manage their behavior. Students are organized into teacher-selected buddy pairs or dyads. Buddy pairs are then instructed about what kinds of behaviors to look for and praise or point out (POPO). These behaviors can be specific to a lesson, similar to those posted on the expectation chart, or just about anything. Tell buddies they are not only responsible for their behavior but the monitoring of their buddy. Some teachers use this technique by setting a timer and designating Buddy A or B as the "checker." At the tone, Buddy A praises or points out Buddy B's behavior. Of course, students need to be taught how to recognize and praise and point out specific behaviors.

Tactic: Collect, Chart, and Chat

This tactic can be done in conjunction with the buddy system or alone. The purpose of this tactic is to teach students to monitor their behavior, record it, and be prepared to conduct a 60-second conference to discuss it. This tactic allows the students to monitor and devise ways to increase behavior (e.g., more participation in classroom discussion, hand raising, etc.) or reduce or remediate behavior (e.g., talk outs, out of seat). Target behaviors are recorded on an index card and given to the student. The teacher (or buddy) holds a similar card. At designated times or throughout the lesson, the student, teacher, and/or buddy record behaviors by tally marks. At the end of the class or at specified times, the tallies are totaled and charted, and the student gets ready for a 60-second conference with his/her buddy or teacher. These conferences should initially be held immediately after the lesson to provide feedback and opportunities to practice. Later they can be held throughout the day. For example, after lunch a teacher can chart and chat with a student regarding period 2.

Tactic: Have Students Provide Their Own Feedback

Present students with data about their performance in chart or graphic format. Make sure that improvements or regressions are apparent. Rather than telling the students what the graph means, ask the students to interpret it. Charts or graphs that do not show strong trend lines provide an opportunity for teacher-student planning for what needs to be focused on to facilitate growth. Give verbal prompts to the student, who should then finish statements such as, "I showed improvement in ...," or "I need to focus in/on ..., by doing ...." This tactic can be used for both academic and behavior performances.

principle

Use Time Productively

The concept of "time on task" has driven effective instruction for some time. Grounded in the idea that students need ample opportunities to respond to academic and other classroom tasks, time management strategies have become central concerns for effective teachers. Establishing routines and procedures, organizing the physical classroom space, giving task directions, making transitions between work sessions brief, allocating time to academic activities, and maintaining a strong academic focus are strategies effective teachers demonstrate when they use time productively.

strategy

Establish Routines and Procedures

Effective teachers set up and frequently communicate routines, procedures, and expectations for classroom behavior. While these may vary class to class, routines and procedures are keys to managing an effective and efficient classroom. Keeping student attention, regulating participation, and providing support and feedback are important components of effective classrooms. Effective teachers have procedures to minimize distractions (e.g., talking out of turn, entering the classroom after the start of the lesson) and manage behaviors (e.g., error correction procedures, transitions) for both large and small group presentations and independent practice. While tactics for establishing classroom routines and procedures seem straightforward, they are often the most overlooked.

Tactic: Use Rules, Routines, and Resources

Effective teachers plan and teach the rules and routines for their classrooms. Students often see several teachers every day, each with their own set of requirements and procedures. Here is a tactic to help students keep classroom demands straight. Provide students with a sheet of typical questions they might ask, and give them the answers according to your classroom. One teacher put together a "Standard Operating Procedures" bulletin board and gave students personal copies of the procedures for their notebooks.

For example, "What do I do if I arrive at class and realize I have forgotten my notebook?" or "What happens if my homework isn't done?" "How do I reenter the room when a lesson is going on?" For younger students telling the routine for lunch line up or bathroom breaks can proactively manage potential confusion and misbehavior. Providing this information to students on the first day of class and reviewing as needed allows students to be aware of classroom rules, routines, and procedures for your class and saves you time and energy in the long run.

Tactic: Teach Transitions

Student achievement in school is linked to the amount of time spent actively engaged in learning tasks. Often much learning time is lost during transition times and behavior problems occur. Transitions between activities can range from several minutes to 20 minutes. Since the typical classroom may have several transitions per class period or day, effective teachers teach students what is expected during transition times.

For example, take the typical elementary school class. It may have 5-10 transitions per day. If the class completes an average of 10 transitions a day at approximately 8 minutes each, that is a loss of approximately 80 minutes of instructional time, or 20% of the school day. That adds up to an entire day per week of potential academic activity lost to transition time! Here's how to better plan for transition:

Transition time needs to be quick and quiet. There are four basic rules for transition:

1 Move quickly and quietly.

2 Put your materials away and get what you need for the next class/activity.

3 Carry your chairs to your group and/or move your desks quietly.

4 Keep your hands and feet to yourself.

Effective teachers use direct instruction to demonstrate, practice, and perform the transition periods. Students are given the opportunity to model examples and nonexamples of transition. It is important to actively reinforce students for correctly following the steps. For example, "Bob, nice job—you did not talk during transition time and you did a great job quietly moving your chair to your cooperative learning group!" Once students are proficient with the steps, teachers can simply give the directions for the next activity and follow it by saying, "OK, it is time to transition. Ready, go." Some teachers time and record the transition time and report to the students how long it took them to move. Others set a timer and say, "You have 60 seconds to transition." The bottom line is that students will respond when they know exactly what they are to do, how they are to do it, and within what time frame.

Adapted from: Paine, S. et. al. (1983).

Tactic: Vary Transition Activities

Some students transition faster than others, others enter the room from another class, or sometimes the teacher is conferring with another teacher. These are times when transition can be enhanced by providing sponge activities that engage students while waiting for a lesson or class to start. Transition activities can also provide students a planned opportunity to take a mental stretch break. After students have engaged in a lesson requiring intense concentration, break it up with a transition activity. Effective teachers plan for these times and provide students with engaging tasks that meaningfully soak up the wait time. Some activities to try are noodle doodles, palindromes, or visual thinking activities. These are fun activities that can be done individually or in small groups.

* Noodle doodles are simple words, phrases, or drawings that when creatively solved translate into clichés or sayings. For example, write EVELATOR on the board and encourage students to solve the puzzle. (What does this Noodle doodle represent? Answer: elevator out of order). Noodle doodles should take into consideration the age and skill level of the students.

* Palindromes are words, phrases, sentences, or numbers that are the same written forward or backward. For example, what is a five letter word for an Eskimo's canoe? (kayak). A number palindrome can be obtained by adding any two numbers together in a specific pattern. It goes

like this: Add the numbers. If the answer is a palindrome, stop. If not, reverse the answer and add again. Try it for:

23 + 45 = ??.

(23+45=69, 69+96=165, 165+561=726, 726+627=1353, 1353+3531=4884)

- Visual thinking activities are those that stimulate students to problem-solve visual puzzles. For example, how many squares are in a square of squares?

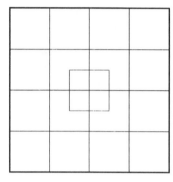

Figure 25

Noodle doodles, palindromes, and visual thinking activities provide students with the opportunity to have fun while they cooperatively collaborate and problem-solve. Have your students make some up and share them with the class during sponge time.

Tactic: Use "Sure I Can" Work

Students do not all learn or complete assignments at the same time. Instead of students sitting idle with down time on their hands, effective teachers provide them with "Sure I Can" folders. This takes planning on the part of the teacher, but the results are worth it! Effective teachers assemble assignments or tasks that students are automatic and proficient at and that can be done without teacher assistance or instruction. Folders can contain worksheets, page and item numbers of text books, or cooperative activities that can be completed with other students who are finished early or also waiting for assistance. Individual student folders can be kept at a designated spot in the room or in a student's desk.

"Sure I Can" work provides meaningful practice related to current or recently taught material or problem-solving skills. "Sure I Can" folders are *not* meant to provide busy work or additional work to those students who finish assignments early. If students view them as such, they will quickly loose the motivation to work efficiently because when they finish they are rewarded with more work. "Sure I Can" folders should contain fun, creative activities that reinforce skills. For instance, try having your students create vanity license plates. Vanity license plates are those you see around that have a catchy riddle or message portrayed in eight digits/letters or less. Have students create them for topics or people recently studied. For example, tell students to create a vanity license plate for a soldier of WWI (e.g., BIG WON), or one that represents their opinion of nuclear power plants (NO

90

NUKES). Sound easy? Try it. Vanity license plates push students to engage in the highest form of thinking and learning. They must synthesize their knowledge about a topic, then apply it to create the plate.

Tactic: Use "Help! I Need Assistance"

Teaching is tough work. In classrooms of 25-35 students the diversity of skill development and behaviors is vast. Since there is usually only one teacher (and/or paraprofessional) in a class, tactics that allow for many students to be provided with opportunities for assistance are needed. This tactic is easy and used during times of independent practice or group work. Each desk or group is given a three-sided card to be taped on a desk. On one side of the card is written, "Looking Good! Keep on Working!" On the other side is written, "I need assistance," or "SOS." The signs are taped to the desk in a way that allows them to be flipped up when assistance is needed. While the student or groups of students are working, the sign is left hanging off the front of the desk, indicating no help is needed. When assistance is needed the sign is flipped up on the desk. The message facing the student(s) is, "Looking Good! Keep on Working!" The message facing the teacher is, "Help! I Need Assistance." (This can be adapted to "We" if used for group work.)

Directions for making signs:

1 Refer to Figures 26 and 27. Using tag board approximately 12 inches wide (it's sturdier than paper), fold it evenly into two 4-inch sections.

2 Then fold two 2-inch sections.

3 Print "Looking Good! Keep on Working!" on one of the 4-inch sections.

4 On the other 4-inch section, write "SOS" or "Help! I Need Assistance" (substitute "We" if for a group).

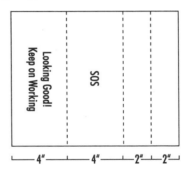

Figure 26

5 If possible, laminate the board.

6 Fold the board into a triangular shape that has two 4-inch sides and a 2-inch base.

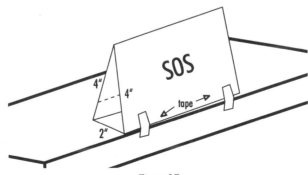

Figure 27

7 Fold the remaining 2-inch strip up inside the triangle, and tape or staple the bottom of the triangle together.

8 Tape the sign along the bottom edge of "Help! I Need Assistance" or "SOS" to the front edge of the desk. This enables the card to be flipped up or down easily.

Once in place on the students' desks, you are ready to implement the tactic. By displaying "Help! I Need Assistance," the teacher is quietly cued that she needs to check in with a student. The student keeps working by moving to the next item of the assignment or his/her "Sure I Can" folder. This tactic encourages ongoing active engagement in learning instead of down time waiting for teacher assistance.

Adapted from: Paine, S. et. al. (1983).

Tactic: Develop a Consistent Daily Schedule

Develop a class period or daily class schedule. The predictability of a schedule or class format helps create anticipation for the class. One teacher listed his class format as follows:

Daily lesson format:

1 We will review what was learned yesterday.

2 We will correct homework and answer any questions about it.

3 Homework papers will be collected.

4 We will begin the day's lesson.

- I model what we are learning/doing
- You show me you know what we are learning/doing.
- We practice together.
- Prove it! You show what you know.

5 We review the lesson.

6 Dismissal.

Often schedules are disrupted by assemblies, emergencies, and late or canceled school days. It is important to tell students that under these conditions there may be an alternate daily schedule that will be discussed prior to the start of the class. Changes in schedule often create confused reactions from students. Accept these and calmly reexplain the reason for the altered schedule. The key is to proactively plan for daily routines and minor interruptions in order to better prepare students for active engagement of learning routines.

Tactic: Give Specific Task Directions

Teaching students to follow directions is a worthy investment of time. While students are expected to follow directions, they are not always equipped with the skills to do so. They often lack in the skills to recognize the need to ask clarification questions. Provide practice by delivering specific directions and allowing students to respond. Here's one idea:

1 Give a series of three or four directions.

2 Ask students to repeat the directions, using oral responding.

3 Then ask a student to repeat the first step.

4 Continue to choose different students to repeat or retell the direction in the correct sequence they should occur.

Variation 1

After selecting the first student to retell the direction, tell that student to pick the next student to retell the next direction, and so on. For example, Joe tells the first step and chooses Mary to recite the second direction. Mary picks Robert to tell the next direction, and so on.

Variation 2

After you are sure students know the sequence of directions and what it is they are to do, randomly ask for the directions out of order. "Paul, what's the second thing we do?" "Kate, what's the last thing we do?"

Use fast-paced questioning to keep students on their toes. Be careful not to frustrate those that process or think more slowly.

Using the specific task directions tactic provides students the opportunity to hear the directions repeated several times, which results in a better chance of following them correctly.

Variation 3

Give students Following Directions Activity Sheets. Use them to teach students the importance of reading all the directions before beginning a task.

Tactic: Follow Directions ... at Home!

Practicing a newly acquired skill or one that needs fluency or mastery work in a variety of settings provides additional opportunities to practice and facilitates generalization of skill. Have students generate a sequence of directions that can be followed at home. This may sound easier than it is. Challenge students to come up with a series of three, four, or even five directions. Be creative. Encourage them to set a time limit requirement for completion. For example, steps for setting the table, steps for making a bed, steps for making a sandwich, etc., all within a set time limit. Encourage family members to get into the act. Have one be the timekeeper. Have them switch roles and complete the directions while the student times them. Make performance comparisons. Who did better? Why?

Tactic: Self-Record to Improve Following Direction Skills

Self-recording is a procedure students can use to decide if they have followed directions in performing expected behaviors. Keeping records of their performance serves as a visual cue of how they are doing. It also provides a systematic way to evaluate following direction skills and plan for what is needed to improve performance or task completion. Although many students automatically know how to follow directions, task completion is increased and confusion is decreased when students are taught to follow directions and how to ask for clarification. Provide students with fun Following Directions sheets requiring them to repeatedly follow a simple set of directions. Or you may want to use the Following Directions sheets as probes and have students keep track of their progress and performance over a number of administrations of the same task. Teach students to generalize their skill at following directions to other class activities using the following self-monitoring questions: What am I supposed to be doing? Am I reading directions carefully? Do I understand them?

strategy

Organize Physical Space

The organization of physical classroom space can have a considerable effect on how students perform in the classroom. Effective teachers purposefully organize their classrooms. The location of student desks, teacher's desk, partitions, materials, and learning stations are key to an efficiently run classroom. Space orientation impacts the quality and desirability of interaction and exchange of information among students and teachers.

Tactic: Consider Student Needs

Student needs are an important factor to consider in arranging physical space in the classroom. For example, some students may need quiet working areas, others may need front row seating, and still others may need space free of movement or distractions. Effective teachers also consider the age and developmental needs of students when they prepare classrooms for instruction. For example, if two groups are working simultaneously, have them face in opposite directions or sit on opposite sides of the room and away from entranceways or windows. Some students work best using headphones, ear plugs, or within partitions to block out noise or distractions. Be aware that some students may feel uncomfortable working with these accommodations. They feel as though they "stick out." It is important to find a place in the room that is comfortable for them to engage in the independent learning tasks.

Tactic: Keep All Areas Visible

When organizing classroom space, arrange areas so that all spaces are easily viewed by you at all times. "Private" work spaces can be created by walling off a section of the classroom with bookshelves or partitions. Although some students will need "private" spaces to work, effective teachers know how important it is to keep these areas in full view, visible from other areas of the classroom. Students working in "private" spaces may need assistance, and you need to be able to see their signals for help. The ability to see all classroom areas at all times is critical for monitoring student behavior. It is a good idea to tell students the reasons behind the class set up. Often these explanations can curb any complaints the students may raise about always being within view of the teacher.

Tactic: Organize Classroom to Influence Learning

Things in any classroom influence the behavior of students. A sponge ball and basketball hoop says "play with me" to some students. To some students a carpeted area says "relax and read," and to others "come wrestle." Careful organization and communication of the purposes of these areas is important in ensuring that materials and classroom space are used as they are intended. Effective teachers set the stage for learning by arranging the classroom by recreational and work activities. The basketball hoop should be away from the learning areas and its use specified. However, one teacher successfully integrates its use by instigating "Hoops for Homework." Students are randomly chosen to shoot a basket. If they make it, no one has homework, or the amount is reduced. Of course, this activity has to be managed for scapegoating (when a student misses), but proves to be a fun incentive for all. Selective planning and use of classroom areas and materials helps establish positive classroom habits and facilitates student learning.

Tactic: Structure Classroom Environment to Increase Attention

During the 1960s, the practice of reducing external stimulation (e.g., bright colors, etc.) was taken to ex-

tremes, making classrooms dull, highly structured environments. However, moderate variations of this philosophy are very effective. For example, one teacher uses each wall in his classroom as an opportunity to post current and upcoming work. The "learning wall," located at the front of the room, contains material that is used to focus attention on current learning activities (past classroom notes, daily assignments, schedules, procedures). A second wall, the "performance wall," displays past work such as classroom charts used in lessons, awards earned, and other records of student progress. A third wall, the "future wall," shows information about upcoming units and activities. This type of organizer helps students see the classroom as a structured place with a purpose, namely, school work and performance.

strategy

Allocate Sufficient Time to Academic Activities

The time set aside for a learning activity is called allocated time. Engaged learning time is the active involvement of a student in a learning activity. Engaged learning time is a better predictor of achievement. Effective teachers systematically designate specific times for academic instruction and communicate the scheduled activities to their students. The typical school day is filled with activities that have a nonacademic focus. Transitions among lessons, sports assemblies, distributing and collecting material, arranging

managing

desks, and moving chairs are all activities that can take up precious learning time. Effective teachers plan for these nonacademic times by allocating time to academic instruction and sticking to the plan. However, while it is necessary to allocate time to instruction, it is not sufficient in providing students the quality instruction and active learning they need. That is, engaged learning time must take place during the allocated time for instruction. For example, it is not enough to allocate 40 minutes for social studies instruction. How often do you hear comments like, "I don't understand why the class did so poorly. I covered this material. They have social studies every day for 40 minutes!" Scheduling or allocating time for social studies and "covering" material is not the same as having students actively engaged in learning the material.

Tactic: Use Allocated Learning Time Effectively

Allocated Learning Time (ALT) is defined as the amount of time set aside for engaged student learning. Effective teachers understand the value of planning for ALT. Classroom daily schedules are created that take into account three basic components to ALT.

1 The percentage of the day or class period allocated for student learning should be about 70%.

2 The amount of time a student should be actively engaged in learning activities should be about 85% of the day or class period.

3 The rate of accuracy of students' work during the active engaged learning should be about 80%.

Use this quick and easy formula to check out your daily schedule:

Formula: Total amount of time in an instructional day x .7 = ALT needed

Example: Full-day class of six and one-half hours
6.5 hours in school day x .7 = 4.6 hours needed (or about 5 hours ALT)

Example: Class period of 45 minutes
45 minutes x .7 = 31.5 minutes (32 minutes ALT)

After determining the amount of ALT required for each day or class period, plan activities that will keep students actively engaged in the learning process for at least 85% of the time. Make sure you give lots of thought to students' levels of proficiency, prior knowledge, and types of knowledge they are using. Planning for these will allow you to provide learning that allows students to achieve the desired 80% accuracy rate. (See Figures 28 and 29 for sample schedules based on the ALT formula.)

It is important to take into account, among other things, set and variable activities and schedule changes, transitions, and attentiveness.

Adapted from: Rhode, G., Jenson, W., & Reavis, K. (1993).

Sample Period Schedule Based on ALT Formula		
Science Class 1:00 PM - 1:45 PM	The Schedule	The Tally
1:00 - 1:05	Get settled, take attendance	
1:07 - 1:15	Review material from yesterday	8 minutes
1:17 - 1:40	Teach lesson	23 minutes
	Guided practice	
	Independent practice (IP)	
1:43 - 1:46	Start homework (con't IP)	3 minutes
1:45 - 1:50	Daily review, wrap up, dismissal	
(Total 34 minutes ALT)		

Figure 28

Sample Daily Class Schedule Based on ALT Formula		
School Day 8:00 AM - 2:30 PM	The Schedule	Minutes
8:00 - 8:10	Attendance, lunch count, announcements	
8:13 - 8:30	Peer tutoring activity (Reading or Math)	17
8:35 - 9:15	Reading groups/independent practice and seatwork	40
9:15 - 9:30	Break time	
9:35 - 10:15	Math lesson/independent practice (Peer tutoring teams)	40
10:18 - 10:40	Language Arts/Spelling practice (classwide peer tutoring)	22
10:43 - 11:08	Writing	25
11:10 - 11:40	Lunch	
11:50 - 12:20	Social Studies	30
12:25 - 1:00	Specials (Art, Physical Education)	35
1:05 - 1:15	Break	
1:20 - 1:55	Science	35
2:00 - 2:25	Social Studies (M, W, F) Music (T, TH)	25
2:25 - 2:30	Clean up and prepare for dismissal	
(Total 4.5 hrs ALT)		

Figure 29

Tactic: Maintain an Academic Focus

Students are masters at bringing up unrelated or irrelevant material during academic lessons. Effective teachers are prepared to redirect these attempts back to the topic at hand in order to minimize the effects on instruction. It is not uncommon for this to occur when a student has been asked a question they feel unable to answer. To avoid the feeling of being incorrect, students will answer a question with another question, sometimes totally unrelated. Effective teachers turn these occasions into opportunities for instruction.

Variation 1

After an incorrect or unanswered question, provide the correct answer while pointing out how you arrived at the answer. Ask the question again to provide the student a self-correction opportunity. You may even ask a second question to the same student and provide a second chance at demonstrating knowledge. Make it a point to ask questions the student will be able to answer correctly. Take into consideration the level of complexity of questions. Carefully structure interactions as this provides ample opportunities for students to practice and receive supportive feedback in a nonthreatening way, thereby maintaining academic focus during a lesson.

Variation 2

Acknowledge the student's question. If it is unrelated, tell them, "That's an interesting question. Write it on a question strip (scrap piece of paper) and put in our question can."

 Tactic: Monitor Group Process and Instruction

Effective teachers know the value of using a tape recorder to monitor classroom instruction. Use tape recorders to monitor your instructional presentations. Check the level and types of questions being used with students, and the modification of directions or rewording of information for those who need it. Look for patterns. Identify those students who actively participated and were asked questions, as well of those who were not heard. Check for the number of positive praise statements used, reprimands, repeats of directions, amount of down time, and the clarity of information delivery. While some teachers use these tapes to critique their teaching, others use them to provide students who are absent with the lesson they missed. One teacher creates a library of tapes for students who are absent for medical reasons. Upon the student's return the lessons can be caught up on either during or after school hours.

Tactic: Develop Awareness of Nonacademic Time

Using a tape recorder is one way to monitor and assess the amount of time spent in instruction. Another is using a stopwatch. To develop an awareness of academic focus within a lesson or class, use a stopwatch and record the amount of time spent in active engaged learning time and/or nonacademic activities (passing out papers, arranging groups, transitions). This deliberate check will show whether an intervention is needed to reduce the amount of time spent on nonacademic activities. Collection of data on a high amount of nonacademic time over several classes or teachers suggests the need for a multilevel or school-wide change or refocus on the elements of effective instruction lesson delivery.

Tactic: Provide Quick Assistance During Independent Work

Automatic correct responses are the goal of most academic instruction and are less likely to occur if students are struggling with tasks at hand. Effective academic focus is maintained when you have a system for helping students find help quickly. Effective teachers have procedures students can follow to find assistance during independent practice. For some it means the students raise their hands and the teacher responds. For others, students are given the means to initiate the request for assistance (e.g., flip the "Help! I Need Assistance" sign, write initials on board, etc.). The key is to provide assistance quickly so that students can continue with assignments rather than wait, lose interest in what they are doing, or engage in inappropriate behavior. Remember: Down time can cause problems, so keep students engaged!

Tactic: Use an In/Out System

This tactic is useful for classrooms where students come and go in a steady steam all day. Schools offer a variety of programs throughout the day—music lessons, chorus, social skills groups, and remedial classes. Save time and avoid disruptions by having students

check themselves "In" or "Out" each time they leave and reenter the classroom. Here's how:

1 Use a piece of poster board and paste a pocket (one with each student's name on it) on the board. (See Figure 30.)

2 Inside each pocket place a slip of cardboard. On one side write the word "In," and on the other the word "Out."

3 Instruct students that upon arrival to the classroom they are to turn the card to "In," and when they leave at any time they are to turn it to "Out."

Some teachers put the student's names on the in/out cards and laminate them for use throughout the year. This saves having to recreate a new poster board each year.

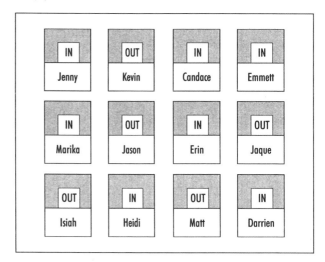

Figure 30

Variation 1

For those students who attend other classes or activities on different days, consider writing down the days and times students go to these. When the student is "out," you can simply pull out the card and read the day and time of where this student is.

Adapted from: Algozzine, B. (1993)

Tactic: Model Importance of Learning Time

Teachers are role models 100% of the time. Therefore, they must effectively model the importance of learning time. The amount of time allocated to academic instruction models messages to students. For example, if chat time or recess periods are extended five to ten minutes beyond scheduled time, but physics or reading classes always end on schedule or slightly ahead of schedule, students begin to make some inferred assumptions about what is important. Make sure you model what you mean.

principle

Establish a Positive Classroom Environment

Most students respond and perform better when teachers are supportive and helpful during learning activities. Student motivation is also more positive when teachers show sincere interest in their work (e.g., what they are teaching) and the work of their students. Effective teachers carefully assess the learning atmosphere in their classrooms; they "read" their students and strive to make the classroom climate comfortable and supportive. By making their classrooms pleasant, friendly places, effective teachers keep interactions positive and their students respond and participate in learning activities. By accepting individual differences, keeping interactions positive, establishing supportive cooperative environments, and making students participate, effective teachers make their classrooms positive learning environments for all students.

managing

Make the Classroom a Pleasant, Friendly Place

Most people perform at their best when they are in safe, organized, and clean environments. Being in an environment that allows a student to concentrate on tasks at hand, rather than worrying about the classroom bully, means a lot to students. Likewise, students tend to be more active learners when they believe their presence, efforts, and opinions are valued. Effective teachers go that extra mile to make sure their classrooms are pleasant, friendly places to learn. Even when the physical condition of the room is less than desirable, teachers make up for it in the way they interact and teach their students. Teachers are different in many ways and so are their methods of creating warm, wonderful learning environments for students. The tactics that follow may help to put a spark in your classroom environments.

Tactic: Greet Students When They Enter and Leave Your Class

Greeting and welcoming your students to class each day makes a difference. Notice students for who they are. Use positive phrases like, "Way cool shirt, George," or "You've got those super sonic sneakers on again, Ina. Could you turn off those colors? Ouch, my eyes!" Let students know you care, notice them, and want them in your class. For some students, these are the only times they are recognized by any adult in

their life, in a positive way. Send the message, "You don't need to get in trouble to get my attention." It is a valuable lesson your students can learn from you every day.

Tactic: Use Positive/Negative Sandwiches

How positive is your classroom? How do you know? How do your students know? Have you asked them? It has been shown that very often the rate at which positive statements are delivered is less than the rate for negative statements. Typically, there is one positive comment delivered every 20 minutes, and one negative statement every 2-5 minutes. Most of the time when students do exactly what is asked of them, their behavior goes unrecognized. Check your ratio of positive to negative statements. How often do you give positive statements to your students? Negative? Students will probably always make mistakes and therefore need feedback on them. Use the sandwich technique to soften the delivery of negatives: sandwich a negative feedback between two slices of praise. For example: "Carlos, you are a wonderful human, however, I need you to sit in your seat now. I know you will stay there until you are told otherwise, because you are such a bright guy." Or, "You know, Hyeonsook, you always do such wonderful work. Let's take a look at these algebra problems and see if we can pick up on a few of your rare errors." By setting the stage with a positive, the negative can be more gently delivered and have less of a negative impact on students. Think about it as an adult. What would you rather hear: "Gee, Stu, you know I love your cooking, and you amaze me with the recipes you try, but I think you may have missed on this one, or the magazine that published this recipe must have left a few steps out!" or, "You know, Stu, cooking obviously isn't your thing."

Tactic: Use Positives Frequently

During every class period deliver at least four general positives to your class. That does not mean four per student, but at a minimum, at least four to the whole class. In addition to these, give positive praise to individual students. Chart your positives—you'll be amazed at what you do and do not deliver to students. Some teachers post a big number "4" in the back of the room in bright florescent colors to remind them of the four or more goal. It's as easy as: "This class is making amazing progress in this unit. I am honored to be your teacher!"; "Excellent work today! Turn to your neighbors and congratulate them for their efforts."; or "Hang in there, I know you can do it, because you are the best!" Get students into the act by having them (or one or two) count the number of times you deliver positive praise to the class. Both you and your students will become more aware of their use and the good feeling that results from the use of positive praise statements.

Tactic: Use Musical Backgrounds

Music "soothes the savage beast," or so the saying goes. Likewise, some students focus and learn equally or better when music is played in the background. Research has shown that students perform better when classical music is played during their work time. How-ever, not all students would tolerate the playing of classical music, given the rather wide range of diversity in the music scene today. Talk to your students, find out what they think would work, and negotiate a schedule of music use. Some teachers only offer musical background options on Fridays during the last ten minutes of class, or on Mondays during the independent work time. Students negotiate the types of music they can bring in for the class. Explore what works for you and your students.

Tactic: Use Honest I's

Students, especially older ones, are easily able to discern honest, genuine positive praise from "puffery." That is, when a teacher gushes praise, hype, and excitement over answers that students give. Often students are led to think things like, "Gee, the teacher must think I am really stupid. Who wouldn't know the square root of 4 is 2." In addition, students pick up on positive praise statements that are used in a manipulative sense. For example, "Look how wonderful Row One looks." Be careful, overuse of this tactic can send the message that it's okay to manipulate people like things. Examples of insincere praise or use of this tactic are: "Wow, Sarita, you did a superb job." (Message: Teacher is making a judgment of Sarita's performance—"YOU did a …."); "Give yourself three extra bonus points, Roberta." (Message: Teacher has recognized the work—not the excellence of the work.)

Using Honest I's delivers a distinct message to students. Use specific and direct Honest I's as follows:

- Thanks for doing what I asked.

- Thanks, I appreciate that.

- Excellent. I like the way you phrased that.

- I know you are uncomfortable with that decision. I sure respect your ability to make that decision given your dilemma.

- That one was a toughie, but you did a great job attempting to figure it out!

- Nice try. Let's take a look at the answer you just gave. Although it isn't correct, I like the problem-solving steps you used.

Notice these statements are specific and recognize students' effort through the use of "I" statements.

Adapted from: Harmin, M. (1995).

Tactic: Smile Before November!

It is dangerous to smile before November, under any circumstances. Myth or truth?

It's hard to believe some folks still believe this **myth** to be true. Effective teachers communicate the importance of teaching and learning through many vehi-

cles. For example, rules and routines for the classroom are taught, posted, and reviewed from Day One of class. But the simple presence or lack of a smile does not maintain classroom discipline. So as long as you have established classroom rules, expectations, procedures, and consequences—go ahead and show those pearly whites! Let students know you are about the business of learning and that you appreciate their cooperation and presence in your classroom.

Tactic: Use Frequent Reviews to Foster Confidence

Work toward making every student feel an important part of class. Reduce students' levels of concern around learning and tough topics by bolstering their confidence first. Provide reviews of previously learned material. When introducing a new fact, concept, or strategy skill, review material students have previously mastered to allow them a successful "show what you know." Encourage students to think back to how hard they thought the topic was when they were at the initial stage of learning or acquisition—and now look where they have come. Reinforce the notion that new material is new because they have had little or no exposure to it. So it would be unreasonable to expect them to be automatically brilliant or accurate 100% of the time (although this does happen). Allow students to relax and embrace the new learning experiences.

managing

Tactic: Make Classrooms Look Inviting

Bulletin boards can be time consuming. Lots of planning and work goes into each one you create for a topic of study. However, the time spent up front pays off in the end. Things posted in your classroom have a purpose. They help make your classroom an inviting, pleasant place to learn. Even something as simple as a poster or two can perk up bare walls (and they provide a great cover for peeling paint!). One teacher allows students to bring in their personal favorite posters. Rules, procedures, and criteria are developed for the students' poster wall. It's hard to believe, but some of the posters that are sold in stores today are just not appropriate for a classroom wall (or any wall, for that matter!). One of the poster wall rules is that a poster has to be approved and initialed by the teacher or an administrator, on the back, in order to get posting privileges. Posters are only posted on the back wall of the room and are rotated on a monthly basis. Not surprisingly, the rules and procedures reduced the potential distraction factor one might think would occur with such a classroom activity.

strategy

Accept Individual Differences

Diversity in the schools has never been greater. Cultural backgrounds and first and second language skills are a part of the planning of every lesson for many teachers. Classes are filled to capacity and resources are often few. Yet effective teachers know the importance of recognizing and accepting individual differences among students. Effective teachers know that there are huge ranges of skill and ability within every class they teach. Accordingly, they make adjustments and plan learning activities to accommodate individual differences rather than to exclude, avoid, or even punish students for them. What constitutes student progress is relative. While learning outcomes or products may be static, the rate at which they are achieved is not. Today, standards drive instruction, which is driven by assessment. Teachers need to visualize and work toward a system where learning is the constant and time is the variable instead of the reverse (which for most is the prevailing model of student learning). Students become casualties of the curriculum and time constraints of learning and are often recommended for placement in special education to "catch up." These students are curriculum disabled, not learning disabled. Teachers must close the gap between the amount of time a student needs to learn material and the amount of time allowed. Teachers must understand that students are not deficit in everything all day long, just as those that are dubbed "gifted" are not gifted in everything all day long. Awareness of individual differences, cultural, learning, or language-based, allows effective teachers to plan and manage instruction to meet the diverse learning needs they are faced with on a daily a basis.

Tactic: Watch Your Biases

Biases are prevalent everywhere. In schools they range from biases in instructional material and methods to particular students, colleagues, and classes. Biases are often subtle and undetected by the biaser. Know yourself and be honest about any personal biases that exist. Self-evaluation on a regular basis is not only important, but healthy and vital to the instructional process. Does the addition of one more student to your class roster cause feelings of resentment to the scheduler or, even worse, the student? Does a personal conflict with a community member, outside of school, lend itself to bias toward any student who is from the same community or political or cultural affiliation? Does the textbook committee's decision to use a specific textbook series cause serious reluctance and lack of effort to teach from it? Did you smile at every student today? Were you especially critical of any particular student? If Beth was disruptive today, can you wipe the slate clean for the next class or tomorrow? And the list goes on. Be aware of your biases and feelings that might interfere with the equitable treatment of students, classes, or colleagues. Do not allow biases to creep into your classroom or instructional process.

Tactic: Permit and Monitor Individual Progress

What constitutes as progress and achievement is relative. Students progress through the curriculum at different rates. Some students need more opportunities to practice than others. Effective teachers know and proactively plan for this. And, they recognize and praise both the student who proceeds at a slower rate and those that are ahead of the game. Slight improvements are recognized and celebrated. Teach students

to keep track and monitor learning and progress. It is important to observe and notice individual differences and deliver positive praise to students deliberately, genuinely, and effectively.

Tactic: Use Instructional Accommodations

Because students acquire skills at different rates, expect that they will perform at different rates as well. Evaluate and provide instructional accommodations for students who need them. It is important to decide what the student needs to accurately learn according to strengths, not weaknesses. Once you have ascertained that, decide how you will accommodate these students during the instructional process. For example, some students (and adults) need tasks broken into smaller, more manageable parts. Think about it—how often do you break up paper work, grading essays, calculating grades? Of course, some breaks are interruptions, but others are planned. How much easier is it to return to the eye-blurring task of grade calculations after a planned break? Students are no different. Here are but a few instructional accommodations:

- Offer extended time for completion of assignments.

- Use a buddy system to help on difficult assignments.

- Provide multiple prompts, opportunities, and methods to allow for diverse student needs.

- Shorten long assignments—decide how much is enough.

• Break assignments into smaller pieces.

• Allow students to use tape recorders to tape oral reports.

• Allow students to use tape recorders as an alternative to writing a report.

• Provide sufficient "wait" time, allowing slower processors to produce an answer.

• Provide mental and physical stretch breaks for those who need them.

Tactic: Use Assessment Accommodations

Just as it is necessary to accommodate students during instruction, it is also important that these accommodations roll over or flow into assessment. However, assessment accommodations are often viewed by teachers, administrators, and sometimes parents as providing an unfair advantage to one student over another. If used as intended, this is definitely not the case. The purpose of assessment accommodations is to provide equal footing to students who need it to show what they know. Not providing students with needed assessment accommodation means only their deficits or weaknesses are tested. A major point here is to differentiate the difference between need versus benefit. For example, right now, you could generate a list of things you know for sure would help you benefit in a testing situation. If you are wearing glasses to read this text, take them off and continue reading. How easy is it? Are you as efficient or fast? Does the lack of having a clear view of the words impact your reading comprehension? Not providing assessment accommodations to students who need them is like saying to you, "Take off your glasses, we are having a test." Now that is unfair. All students and adults can benefit to some degree from some assessment accommodation.

Tactic: Teach Students to Set Individual Work Rates

Students often perform more efficiently when they are given the opportunity to set their own standards or rates for completing tasks. Teaching students how to set timelines and deadlines raises their awareness of what they need to do or not do to get work done on time. Keeping records of these effort-setting goals can prove to be a useful tool for monitoring work completion and impediments, and for offering suggestions for setting different or more efficient work completion rates. Once visual data is collected by having students chart behavior (see Figure 31), use this information to set up an Aim Star goal. Aim Stars are extremely useful ways to have students keep track of their progress toward their goals. (See Delivering: How to Teach; Monitor Performance; and Replan Instruction; Use Data to Plan Subsequent Instruction.)

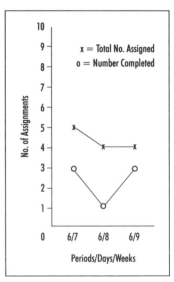

Figure 31
Behavioral Record

Establish Supportive, Cooperative Learning Environments

Often students see teachers as adults that "do things to them." Students who feel this way struggle to gain a sense of control through passive resistance—not arriving to class on time, not doing homework, not listening. This lack of effort soon translates into a cycle of failure. For many students, learned helplessness and the failure cycle are only too familiar. These students are quick to feel dumb or insecure in their learning efforts or task completion. It is vital to create supportive, cooperative learning environments for all students. There are times when individual, independent approaches to learning are not only appropriate, but necessary. The relative ease with which students embrace these approaches can be dependent upon how they are seen by other members of the class. If Joy needs to relisten to today's lesson on quadratic equations, she is more likely to dive into the tape if others do not see this accommodation as one for "kids who don't get it." In the same manner, day-to-day school activities and routines can become tedious and tiresome for both teachers and students. Effective teachers keep routines and procedures upbeat by providing opportunities for positive interactions, varying the approaches to instruction and practice and structuring activities for high levels of success and feedback. Finally, effective teachers know that social learning theory is not dead. Modeling the desired and expected classroom behavior is an effec-tive and empirically proven way to teach students what you expect them to do.

Tactic: Use Student De-Stressors

Students show their distress in many ways, from a furrowed brow to acting-out behavior. There are numerous reasons that students feel distress—family conflict, girl/boyfriend problems, grades, assignments, peer conflict, and so on. Effective teachers know they can relieve or ease students' stress or concern by simply checking in with them in a supportive, unobtrusive way and modeling stress reducing behaviors. For example, modeling what to do if you have locked your keys in your car is a wonderful way to teach students anger control and cool-headed problem solving. Talk the students through your thought processes.

> *Well, this is definitely not a permanent or fatal situation. It won't last forever, and I'm certainly not in any danger. Well, I guess I'll call to see if my neighbor is home and able to stop by with the extra set of keys. Or I suppose I can call the local locksmith. I guess I won't be going anywhere too soon. I'll just have to reschedule that appointment I had. So how can I avoid this from happening again ...*

Think how useful this modeling is for students who receive assignments or test scores lower than expected and proceed to fall apart at the seams. Here

managing

are some casual ways to reassure students and offer them an opportunity to talk about their stress:

- Hey Jearaux, you look a little stressed, want to talk about it?

- Take your time, Becky, we'll get you caught up, no matter what!

- Tom, you may have failed this test, but it is not the end of the world. You may not feel great, but you certainly are going to make it. Let's talk about what we can do to get you back to feeling better. You're worth it!

- I'm with you, Pat. I had a similar experience last week ...

Tactic: Use Parental/Guardian Support

Research has shown over and over again the valuable effects parental involvement has on student learning. Students often work best when they know that everyone has their best interest in mind. Use parent/guardian volunteer help in the classroom. One teacher uses a "parent of the morning" theme. This provides the students the opportunity to work with other adults in the classroom setting. It also gives the parent/guardian the opportunity to see what the class is really like in full swing. Everyone gets a better view and appreciation of others' styles and methods. However, some parents themselves need a supportive, cooperative classroom environment as well. It is not uncommon for some of your students' parents to

have been your student or someone else's student in the building. It is also not uncommon for parents themselves to have had a less than pleasant experience in school. Therefore, not all parents will feel comfortable entering the classroom as a morning volunteer. Proactively plan by keeping helping tasks relatively easy and uncomplicated (supervising morning work time, assisting students during a lesson, etc.). Provide opportunity for structured supervision at a helping station. Make sure parents have the answer key. One teacher even sends home a "morning agenda" and example copies of the work the students will be engaged in. This provides parents an opportunity to be ready, even if mentally, to be the morning volunteer. Make your classroom a supportive, cooperative learning environment for all!

Tactic: Use 100% Role Modeling, All the Time

Effective teachers know they are "on stage" 100% of the time. They know the power and importance of role modeling desired, appropriate behavior(s). They don't use the old cliche, "Do as I say, not as I do," but rather, "What's good for the goose is good for the gander." If the first rule on your rules and procedure chart is "be on time" for class, how can you monitor it if you aren't in class when the bell rings? If the next day you are on time and you deliver a reprimand to someone who was on time yesterday but late today, you are being a poor role model. Or consider this—Kip drops a full box paper clips all over the floor and proceeds to kick half of them across the floor. Dr. Vaye responds with "Gees, Kip, did you have to drop and proceed to spread my paper clips all over the floor? Nice mess. We'll all have to wait for you while you pick them all up before we can continue with this lesson." Meanwhile, Mrs. Peterson walks in, sees Kip picking up the clips, and says, "Kip, you'll be here all day. Let me help you. Mr. Vaye, I have a question for you …" (Mrs. Peterson continues to ask the question while helping Kip pick up the clips). Which teacher models supportive, cooperative behavior? You be the judge. The bottom line is use 100% role modeling, 100% of the time.

Tactic: Stay Calm, Remain Cool, and Deliver Reminders

How many times have you had to stop or interrupt the flow of a lesson to answer or repeat a direction? What if you have forgotten the direction/procedure? If done often enough this interruption cycle can create frustration and resentment on your part toward the student. Effective teachers proactively manage this in a number of ways. Instead of responding with "Excuse me, Julio, were you on Mars when I gave directions?" they respond with, "Julio, I'd like you to look around at your neighbors to see what page we are on." Other ways of using this tactic include:

- "Kerri, I'd like you to read our daily schedule before you ask a question about what's next."

- "Don, when the sign is flipped to "IN" that means everyone is in the classroom and no one is using the lavatory."

- "Peggy, when I give the sound signal it means mouths closed and eyes are directed toward me."

The manner in which these reminders are given are calm and intended to preserve student dignity. After all, everyone occasionally forgets where they are or what they entered the room to find.

Tactic: Use Next Time Messages

It is often too easy to pick out and criticize things that have gone wrong, when in fact there is nothing to do but work to avoid it from happening again (the old "spilled milk" routine). Effective teachers know they can choose how to correct and remind students in a way that delivers the message in a matter-of-fact way and communicates a "next time, think before you do" message. Effective teachers consider this a delivery of a nonthreatening reminder of what is expected or desired next time. For example:

- "Marisol, remember to pick up the papers you miss when you shoot them for the wastepaper basket."

- "Susan, next time ask to water the plants."

- "Mary Pat, next time you bring food to class be sure you have enough for everyone."

These comments deliver gentle "next time" reminders while acknowledging what behavior just took place. Of course, if it is something that is intolerable and not allowed, this tactic would not be used.

Adapted from: Harmin, M. (1995).

Create a Nonthreatening Learning Environment

After you have made your classroom a pleasant atmosphere to learn in, accepted and planned for individual differences, and established instructional methods and routines for a supportive, cooperative classroom, the final piece is providing a nonthreatening learning environment that ties the other strategies together. Effective teachers know that bulletin boards, posters, and routines meant to facilitate a positive environment are not the driving force behind student participation. It is a student's intuitive sense of whether all these components are genuine and can be trusted. After it is all said and done, students themselves are the ones that make participation decisions. Your body language, the way you conduct yourself in a less than pleasant situation, your interaction with students who do not follow rules, your response to questions—all go into these decisions. Let your students know that everyone can learn from their mistakes. Give feedback that stresses the positive aspects of performance, and handle errors in a supportive, matter-of-fact way. Acknowledge the effort that students are making. Use specific and powerful positive praise and feedback statements.

Tactic: Help Students See Their Strengths

Often one of the most difficult things to do is to identify "good" qualities and skills we have to offer. Think of the job interviews you've had where you've been asked, "Why should we hire you?" For most, it isn't a very comfortable question. Likewise, helping students recognize their strengths isn't easy, but it is important. Teach them they are worthy humans and have much to offer. Provide students with the opportunity to privately compile a list of "I" statements that describe or affirm their strengths. These can be focused on a content area, activity, or nothing at all. Hold private one-minute conferences with them to confirm and give feedback. "Great job, Dorene, but you know I also see you as a dedicated worker." Student comfort is the key to facilitating student participation and risk taking in your classroom.

Tactic: Acknowledge Emotions, Feelings, and Qualities

Some students only know two feelings: being in control and being out of control. Teach and model how to moderate these feelings. Acknowledge students' feelings about situations, and assure them that it's normal to feel angry, sad, etc. When appropriate, use situations from the students' lives to initiate a lesson about feelings. For example, one teacher used the death of a classroom pet to teach about feelings. Use a wheel or spinner with feelings placed in various sections to encourage students to describe times they had the feeling. If the spinner lands on "excited," students talk about times they were excited. If the spinner lands on "furious," students are taught the meaning of the word and are asked of examples when they might be furious. Another teacher has the class brainstorm things they are "good" at. Students are encouraged to identify other classmates' skills as well as their own. For example, "I think Gloria has a beautiful singing voice." The word "singing" is written down. After the brainstorming is completed, one word qualities are written in the wheel. The wheel is spun and students are told to stand up, raise their hand if it is a quality they have, or if they know someone with this quality or skill. Be sure to laminate the wheel so it can be reused. You can move to a new set of feelings by wiping off the old and writing in the new.

Tactic: Use Brag Boards

Use students' work to point out positive qualities of a student. Assist students in creating biographical sketches of who they are and what they are about. Select one student to be Star of the Week (or VIP). Post the student's picture on the Brag Board along with his/her sketches and anything else the student would like to use to tell lots of good things about himself/herself. Be careful, some students will not feel they can offer much or compete with other students. Know your class and set parameters so that all students, regardless of their situations can participate comfortably. When determining what privileges to award the Star of the Week, remember that any student, young or old, enjoys the opportunity to call roll, call line ups for lunch, decide on how much homework or problems on a page students will complete. You decide what privileges VIP students will get and what works for you and your class. Make everyone feel special.

Tactic: Provide Options for Answers

Sometimes students are reluctant to respond in class because they are uncertain of their ability to be correct. One strategy that will allow them to respond with confidence is to provide a multiple choice answer option. For example, "Did the war of 1812 begin in 1902 or 1812?"; "Is the abbreviation for September Sept. or Spt.?"; "Is a peanut a fruit or a vegetable?" By providing options you also provide prompts or cues to trigger knowledge of the facts being asked. Likewise, these options can be used for behavior options. "Doug, would you like to do the assignment now or during lunch?" The choices provided should be adjusted for individual students. Some will require more hints than others. When students are very uncertain or low in their level of achievement or functioning, you can provide for error-free responses—"Joshua, is a peach a fruit or an animal?"

Tactic: Recognize Effort and Participation

Provide incentives for participation and effort. Teach students "problems are our friends." All efforts are recognized and sometimes rewarded with incentives students have selected. These are not linked in any way to the correctness of answers. Rather, they are directly correlated with individual and group effort and participation in activities and learning tasks.

Tactic: Use Silent Notations

Make a mental note of learning needs and behaviors that require further instructional consideration.

Sometimes the best reinforcement is no reinforcement. Likewise, sometimes no response is the most appropriate response. Effective teachers who use this tactic make a mental note such as, "Ah, I think there may be a problem here." You decide at a later time whether anything needs to be done to address the "problem." For example, a brief skirmish between two students may draw such a mental note. The circumstances that precipitated the skirmish may disappear all by themselves or may need some mediation at a later time. Be assured that responding to a misbehavior using the silent notation tactic is in no way an indication of an ineffective teacher. Rather, it is the sign of an effective one who is wise enough to know when to intervene and when to monitor. Of course, effective teachers know never to use the silent notation when there is physical danger or a potentially damaging situation brewing. Important things are modeled and portrayed using the silent notation:

- You model personal security, someone who is unafraid, not worried or reactive to a situation.

- You communicate confidence in the ability of your students to problem-solve a situation and/or use self-management skills to resolve issues (after you have taught them these skills).

- You provide a rich environment for students to collaborate and cooperate together, not directed by an ever-present authority figure.

- You provide an opportunity for students to generalize problem-solving and cooperative skills to other situations.

- You avoid escalating tense situations.

- You avoid singling out students and placing them on the spot. It's better to have a private conference to discuss the problem situation, whether academic or behavioral.

- You allow yourself the opportunity to pick your battles and act instead of react.

Silent Notation allows effective teachers to reteach or review skills or rules and procedures that need reinforcement. It allows you to choose where you will put your energies now and later.

Adapted from: Harmin, M. (1995).

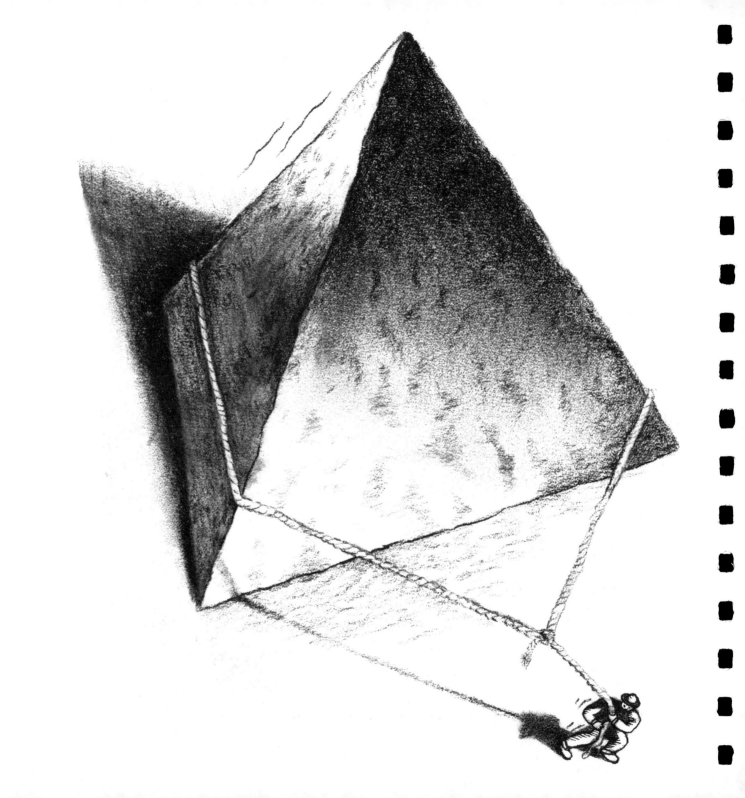

delivering

Teaching is systematic presentation of content assumed necessary for mastery of subject matter being taught. Good teaching doesn't just happen. It involves careful planning to decide what and how to teach, and how to communicate realistic expectations. It involves effective managing of classroom interactions to reduce disruptions and increase time students are productively engaged. It involves delivering lessons that introduce and extend levels of understanding of specific content. Delivering instruction is a key component of effective teaching.

Delivering instruction involves presenting information and keeping track of the extent to which the content represented by it is understood or acted upon by students. This means that effective teachers make decisions about how to present information as well as how to monitor and adjust their presentations to accommodate individual differences and enhance the

delivering

Component	Principle	Strategy
Delivering Instruction	Present Information	**For Presenting Content** Gain and Maintain Attention Review Prior Skills or Content Provide Organized, Relevant Lessons
		For Motivating Students Show Enthusiasm and Interest Use Rewards Effectively Consider Level and Student Interest
		For Teaching Thinking Skills Model Thinking Skills Teach Fact-Finding Skills Teach Divergent Thinking Teach Learning Strategies
		For Providing Relevant Practice Develop Automaticity Vary Opportunities for Practice Vary Methods of Practice Monitor Amount of Work Assigned
	Monitor Presentations	**For Providing Feedback** Give Immediate, Frequent, Explicit Feedback Provide sPecific Praise and Encouragement Model Correct Performance Provide Prompts and Cues Check Student Understanding
		For Keeping Students Actively Involved Monitor Performance Regularly Monitor Performance During Practice Use Peers to Improve Instruction Provide Opportunities for Success Limit Opportunities for Failure Monitor Engagement Rates
	Adjust Presentations	Adapt Lessons to Meet Student Needs Provide Varied Instructional Options Alter Pace

Figure 32
Three Principles of Effective Delivery

learning of all their students. As illustrated in Figure 32, there are three principles of effectively delivering instruction:

1 Present information

2 Monitor presentations

3 Adjust presentations

Each of these principles implies a set of strategies that teachers use when delivering instruction.

Present information involves making decisions about how to present content, how to teach thinking skills, how to motivate students during content presentations, and how to provide relevant practice. When presenting content, effective teachers gain their students' attention, review previously covered material, provide organized lessons, introduce new material by relating it to known content whenever possible, and interact positively with their students. When teaching thinking skills, effective teachers model ways to solve problems and present alternative ways of finding answers as they deliver instructional presentations. When motivating students, effective teachers focus on using intrinsic (i.e., internal sources of satisfaction) as well as extrinsic (i.e., external sources of satisfaction) rewards with enthusiasm and interest. When providing relevant practice, effective teachers help students develop automatic responses, vary opportunities for practices, and provide ample time and relevant, varied activities for guided and independent practice. The goal in presenting information is to teach students something they do not know.

Monitor presentations involves making decisions about how to provide feedback and how to keep students actively involved when delivering instruction. When providing feedback, effective teachers provide immediate, frequent, explicit information that supports correct responses and provides models for improvement of incorrect responses. When keeping students actively involved, effective teachers regularly monitor responses during instructional presentations, use peers to enhance engagement, and provide ample, varied opportunities for supporting success and correcting failure. The goal in monitoring presentations is to ensure that students are learning the content as it was presented.

Adjust presentations involves making decisions about how to change instruction by modifying lessons, by using alternative instructional options, and by using differing levels of pace to meet the individual needs of students. Effective teachers teach skills until students master them, and they use information gathered during instructional presentations and practice sessions to decide when and how to modify their teaching so that all students can be successful. The goal in adjusting presentations is to make any changes needed to ensure that all students benefit from instruction.

These three delivering principles are addressed in this section. An overview is provided for each, illustrating how it relates to effective delivering, and describing a set of specific strategies that effective teachers use when focusing on it. The main content of the unit is a set of tactics that illustrate specific ways to actively address each principle and strategy when providing effective instruction.

delivering

principle

Present Information

Delivering instruction (teaching) involves presenting information for students to learn. When presenting information, effective teachers use different strategies to present content, teach thinking skills, motivate students, and provide relevant opportunities for practice.

When they present content for their students to learn, effective teachers gain and maintain their students' attention before reviewing prior skills or lessons. They provide organized, relevant lessons that maintain their students' interest.

When they teach thinking skills, effective teachers often model or show students how to do what they expect them to do. They also directly teach fact-finding skills, divergent thinking skills, and learning strategy skills to their students.

Most teachers recognize that people learn better when they are motivated, and they use the following strategies to motivate students: They show enthusiasm and interest, they use extrinsic rewards effectively they consider the level of skills and student interest, and they interact positively with their students.

When they provide relevant practice, effective teachers strive to develop automatic responses by varying the

ways their students perform what they have been learning. They use seatwork effectively and monitor how they use it. They also vary the methods they use when students are practicing what they have been learning.

delivering

For Presenting Content

So much content, so little time. Today, teachers are being required to teach to higher academic standards. Students are being held accountable for learning by showing what they know through a variety of performance assessments. Effective teachers recognize the importance of presenting instruction (e.g., facts, concepts, strategies) using a multifaceted approach. Delivery of content is key to providing students the foundation upon which learning occurs. Effective teachers know that some students have an easier time learning facts, while others grasp strategies more readily. Some students learn best with material delivered using concrete examples, others prefer abstract examples. Proficiency is yet another matter. To what level or degree of accuracy, mastery, and automaticity are students required to learn material? Planning for these variables and presenting content that considers them is a key to student learning.

strategy

Gain and Maintain Attention

It isn't difficult to understand how inattention can interfere with students' ability to successfully complete a task. Effective teachers recognize the importance of student attention to tasks and use a variety of tactics to gain students attention before and during instruction. Sounds so basic and practical, right? Take note

of your teaching behavior. How do you gain all of your students' attention? How do you know you have their attention? For some, it is making sure "all eyes are up front." But what if making eye contact is culturally inappropriate? What do you do to maintain student attention once you get it? Here are some tactics to help.

Tactic: Teach Listening as a Skill

The average student spends over half his/her time in school listening. That means students give more time and energy to listening than to lots of other things in school. For many students listening does not come naturally. For others it is as natural as walking or eating. Hearing is an ability, but listening is more than just hearing. Listening means directing your attention to what you are hearing and trying to make sense of what you've heard. Listening is a skill. Like any skill, it requires learning and practice. To be a good listener is to be an active listener: Keep your thoughts directed to what you are listening to. In general it is estimated that students can think at a rate of 4,009 words per minute. People can speak at a rate of 125 words per minute. Therefore, the speaking rate is approximately three times slower than the thinking rate. In order to gain and maintain students' attention, they need to be listening first. Have students inventory how well they listen and use the results to teach the skill of listening.

delivering

⏲ Tactic: Use Speak, Listen, Respond

When delivering any amount of information it is important to check in with students to assess whether they are actively involved in the lesson and understand the content. Before you start your lesson write on the board or post a chart:

1 Summarize

2 Questions

3 Reactions

4 Miscellaneous

Tell the students that after a period of time you will stop the lesson and ask them to respond in one of the formats listed above. At a likely time in your lesson, stop and say:

> *Take a moment and respond to one of the four choices on the board. You can (1) **summarize** the important points you just heard, in your own words; (2) record any **questions** you may have about the lesson so far; (3) respond or **react** to anything you heard; or (4) record, draw, or write any other **miscellaneous** things that help to capture your thoughts about our lesson.*

Tell the students they will have about two minutes to write. Monitor student progress by wandering around the classroom. During this time students may want and need clarification on presented information. This can be handled many ways. One way is to directly answer the questions. Another is to have students write the questions as per option 2. Another is to have students ask a partner or study buddy for clarification. Be careful that the partner format does not preclude these students from recording their responses to one of the four choices.

Some teachers have students keep a daily Speak, Listen, Respond log for each class and periodically collect them for review. Other teachers use the log to start the next day's lesson by soliciting information from any of the four choices. Still other teachers have students break into base or cooperative learning groups and share their Speak, Listen, Respond logs.

Adapted from: Harmin, M. (1995).

Tactic: Use Clap Patterns

Here's a fun, quick way to gain students' attention. Anytime students are engaged in a small group or large group activity, it is always a challenge to pull them back together as a group or to simply regain their attention. Simply choose a clapping rhythm and demonstrate it. Then say, "If you can hear me, clap my clap." Students who can hear you will repeat the rhythm, drawing others' attention to it. Soon the entire group will be clapping the clap or simply attending to you for their next direction. For example, try this

delivering

rhythm: 1-2-3, 1-2-3, 1, 2, 1-2, 1-2-3. (Saying this pattern in your head may help you hear the rhythm.)

Tactic: Give Zero Noise Signals

The zero noise signal is made by curling your fingers into a zero and resting them on your thumb. Explain to your students that anytime they see you give the zero noise signal they are to stop what they are doing, stop talking, look at you, and mirror the signal back. This tactic is especially useful when students are engaged in activities that require them to be spread over the space of the room, some with their backs to you. Simply raise the zero noise signal over your head. Students who are facing you should respond by mirroring the signal. Other students who may not be able to see you will see these students and are cued that the signal has been given. Note: It is important to remember that different hand gestures or signals connote different things in different cultures. For example, in one culture the zero noise signal connotes a rather offensive word. In this case a better alternative might be a "thumbs up" signal. Be sure you check the signals out in respect of the cultural differences your students may bring to class.

Tactic: Teach How to Listen, But Good

Teach students how to listen in fun motivating ways. Use riddles or brain teasers. Students will become all ears when they are faced with an ear bending puzzle. Have students work in groups and collectively problem-solve. Use teams or let students try their hand at them first before moving into groups. For example:

Question: Why can't a person living in Lexington, Kentucky be buried west of the Mississippi?

Answer: Because a person who is living can't be buried!

Effective teachers use these exercises to teach students common causes for listening errors:

▲ Focusing on a single word rather than the entire direction, question, or sentence

▲ Jumping to a conclusion based on your expectations rather than what is actually being said

▲ Not paying attention to or asking for clarification of key words

▲ Switching or hearing the order of the words differently than what is spoken

▲ Overlooking verb tense or other clues that tell something has happened

Effective teachers take time to process students' correct and incorrect answers to reinforce and model listening and thinking skills.

Tactic: Vary Presentation Formats

Effective teachers vary the way they present their content. For example, one teacher starts his lesson using pantomime of what he wants students to do to get ready for the lesson. Other teachers use whispering. One teacher used the whispering technique as

delivering

follows: "The first answer to Friday's social studies test is …" There was an immediate hush that fell across the room. Other times she tells a joke or riddle for students to solve. Start a lesson with an unusual prop! One science teacher wraps himself in plastic packing bubbles to start his lesson on plastics. Use drawing, role plays, and acting to draw and maintain attention to your lesson. Varying the formats of content presentation provides both you and your students a break from traditional verbal or written modes and adds novelty to the lesson.

Tactic: Keep Students Active

Sometimes the easiest way to gain and maintain student attention is by delivering content that requires them to be actively involved. Use choral responding, or have students respond by using signals. Pose questions or problems to the class and have students hold up response cards (Yes/No, punctuation mark, numbers, vocabulary words, etc.) Some teachers find individual chalkboards or magic slates to be the novelty students enjoy best. They provide all students the opportunity to show what they know while allowing the teacher to do a quick check of student understanding and progress.

Tactic: Use Quick-Paced Instruction

The simple use of brisk-paced instruction helps maintain student attention. Varying question formats, who you call on, and how you call on them has a positive impact on gaining and maintaining student attention. Use of random questioning formats is best. No

predictable patterns can be noted. All students will be more likely to attend if they don't know who you will call on next. For example, ask Ron to repeat the directions and Amanda to put them in her own words. Then have Jacob show the class what they are to do, while Robert evaluates if the directions were followed correctly. This format can be used for classroom procedures, instructional tasks, strategies, and other tasks that require completion.

Tactic: Catch'em While They're Hot!

Use errors to motivate students. Deliberately make an error in a written lesson or procedure and reward students who catch it while it's "hot off the press." One teacher makes a tally sheet called "Hot Pursuit." Tallies are kept for the students who are in "hot pursuit" of teacher-made errors. Students are considered "hot" on the trail of attending if they catch the teacher's error. It is important to have the student tell what the error is and how to correct it. This tactic provides teachers the opportunity to model error correction procedures while checking on student understanding of the fact, concept, or strategy that was in error.

Tactic: Use Response Sheets and Format Organizers to Focus Attention

For some students maintaining attention to tasks or lesson presentation is an especially challenging task. Help students by providing them a written outline of major points you will be making during you lesson. Have these students check off each point as it is cov-

delivering

ered in the lesson. During the delivery of the lesson, stop and review with students what points have been covered thus far. It is also helpful to show students the sequence of your lesson by writing the format that will be followed on the board. Allowing students this overview and framework for a lesson helps them see the big picture and anticipate what's coming. For many students putting the lesson format on the board provides a level of comfort. The lesson routine is sequenced and predictable for both you and your students.

Tactic: Cue Important Points

Effective teachers use a variety of ways to draw students' attention to important points in a lesson. One way is to use voice inflections. Another is to use words to highlight. For example, "Here is a point you will want to remember," or "The key fact to remember in this passage is …" Or perhaps the combination of both: Whisper to the students, "This is really important to write in your notes." A high school soccer coach who teaches health raises a yellow card to signal students to highlight the fact they need to know. In the game of soccer, if a referee holds up a yellow card over a player, it means that player has been issued a game warning. For this well-known school coach the use of the yellow card is a novel signal that he can hold up, signaling an important point for students to be sure and note or highlight, while not missing a beat of lecture.

Tactic: Use Wait Time Effectively

Effective teachers know the importance of using wait time during the presentation and delivery of instruc-

tion. It is not uncommon for teachers to move too quickly during questions and answers, or choose the class pacers or those students who the teacher can count on to give the correct answer. In the meantime, the other students may be lost, unable to transition as quickly from one question to the next. This in turn can cause frustration for many students, and they may loose interest in the lesson. Effective teachers are cognizant of the importance of waiting at least three to five seconds for students to respond. It is important to watch students and monitor their use of wait time. Some students are inherently slower to think and respond than others. The effective use of wait time encourages optimal levels of student response.

Review Prior Skills or Content

Prior knowledge is one of the most important variables of student learning. The prior knowledge a student brings to each lesson, no matter what content area, is key to linking to other learning. Automaticity of task completion and the application of content knowledge to other tasks is an ultimate goal of effective instruction and student learning. Effective teachers do not make assumptions about students' prior knowledge or experiences. Rather, they plan for them. The beginning of every effective lesson should start with a review of content or skills from the previous lesson. Students are actively engaged in this review and student understanding is checked. Often instructional

delivering

124

skills are hierarchical in nature. That is, they build upon each other. Therein lies the importance of reviewing content and skills. Skills that are needed for current and future lessons need to be checked for accuracy and acquisition, and retaught if necessary.

Tactic: Use Distributed Practice

Have you ever "crammed" for an exam? Pulled an "all nighter" to study for a test? Known anyone who has? Think back to how much information you remembered after you left the exam room. You basically stuffed information in your head for the test and then forgot it as soon as the pressure was off (that is, if you "crammed" for the test). This is not the way students should study or show what they know. The educational term for "cramming" is massed practice, where practice or studying is done all at once. The most effective way to study and retain information is to use distributed practice. In distributed practice, review and studying are done daily and frequently. Over time the information reviewed becomes automatic and can be called up from memory with little effort. Beginning each lesson you teach with a review of what was learned the day before provides for distributed practice.

Tactic: Use Mnemonics to Cue Prior Learning

Mnemonics are tricks or strategies that can be learned and are useful for remembering specific facts and details. Learning with mnemonics is a process of linking what you already know (old stuff) with what you want to learn (new stuff). One form of mnemonic is the use of mental pictures. These work best when they are exaggerated, humorous, and ridiculous. For example, you can never remember Jeff Young's last name. So you use a visual mnemonic. You picture a baby with an index card that says "Young" pinned to its diaper.

Likewise, some of the details students learn to remember are or become habitual (remembering locker combination, class period times), while others require a conscious effort. Although effective concentration necessarily contributes to success in remembering facts, it is not sufficient. For example, most 16-year-olds are interested in learning the material in a driver's manual, because passing the test and getting a license is important. However, the concentration needed to learn the information is necessary but not sufficient for passing the driver's test. One needs to practice remembering by doing. When students find a subject or topic dull and boring, concentration becomes even more difficult. Teach students to enter a state of concentration by relaxing, breathing deeply, shrugging shoulders, and paying attention to their feelings and thoughts.

delivering

Tactic: Use Tips for Remembering

Encourage and teach students to integrate isolated facts into a whole. Things are more easily remembered in the gestalt. Encourage students to become personally involved in their learning. Here are seven tips to teach your students to remember things:

1 Review in your mind what you will need to take with you before you walk out the door. Ask yourself, "Do I have everything?"

2 Wear your watch, ring, or piece of clothing in an unfamiliar way. The strange feeling may help you remember that you have something to remember.

3 Ask a reliable person to remind you.

4 Write it down and prioritize your list.

5 Repeat each item you have to remember at least five times.

6 Create a picture of what you're trying to remember in your mind. Visualization helps you store what you're trying to remember.

7 Make up a formula or sentence. For example, Every Good Boy Does Fine is a way for musicians to remember the lines and spaces on the treble clef (E, G, B, D, F).

Tactic: Use Memorization Strategies

The brain can hold an amazing amount of information. There are intriguing ways to make memorization much easier. By using association strategies, things can be easily remembered because you must associate what you're learning with something already known. For example, you are having trouble remembering Mr. McDonald's last name. Try visualizing that person in a Ronald McDonald® suit eating a huge hamburger! Or perhaps you are trying to learn how many times "s" appears in the word that means something very sweet and delicious. Associate the correct spelling with wanting two helpings of dessert! Okay, one more. You are trying to teach your students to remember a characteristic of the Chou dynasty of China. Have them think of the chow dog. They are usually aggressive animals, reddish or rust in color. It just so happens that the Chou dynasty was fierce and warlike (aggressive animal) and is the era when the Iron Age began (rust in color). Can you see it now? Here are some specific association strategies to help improve memory:

▲ Use images. Produce a mental picture of things previously seen or that can be visually imagined. Make it unusually large or exaggerated. Make it move. Make the image unusual, bizarre, or even ridiculous.

▲ Use index cards. Write one piece of information on the front of the card and associate it with a piece of information on the back.

delivering

▲ Use a linking system. Create mental pictures between two items at a time. The first item helps to remember the second, the second helps to remember the third, and so on.

▲ Use comparisons. Find points of similarity between two things that must be associated.

▲ Use place. This entails making a mental map of a place that is familiar (classroom, bedroom, baseball diamond, etc.), and the items to remember are associated with certain landmarks of the room. For example, in teaching students to remember five advantages the North possessed in the Civil War, a teacher has her students visualize a baseball diamond. At home plate is a picture of a railway station or terminal, at first base are factory exhaust stacks, at

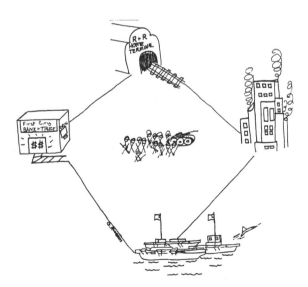

second base are ships on water, and on third is a bank. Inside the diamond are soldiers and a tank. The thought process becomes: railway system, factories to produce arms, water access to land, money, and lots of soldiers and ammunition.

▲ Use rhymes. The rhyme of a song or poem is a powerful tool for remembering. "Thirty days hath September, April, June, and November …"

▲ Use breaks in patterns. Create an abnormal circumstance to "jar" your memory (e.g., walk to class a different way, carry a different book bag).

▲ Substitute words. Similar to imagery, try to associate a well-known word that does have an image that sounds like part of the word to be remembered (e.g., Minneapolis is one of the Twin Cities of Minnesota—mini-skirt).

▲ Use clustering strategies. Outlining, coloring, grouping, alphabetizing, and sequencing are all ways of putting information in clusters of things to be remembered.

Tactic: Play Bingo

Information review doesn't have to be boring (and shouldn't be). Use Bingo to stimulate student learning and review. All you need to do is create a Bingo board using the facts, concepts, and strategies you want your students to review, and provide chips to cover the spaces. Be sure that the answers to your questions are somewhere on the student boards. For

delivering

example, Bingo can be used to review abbreviations of the periodical table, musical note values, historical dates, products and quotients, vocabulary, grammar, punctuation, and just about anything else. It's fun, easy, and engaging.

Adaptation

Vary the cells of the Bingo boards. For students who need more immediate feedback and recognition of efforts, start with a Bingo board that has three cells across and three cells down. Then gradually increase the number of cells to four across, four down, then five across, five down, and so on.

Decide what (if anything) the students will earn for the winning Bingo card. For some students the simple fact they get to yell "Bingo" first does the trick. Others may desire a more formal record or posting of winning efforts. Be sure to consider asking students what they think when designing the recognition or reward system.

Tactic: Teach Students How to Create Review Procedures

Have students create ways of reviewing previously taught content material or skills. First teach them what the purpose of review is for. Model how review can be conducted and what should be included. Then set them loose to create class reviews for content delivered. This can be done for extra credit, or just because. Review fact sheets or activities can be created by individuals or groups of students on a random or rotating basis. It can be assigned as home-

work or classwork. Once students have the general idea of what and how review is conducted, student-developed reviews become easy and fun to create. Remember, review is quick, to the point, and serves as a monitor and check of whole class understanding of content and/or skills taught.

Tactic: Use Numbered Heads Together

Numbered Heads Together is an alternative question technique and format that provides students the opportunity to actively engage simultaneously in learning. It provides a structured opportunity for students to collaboratively discuss content or related information. Finally, it instills individual and group accountability, because individuals are not only responsible for their own learning but the learning of all group members. Here's a brief overview:

1 Divide students into random heterogeneous learning teams of four.

2 Number students within teams 1-4.

3 Ask a question of the entire class. Then say, "Put your heads together and find the answer. I will call on a number from 1-4. That number (person) will be responsible for answering the question. Therefore, it is important that everyone know the answer to the question."

4 After a sufficient amount of time has passed, say, "All the number ___s that can answer the question raise your hand."

5 After the selected numbered student has given his/her response, say, "Are there any other number ___s that can expand or add to that answer?"

6 It is important to randomly select the numbers. Be sure that all numbers are called, but avoid calling the numbers in sequence to avoid predictability.

Source: Kagan, S. (1994).

Tactic: Use "Chart It!" for Review

Effective teachers know the value of providing students with activities that allow them to move around with structure and a purpose. Using Chart It! as a review procedure provides students with the opportunity to show what they know about a topic. The charting exercise allows for relearning, review, and the opportunity to integrate knowledge about several topics or issues about a single topic. Here's how:

Materials needed:

Chart paper or butcher paper large enough for several groups of students to record their responses. One chart per group.

Procedure:

1 Divide the class into groups of four or five students. There should be as many groups as there are questions or topics. That is, if you have five questions there should be no more or less than five groups.

2 Before class, write a topic or question across the top of each chart paper. Each group gets a different chart. Each chart has a different question or topic.

3 Tell the students:

Each group has a chart with a question (or topic) across the top of it. When I say "start," you will have approximately two minutes to write as many responses to the question (or topic) on your chart. After the time has passed, I will say "switch." You are to pass your group's chart in a clockwise direction to the group on your right.

note: The exact direction doesn't matter, just make sure students rotate the charts in the same direction each time the "switch" direction is given.

As soon as you receive your new chart, begin working on it. We will continue this process until all the charts have been rotated around to each group once. You should end the activity with your group's original chart.

delivering

4 Once the charts are back to the original owners, give the following instructions:

> *Review the list of items/responses on your chart. Together as a group, select by consensus the top three responses you feel best represent the given topic. You will have about four or five minutes to do this.*

This process entails some discussion and prioritizing of responses.

5 After this is completed (approximately five minutes), instruct each group to choose a spokesperson to briefly summarize their chart to the rest of the class.

6 After the activity is complete, the charts may be posted in the classroom for later use, additional review, or to help students that missed the lesson.

The information and processing that Chart It! calls upon is amazing. Students usually comment as to how much harder it is to think of things to add to the chart after it has been to other groups—most ideas have been recorded by other groups. As a bonus, you now have a student-developed review chart for a test, or an informal assessment of student understanding of a topic.

Variation

Instead of switching the charts in a clockwise motion, have the students walk as a group to the next chart.

For either format the charts can be placed on the floor, a table, or taped to a wall. Be sure to give each group a different color marker to use. It is easier to keep track of groups' responses when they are color coded.

Adapted from: Kagan, S. (1994).

Tactic: Assign Student Reviewers

Students of effective teachers know that every lesson starts with a review of the previous day's lesson content. These reviews are brief, fast, and engaging. They serve as a launching pad for the lesson that immediately follows the review. Assign students to conduct the review. Encourage creativity. Allow students to vary the format as long as the goal of the review is accomplished. Have review sign ups. Encourage students to take the lead in at least one lesson review a month. By using a sign-up sheet, you are able to hold brief planning meetings with student reviewers to make sure the students understand the review format, content, and time in which the information must be delivered.

strategy

Provide Organized, Relevant Lessons

Effective instruction and learning are more apt to occur when information is delivered in an organized, coherent manner. When clear directions, adequate examples, and practice are provided in a relevant context for students, making connections and learning is

delivering

more successful. Effective teachers provide concrete and relevant examples when presenting content and provide practice to facilitate mastery. Helping students link what is being taught to their prior knowledge and daily living experiences keeps students engaged and motivated in the learning process.

Tactic: Use a Model of Effective Instruction

Teaching is hard work. Learning can and should be challenging to students. However, the perfect blend of learning and challenge is important if effective instruction and learning are to take place. Here is a brief list of things to remember when presenting content to students:

1 Tell students what the lesson objectives are.

2 Review material learned the day/class before.

3 Deliver information.

4 Demonstrate and model the information or tasks you want students to do.

5 Provide guided practice for students. Monitor and deliver immediate and corrective feedback on student performance.

6 Provide students opportunities for independent practice. Support and provide corrective feedback.

7 End each lesson with a summary and recap of what was taught and learned.

This is but a brief list of several of the key components of an effective teaching model. The important things to remember are to provide an anticipatory set to students at the start of a lesson to perk interest and help connect to their prior knowledge of the subject, present the content in a motivating way that provides students the opportunity to respond and practice, and deliver feedback on their performance and efforts. Finally, be sure to summarize what was learned.

Tactic: Use MAPS

Effective teachers use consistent formats in planning and delivering lessons. Effective lesson formats include but are not limited to gathering materials, developing aims or goals of the lesson, delineating the procedures or steps in the order in which they need to occur, and summarizing what was taught and learned during the lesson. For many teachers, the space allotted in plan books is insufficient to record daily lesson plans. Here's a quick and easy way to comprehensively plan a lesson, including what information and steps you will use to deliver your lesson information. This procedure is called MAPS (see Figure 33).

Materials needed for the lesson—These include but aren't limited to handouts, books, materials for class projects, and anything else that is needed during the lesson.

Aim—What is the aim or goal of the lesson you will teach? These are the objectives for learning and instruction of your content.

delivering

---

maps example

M   Overhead, hand-outs, cooperative group lists for social studies.

A   Students will complete hand-out for Civil War in cooperative language groups. By end of class all students will hand in completed sheets.

P   Review yesterday's lesson, answer questions.

     Explain today's procedure:
- ▲ Review hand-out/sheet assignment as a class.
- ▲ Get into cooperative language groups.
- ▲ Complete sheet, and hand in.

S   Review today's lesson.
- ▲ What was purpose of task?
- ▲ What was learned?
- ▲ Any comments, questions?

Figure 33

Procedures—What procedures or steps will you follow in your lesson? For example, introduction and overview of lesson, a statement of objective, review of yesterday's lesson, delivery of information, modeling or demonstration, checking for understanding, guided practice, independent practice, corrective feedback, and so on.

Summary—In the summary section of MAPS you are to summarize or recap the lesson objectives, what was taught, and what was learned. Here homework can be assigned.

Tactic: KISS IT!

Keep it simple, stimulating, interactive, and **tangible.** This statement is so profound it could be considered a golden rule of delivering effective instruction. Keeping it simple means breaking complex facts, concepts, or strategies down into subskills or lessons that are fast-paced and interactive. Sometimes teachers attempt to teach complex skills in one long lesson, even though they build on each other and are hierarchical in nature. However, students get lost along the way. Students need both a break and practice on subskills that build on each other. Anticipating potential problem areas in a lesson and planning for them by providing alternate examples and activities can keep instruction stimulating, interactive, yet tangible for the students.

Tactic: Use Organizational Study Guides

Organizational study guides take many different formats. Lesson outlines, charts, lists of key ideas, phrases, words, structured overviews, timelines, flowcharts, questions, and fill in the blanks are just a few. Study guides may serve as advanced organizers for an upcoming lesson or as a review of what was taught. Regardless, they provide students with materials that enhance and facilitate learning. Here are three variations:

Variation 1

Make a list of all the important facts, concepts, and strategies you want students to learn as a part of your lesson or unit of instruction. Develop the list into a set of questions for students to answer. Students know that anything on the question sheet is fair game

delivering

for a test and, at a minimum, is required learning for the unit or lesson of instruction. Give these guides out before you start instruction. For example, a study guide for a lesson on the Apollo 13 space mission might look like:

Study Guide: Apollo 13 Space Mission

1. What year did the Apollo 13 space mission take place?
2. In what state was the launching pad?
3. What are the names of the Apollo 13 crew members?
4. Define orbit.
5. Discuss the principle of weightlessness in space.
6. Who was the first man to walk on the moon?
7. What was said by the astronaut as he/she stepped onto the face of the moon?
8. What was accomplished during the Apollo 13 mission?
9. What is the name of the ocean where the spaceship fell from orbit?
10. Describe an astronaut's diet while in space.

Variation 2

Provide students with a similar format as above. In addition, include text page numbers where the information can be located.

Variation 3

Use the same format as above, but have the students answer the question and provide the page number where they found the answer. Inferential answers will need to be supported by providing the thoughts or information that led students to their inference.

Tactic: Use Advanced Organizers

Advanced organizers are content outlines and lists of key information (facts, concepts, strategies) that will be presented during a lesson. Advanced organizers cue students to information they should watch for. This can take many formats. The important point is that they help students get a handle on what's ahead and what to expect. Here are a few variations you could use:

Variation 1

Provide students with a topical outline of key vocabulary, facts, concepts, and other important information. For example:

Area of Study: Inline Skating Safety

Key Vocabulary:

1. Protective equipment
2. Wrist guard
3. Bearings
4. Helmet

Key Concepts:

▲ Always skate in control
▲ Always wear appropriate protective equipment
▲ Check and keep clean skate bearings and wheels
▲ Practice stopping

Other Important Information:

▲ Demonstration sport in the Olympics
▲ Part of some state's physical education class requirement
▲ Most common injury: broken wrists and elbows

---

delivering

Variation 2

Provide students with a template or framework that students are to fill in with information as they learn it. Decide whether you want to provide the exact number of spaces for information. For example, there are four key vocabulary words students will need to know. Students must pay attention in order to find out which words they are.

Area of Study: Inline Skating Safety

Key Vocabulary:

1.
2.
3.
4.

Key Concepts:

▲
▲
▲
▲

Other Important Information:

▲
▲
▲
▲

Variation 3

Here is another example of a content advanced organizer. This can be tailored by you to cover the breadth and depth of the content to be delivered.

Outline for Inline Skating Safety

I.

   A.

   B.

II.

   A.

      1.

      2.

   B.

      1.

      2.

Tactic: Use Graphic Organizers

Graphic organizers are visual outlines of information students are responsible for learning. Graphic organizers are usually provided in sequential and linear order. You may have students complete these as you teach a lesson, immediately after, or for homework. They can be completed independently, in small groups, or as a whole group process. They can be developed as follows:

1 Identify and list the facts, concepts, and strategies you want students to know.

2 Place them in a sequential and linear order.

3 Create a visual outline or framework for the information.

delivering

Variation 1

Use the same format as above, but provide students with partial information and reference points filled in. They are responsible for finding and filling in the remaining information.

Variation 2

Provide students with a completely filled in graphic organizer. However, intermix correct and incorrect facts and concepts. Students are given the task of checking and correcting the graphic organizer based on lesson information.

Variation 3

For those students who exhibit near point or far point copying difficulties, written organization problems, and/or graphic motor problems, provide a correctly completed graphic organizer. Have these students follow along and highlight the facts and concepts as they are introduced and appear in the visual outline.

Tactic: Provide Notetaking Templates

After you have taught your students how to take notes, you may still find there are many students who have difficulty listening and writing down key points and information. Effective teachers provide these students with notetaking templates. Notetaking templates are outlines of the content you will be teaching during a lesson. They include information you expect all students to write into their notebooks. Notetaking templates require you to have your lessons pre-planned well in advance so that the templates can be

created. You may wish to give notes to all your students in template form. Simply write on the board or overhead the template of information you will be speaking to and then fill it in as you go. Students really appreciate notetaking templates.

Name of Fish	States Where Found	Most Successful Fishing Technique	Best Time of Year

Tactic: Model Desired Response or Behavior

Most often school success is correlated with students' ability to follow directions correctly. Effective teachers not only deliver clear directions, but teach students how to follow them. Modeling is an effective way to provide students a concrete, visual example of what written or orally presented directions say to do. Providing a model and saying or verbalizing the actions or steps of a process (a think-aloud process) accommodates a variety of learners and assists students

delivering

who may have difficulty following directions because of language or memory problems. For example, complete an algebraic equation on an overhead while talking through the steps and calculations aloud. Or show students how to complete a lab report they are expected to produce as part of a project or test.

Tactic: Facilitate Following Directions

Here are some tips to remember when giving directions to students:

▲ Cue students that directions are about to be given.

▲ Use simple terms and phrases.

▲ Speak softly, slowly, and keep verbiage to a minimum.

▲ Check for understanding.

▲ Have students repeat the directions using their own words.

▲ Say and write directions on the board.

▲ Break directions into easy steps.

▲ Use a buddy system to help clarify directions.

▲ Limit the number of directions given at one time.

▲ Use eye contact and close proximity to help focus student attention.

▲ Prerecord the directions for later review by students.

▲ Say, write, and model the directions for students.

Tactic: Take Time to Show Content Relevance

It is important to plan ways to relate content material to your students' lives or experiences. How often have you heard students say, "Why do we have to learn this?" or "When will I ever use this stuff?" Effective teachers take time to communicate the importance of learning material covered. For example, show students how learning percents in math can save them money when shopping for clothes, CDs, etc. One high school teacher works with students who read slowly and sporadically. To teach reading fluency, she uses one-minute timed readings. Resistant learners argue against the need for the task. This teacher relates it to driving on a street or expressway. The need to read quickly is evident when you need to read street signs or road signs. To make her point more relevant she shows a video she made of a typical trip on an expressway, including entering and exiting traffic lanes. Her students can see the importance of being able to read fluently and accurately.

Tactic: Help Students Organize Thoughts Ahead of Time

Many students have the best intentions of getting an assignment done, but lack the organization skills to do it. Effective teachers teach students ways to get organized for a task. This is apparently more difficult for students in the area of writing succinct paragraphs, essays, and compositions. Here is a quick and efficient way to teach students how to organize their

delivering

thoughts ahead of time when they write. Have them follow these steps: D-E-F-E-N-D and S-E-A-R-C-H.

D ecide on position.
E xamine reasons and details for position.
F igure best order of reasons and details.
E xpose position in first sentenced.
N ote each reason.
D rive home position in last sentence.

Students can use this acronym for defending a position or writing a factual piece.

S ee if it makes sense.
E ject incomplete sentences.
A sk if it's convincing.
R eveal capitalization, punctuation, etc.
C opy over neatly.
H ave a last look.

For Motivating Students

Students learn three to four times more when they are in a good mood. Effective teachers know that students learn best when teachers are enthusiastic about the content of their instruction. Effective teachers not only show interest, but get excited about the process of learning. They communicate the importance of what they are teaching and help students make connections to prior knowledge and experience. Students know a well planned, managed, and delivered lesson when they see one. Model the importance and value you want students to put on learning. Show them the significance of the learning process.

Show Enthusiasm and Interest

Today, students come to school with more and greater needs. These needs go beyond academics. Many students need nurturing and good old-fashioned tender loving care. Effective teachers recognize the importance of maintaining positive and trustworthy interactions with students. Students work harder and are more likely to take learning risks for teachers they like, respect, and trust. And, students learn better when teachers are excited and enthused about the content of their instruction. Use spunk and drama to get your points across. Stand on your head if you need to. A bit of drama goes a long way.

delivering

Tactic: Catch'em Being Good!

Do not leave well enough alone. Recognize and reinforce students for demonstrating appropriate and expected behavior. Research has shown that 85% of the time that students do exactly what they are told, they are not reinforced. It has been shown that, on the average, negative verbal reprimands are delivered once every 2-5 minutes. Positive statements are delivered once every 20 minutes. Effective teachers deliver at least four positive praise statements to their class of students per class period. Just for fun, keep track of how many positive statements you deliver per class and/or per target student. You may be surprised. Some teachers plaster a big "4" at the back of their classrooms as a reminder to deliver at least that many positive statements. If you're brave, select a student monitor or two to chart your behavior. Don't be afraid to increase those positive praise statements. Let your students know how much you appreciate and care about them.

Tactic: Empower Students

While educators are taught to recognize student academic and behavioral efforts there is another, often neglected, area of responsibility. Teach students about dignity, inspire them to achieve it, and recognize it when they do. Life is not always about producing the best, making the best grade, or looking the sharpest, but about courage, effort, citizenry, self-management, and awareness. To inspire these qualities they first need to be taught, modeled, and widely recognized among students (and some adults). Modeling or using simple statements as those listed below can help facilitate growth in this area.

To support student **courage** or **dignity**, consider these statements:

- ▲ "You really show your commitment to what you say."
- ▲ "Nice job making your point in an eloquent manner."
- ▲ "You did a superb job sticking up for yourself."
- ▲ "That's the way to stick by your beliefs (or a friend, etc.)."
- ▲ "I know how hard it can be to stick to your beliefs when others oppose you."

To support student **effort** and **energy**, consider these:

- ▲ "Way to use that brain!"
- ▲ "You really shine when you put forth your effort!"
- ▲ "Remember to stay focused in a moment of frustration."
- ▲ "Just when you think you can't do it anymore (figure it out, put up with it, etc.), give it one more try."
- ▲ "Even though I know it is sometimes very difficult for you, I admire your effort to get to bed at a reasonable hour."

delivering

To support student **self-management** skills, try these:

- ▲ "I really appreciate the way you …"
- ▲ "Try not to jump at the first thought that comes to mind; think it through."
- ▲ "I always remind myself of the phrase, 'Act, don't react,' and find it helps me when I am annoyed."
- ▲ "I like the way you ask for help when you need it."

To support student **citizenry**:

- ▲ "Thank you for volunteering to help."
- ▲ "You really show your respect for differences by allowing others to speak their opinions without interruption."
- ▲ "I always like to make the effort to welcome newcomers."
- ▲ "I like to show my appreciation to others by …"

To support student **awareness**:

- ▲ "Thank you for keeping an open mind."
- ▲ "We all get blue sometimes, we just need to try different ways to pull ourselves back out of it."
- ▲ "You really picked up on the nonverbal messages."
- ▲ "Thank you for noticing he/she needed help."

These statements show how and to what degree you can support and integrate the development of student dignity, effort, self-management, citizenry, and awareness in your day-to-day dealings with students.

Adapted from: Harmin, M. (1995).

Tactic: Make School Fun!

Teaching should be fun, and so should school. School is a place where natural interests in learning should be supported. Life is too short to spend it fussing and fighting with resistant students or feeling like you can't teach them. Intersperse "brain buster" lessons with novel, fun "brain breathers." For example, break up cognitive and heavy academic learning with fun ways to practice and reinforce student learning. Use Bingo, visual thinking, riddles, student reviews, vanity license plates, and cooperative learning tactics, just to name a few. School is not fun for some, so you may have to go that extra mile to get those students hooked on learning. Take a minute and think about something you are really good at. Now think of something you are not so talented at. Which of these would you like to do in front of a group of your peers all day long, or even for 45 minutes? Get the point?!

Tactic: Show Enthusiasm and Interest

Have you ever attended a lecture or inservice that put you to sleep? Watched a dreadfully boring movie? What made them so dull? How could they have been improved? More active participation? More interaction? More practice of what was being taught? Hey, even a few jokes and cartoons would have helped! Adult learning styles and environments are no different from students. Students need to be engaged and occasionally entertained too. One well-liked and well-known high school literature teacher is known for her "dress up days." At any time during the reading of a piece of classic literature this teacher might dress

delivering

up in the garb representing the era of the classic. She dresses the part of the villain, hero, era, etc. Students who are not enrolled in her class often take the long way to lunch just to walk by her class to see her in action. Another elementary teacher, when teaching the consonant-vowel-consonant with a silent e (CVCe), dresses as a magician. He wears a top hat, cape, paper mustache, carries a magic wand, and calls himself the "Final e, Silent e Magician." Once into the guided practice portion of his lesson, he allows students to use his props and perform magic on CVCe words. It doesn't take much to draw attention, interest, and enthusiasm to the content of your instruction.

Tactic: Use Proximity Praise and Requests

Research has shown that the best praise is specific praise, delivered "up close and personal." By that we mean within one to three desk lengths from the target student. The same goes for requesting students to do something, like sit in their seats. A typical request may go like this: "You guys in the back of the room, could you take your seats?" When no one responds, you revert to the voice volcano and viper behaviors. The voice volcano is a method where you get right up in a student's face and scream in a loud, forceful voice, "Becky, get in your seat now!" While you are up close, personal, and rather specific in your request, the student has been blown halfway across the room from the volume of your voice (and unfortunately does not land in her seat). So you start with the vipers. That is, you stand in the front of the classroom and proceed to point at students in the back of the room, repeatedly simulating a viper attacking its prey. Ouch! Use specific positive praise statements within close proximity and deliver specific requests in the same manner. For example, "Becky, please sit in your seat now and do not get up until you have received permission from me." You will be pleased with the results.

Tactic: Let Students Know They Have a Teacher Who Cares

Inform students at the beginning of the year and every day thereafter that you are a teacher who cares for each and every one of them. Tell them that it is your responsibility to make sure they all are learning to their fullest capacity. Let them know you are in charge and you will be sure to handle any behaviors and complaints in a swift and fair manner. Tell them there may be times you choose to ignore a student(s) who appears to not want to learn, but will continue instruction with those who do. Let them know that you are very aware of the misbehavior but have chosen to ignore it. Let them know that at those times it is their job to stick with you and ignore the misbehavior too. The goal is to allow the learning process to continue for those who want to learn and for the misbehavior to eventually stop. And, don't forget—smile before November!

delivering

Tactic: Make a Big Deal of Progress and Effort

Effective teachers take time to talk with students about their effort and progress. All of us can use a boost from time to time, no matter what our level of ability and interest in school. It feels good to be recognized and confirmed as a valued member of class. (And yes, this goes for those students you hope are absent so you can get through your lesson.) There are a number of ways to recognize student progress. Effective teachers know the value of being able to say something nice about every student on the class roster, even if it means complimenting them on how well they breathe. The point being, as role models for students, teachers need to genuinely show interest and care for the effort and progress students make, no matter how small. It is always powerful to back it up with data and specific examples. "Hey, Trish, last week you completed two of five homework assignments, and this week you completed three! Keep it up and soon you'll be at five of five." Hold brief conferences with your students (one minute or more if needed) to allow for personal contact and giving feedback. Keep track of your conferences. Record what you talked about and together set mini goals for the next conference. Keep it simple and personal.

Use Rewards Effectively

Some educators argue that rewards and reinforcement are simply bribery and don't belong in the classroom. Some believe students should "just do it." Perhaps teachers should "just do it" and not expect a pay check? Everybody works for something, and something works for everybody. Nobody does anything for nothing. There is always some purpose, or reward to our behavior, be it charity work, chores, or paying bills. Effective teachers know that some students need more incentive to complete work and meet other classroom expectations than others. And while everyone enjoys recognition, not everyone enjoys the same kind of recognition. The incentive is in the eye of the beholder. Effective teachers use different types of rewards and recognition to encourage the best efforts from their students.

Tactic: Use Reward Chains

Get students involved in setting goals for behavior and academics. Use reward chains to show progress toward the goals. Here's how:

1 Have a goal-setting session with your students. Pick one to three behaviors they need to learn, achieve, or improve, such as arrive on time to class, come prepared with needed materials, all homework is complete.

delivering

2 Get some colored construction paper and have scissors, glue, or tape readily available.

3 Hang a rod high from some visible spot in the classroom. This is where the reward chain will hang. The rod can be a yardstick or another utensil that is straight and can be suspended easily.

4 When students display any of the goal behaviors, cut a strip of construction paper, write the goal behavior that was accomplished, and close the strip into a circle or link on a chain. Be sure to fasten the first link of the chain around the hanging rod.

5 After that, every time the target behavior(s) is exhibited, links of the chain are made and connected to those already suspended from the rod. Make sure you, or a student, write the goal behavior(s) displayed and the date on the link of the chain.

6 When the chain hits the floor, a preplanned reward or recognition is delivered. The process is started again with the same or different behaviors.

This tactic is fun and extremely motivating for all ages of students. One high school physics teacher used it with his AP class that was perpetually late and "kiddy." Two goal behaviors were set: on-time, and raise hand to speak. These two behaviors were written on the board. If all students met either of the two goal behaviors, a link was earned. The real honor came when a student was selected to ceremonially

make and connect the link. What did these students earn when it hit the floor? Ten minutes of chat time at the end of Friday's class.

Variation
Take note of the width of the chain links and the height at which the rod is hung. The fatter the strips of paper the faster the chain will hit the floor. However, this may matter little if the rod is hung high enough. When you introduce this tactic it may be a good idea to have wide strips or links made (three inches or so). Gradually reduce the width of the strips. Try randomly cutting the strips of paper beforehand and pull them from a hat. Or, you may choose to gradually slim down the links as you build the chain. The choice is yours.

Adaptation
Reward chains can be adapted for use with individual students.

Tactic: Color My Effort
This tactic is based on a matrix setup. Create matrices that have anywhere from four to twenty or more cells. Have students set individual goal behaviors and identify a desirable reward or recognition for their effort. When a student exhibits his/her goal behavior to a set criteria, that student gets to color in a cell of the matrix. When all cells across, down, or on the diagonal are colored, the student earns a preplanned recognition. For example, Peggy needs to complete her work on a more consistent basis. While the work she

delivering

does is stellar, it is not always completed on time, causing a chain reaction of delay and catch up. Peggy has decided she would like to bring in microwave popcorn to pop for herself and two friends of her choice when she colors her efforts in completely. So, for every assignment Peggy hands in, she gets to color one matrix cell. When any three cells are colored in (3 x 3 matrix) a row or diagonal, she earns her popcorn incentive.

Variation

Instead of all cells across, down, or on a diagonal, require the entire matrix to be colored in before recognition is delivered. But be careful. Some students will not be able to maintain or delay gratification long enough to wait for the entire matrix to be colored. For them it is better to start with cells across, down, or on a diagonal and work toward all cells colored in. With this in mind it is wise to start with smaller matrices of four to six cells and gradually increase the number as students get more comfortable and successful at meeting their goals.

Adaptation

Color My Effort can easily be adapted to Color Our Effort. Use it with small or large groups of students.

Tactic: Differentiate "Earned" From "Given"

When establishing a recognition and reward system with your students, be sure you carefully explain that rewards are "earned" as a result of desirable and ap-propriate behavior, just as negative consequences are "earned" as a result of inappropriate behavior. Emphasize the power of earning by having students tell how and why they have earned the recognition. Remember, recognition and rewards do not have to be stars and stickers. For some students a handshake, a private lunch with you, or a tally mark by their name will suffice. Other students may require more creative and tangible incentives. All students will work for something, not all will work for the same thing. But something works for everyone. If at first you don't find it, keep trying. Be sure to know your students and plan for them.

Tactic: Use Lotteries for Everything!

There are a number of ways to use this tactic. A favorite is to purchase a roll of tickets or coupons that are used as raffle tickets (you can call them lottery tickets), and make a lottery box. The lottery system can be used with spelling words, vocabulary, math facts, story main ideas, expected behavior, current events, history facts or dates, and just about anything else that allows you to write the answer on the back of a one inch by one half inch lottery ticket. Here are some fun ways to use them:

▲ Have students record the main idea of the story you have recently read. Write the answer on the back of the ticket with your name and date, and put it in the lottery box.

delivering

▲ During transition time write a riddle or brain teaser on the board. Have students write the answer, their name, and the date on the ticket and put it in the lottery box.

▲ Give a definition of a vocabulary word and have students write the word on the back of the ticket with their name and date. Put them in the lottery box.

▲ Put a math fact on the board and have students solve it and write the answer on the back of the ticket with their name and the date. Drop them into the lottery box.

note: For the above uses, consider assigning a student to check the answers on the lottery tickets before students place them in the box. Otherwise you may find yourself checking the answers of story main ideas, riddles, etc. forever.

▲ Reinforce students for their appropriate or target behavior (e.g., arriving on time, breathing nicely, smiling, use of appropriate language, etc.). Have them write what behavior they were reinforced for on the back of the ticket along with their name and date.

▲ Set a criteria that a student or class must meet. That is, how many times does the target behavior have to occur before a drawing is earned? For example, students must deliver five genuine, positive praise statements. Or, everytime a student raises his/her hand and waits for permis-

sion to speak, the teacher will put a tally mark on the board. When there are at least 10 tallies, the students have earned a lottery drawing.

Always be sure to have students write their name and date on each lottery ticket.

Lottery drawings:

▲ For those drawings that are answer specific (answers to riddles, math facts, etc.), if the information recorded on the ticket is correct, then that person is eligible for recognition or reward. If the information is incorrect, put the ticket aside and choose another one. Decide if you want to announce whose ticket was pulled but was incorrect, or if the information is to be kept anonymous. While it's important to avoid teasing and scapegoating of those students who gave incorrect information, at the same time you will want to let them know their name was indeed drawn and "you just never know when your ticket will be drawn, so stay on your toes and keep working hard on those tickets."

▲ For those drawings based on meeting set criteria (e.g., tally marks), simply draw a ticket. The name on the ticket wins the incentive.

note: This works well with individuals but be careful if the criteria was met as a group and one person's name is drawn, and "unfair" discussion may start.

delivering

144

Be sure the procedures are clearly understood by all students. This method uses a random schedule of reinforcement. Students never know whose name will be drawn, so they all work hard toward meeting the set criteria.

Variation 1

Pepper the lottery box with premade tickets that have specific rewards or have the entire box filled with incentives students would die for. In the latter case, when students earn the chance for a lottery drawing, they earn a specific incentive. One teacher uses "good for one free trip to the bathroom"; "good for one free homework pass"; "good for one lunchroom treat of your choice"; "good for one discount ticket to a local fast food restaurant"; "all kids win!"; etc. These of course will very much depend on your situation and what students will work for. For example, for students who must be under supervision at all times, the privilege of leaving the classroom unaccompanied to use the lavatory would have significant value.

Variation 2

Use team tickets with the lottery system. If students are working in cooperative groups and one person on a team is praised or recognized for a specific behavior or effort, all the team members' names go on the back of the team ticket. If at any time a team ticket is drawn, then all members on that team are rewarded. Be sure to announce the name of the individual team member who earned that reward for them.

After the day or class is over you can dump all the tickets into a weekly lottery drawing box to be used later in the week. Some teachers do monthly, quarterly, or semester drawings. One teacher went as far as having a super duper year end grand prize drawing. The winner won a portable cassette/radio and got to pick two friends to go with him/her to the ice cream parlor of choice—driven in a local police squad car! Remember, the effectiveness of this tactic is only as strong as the reward or recognition on the other end of the drawing. Establish with students ahead of time what they are working for.

Tactic: Use Mystery Motivators

Mystery Motivators (Rhode, Jenson, & Reavis, 1993) are incentive systems designed to deliver random rewards for appropriate or target behavior. They can be used with individual students, teams, or an entire class.

Here's how they work:

1 All you need are invisible and developer markers, and/or peel and stick dot stickers, and an envelope.

2 Establish with your students a menu of rewards or incentives they are willing to work for.

3 Write one reward item on a slip of paper and put it in a sealed envelope. Post the envelope where all the students can see it (see Figure 34).

delivering

4 Define the behavior you want the students to increase or decrease. The behavior should be specific and able to be observed and measured. For example, all students will raise their hands and wait to be called on before speaking. Make sure your students know what the target behavior is, and post it for all to see.

5 Using a daily or weekly calendar, take an invisible marker pen and write an "M" or any other indication of reward (star, smile face, words) in the day's squares of the calendar or Mystery Motivator form. On the days you decide to make a mystery motivator unavailable, mark nothing. If using peel and stick dot stickers, simply mark an "M" or any other award winning mark in ink and cover it with a dot sticker. All five days of the week should have a dot sticker, even if no reward is indicated.

Figure 34

6 If the students meet the prescribed criteria for the selected behavior, they get to color in the square for that day with the developer pen. For example, suppose the target behaviors for your class are: (1) all students arrive to class on time; and (2) all students have homework completed. Select a student to go to the Mystery Motivator form and color in, or peel off the sticker from the day's square. If an "M" or designated mark appears, the Mystery Motivator envelope is opened, and the reward is delivered immediately.

7 However, if no mark appears, congratulate the students on their behavior and tell them to keep up the great work because tomorrow could be "the day."

hints: In the beginning of using this procedure, be sure to mark at least two or three "Ms" or reward marks per week. This allows the students to become familiar with the routine, while reinforcing them immediately for their efforts. Once students have bought into and understand the routine, thin the reward marks out to one or two per week. Again, this will depend on the motivation level of your students and their ability to delay gratification or reward.

This tactic utilizes the most powerful and potent behavior reinforcement—variable schedules of reinforcement. Similar to playing a slot machine, one never knows when the reward or jackpot will come. This alone reinforces the behavior of pulling the slot

delivering

arm, or in the case of your students, continued efforts in academics and behavior.

Variation

A bonus square on the Mystery Motivator form may provide an additional incentive to the students. A number between one and five is written in the box. At the end of the week the students get to color the bonus box with the developer pen (or peel off a sticker) to reveal a number. If the students have met the criteria for the target behavior as specified in the bonus square, regardless if they have been rewarded during the week's Mystery Motivators or not, a bonus reward is given. This reward may be either predetermined or a surprise to the students.

Adapted from: Rhode, G., Jenson, W.R., and Reavis, H.K. (1992).

Tactic: Combine Lotteries and Mystery Motivators

Use the Mystery Motivator with the lottery system. Follow the same steps described in the lottery ticket tactic, above. When a student's name is drawn, he/she earns the privilege of coloring in a square or pulling off a dot sticker. If there is a reward mark, the student(s) is the recipient of whatever is written on the slip of paper in the Mystery Motivator envelope.

Tactic: What Are We Working For?

When students are aware of a goal or ultimate product, they have something to shoot for. Simply directing their effort, or beginning with an end in mind, drives their behavior. What Are We Working For is a tactic that combines public posting with goal setting. For example, a goal for all students to have all homework assignments complete or obtain at least a 75% on them could be set for a class. Using a graphic chart post the goal and then indicate the progress made toward the goal on a daily basis. Sometimes fund raisers show the local public how the community is doing in its effort to support the cause by posting a thermometer with benchmarks in dollar amounts. The mercury rises to reflect the amount of money raised. In the same manner, a thermometer can be used to publicly display how an individual, small group, or class of students is doing in their efforts to meet a set goal —academic or behavioral. When the goal is met, a preplanned recognition or reward should be delivered. These, of course, need to be planned with these students involved in meeting the goal. Some teachers make an icon out of what the students are working for to use as a marker of progress toward the goal. For example, if students are working for free chat time at the end of Friday's class, make a picture of people chatting together. Have one person equal a day, and color them in as you go. Or if making popcorn is the reward, use pictures of popped popcorn and color those in as you go. For no homework over the weekend—ask the students for an idea! For some students some free time or no home-

delivering

work will do the trick. Set the goal, its timeline, and the recognition with your students. Goal sheets can be kept by individuals and groups or posted in the class for all to see.

Tactic: Use Good Kid Patrol

Here is a schoolwide tactic that can catch lots of students doing good work. At the start of every day, give seven (or more) teachers several brightly colored slips of paper. Have the slips say something like:

> Today, ___Emanuel___ was caught being good by ___Dr. E.___ in ___the Science hallway___ at ___1:15 p.m.___ on ___December 10, 2000.___
>
> Congratulations!
> **Now report to the office!**
>
> Signed by ___R. Erickson___

Teachers are to give out all the slips each day to a student they catch being good or doing a good deed. Upon receipt of the slip, the student reports at that time or some convenient time during the day to the principal or other designee and hands over the slip. In return, the student is given a marker and walked to a laminated board that has 100 squares on it. The students writes his/her name in any open square.

This Good Kid Patrol continues until all the cells on the board are signed in by students (a student's name may appear more than once in a row or column). Whenever a row or column is completed, the principal gets on the PA and announces the names of the students who helped build the winning row or column. They are rewarded by the principal in a pre-planned way. Here are some ideas that have been used by building principals: private lunch time with the principal; principal assistants for a day (roles are defined); some outside school activity at no cost to the students, for example, a movie, field trip to the zoo, fast food restaurant, and the like. You'd be surprised what community businesses and organizations will donate or discount for this worthy cause.

Variation 1

You may want to rotate the teachers on patrol by the week instead of the day. That way the patrol schedule can be published to teachers and planned for. You may want to set the number of slips to be given out per day. The number will depend on the size of your school and the frequency with which you want to reward the student effort. You can always start with more slips and then reduce them to fewer per day.

Variation 2

Give patrol duty to older students. Have older students look for younger students. Or have same aged students look for students. Be sure to proactively manage favoritism and/or bullying behavior that could occur when one student wants the slip "or else."

delivering

148

Variation 3

In addition to signing in the square of their choice, have a Good Kid Postcard mailed home for that day, and/or call home.

Variation 4

In addition to the group reward, have a group photograph taken. Post it where all can see. Make a big deal out of this honor. And be sure to remind students that good behavior is not nerd behavior. It is a cool thing to be caught doing something good.

Variation 5

Vary the number of cells on the board to 50, 75, 100, etc. This number will vary according to different variables, for example, the desire to catch and reward students sooner, rather than later, or the number of students enrolled in the school.

Adapted from: Workshop materials, Jenson, W. (1996).

Tactic: Use Dialing for Deliverables

This is a fun tactic that can be used with an individual, whole class, or a group of students. In any case, a menu of reinforcers of five to eight items are identified and placed on the face of a dial or spinner. However, the dial sections are not uniform. The sections vary in sizes from very narrow to a third of the circle. Anything goes.

Procedure:

1 Together with students generate a menu of incentives.

2 Have students, by consensus, prioritize them from most to least desirable.

3 Starting with the item deemed most desirable, write one in each section of the dial, starting with the thinnest section, and progress to the widest.

4 When students have earned the opportunity to be recognized for appropriate behaviors, they are invited to "dial for the deliverable."

5 Selecting students to dial can be done at random (e.g., pulled from a hat), by class vote, or teacher choice. The chosen student spins the dial. Where the needle lands is the incentive of the moment.

Remember, all reinforcers reach a point of satiation. That is, they no longer are novel or motivating to the students. Effort and excitement begin to wane, signaling a time for change. Keep a watchful eye out. Be ready to replace the Dial of Deliverables with new incentives as needed.

Variation 1

This tactic can be successfully used with whole class, small group, or individual students. The key to its use is the desirability of the incentives. Be sure students identify them, while you moderate the reality of use. For example, one student wrote, $100 for his top pri-

delivering

ority, another wrote sleep in late everyday. You know the routine—negotiate and help students identity classroom-based incentives or those that parents/guardians can deliver.

Variation 2

A quick way to plan for the ever changing reinforcement menu is to create a color-coded or patterned dial. The sections in the dial are still varied, however, the menu of items are placed on a color-coded list or patterned list that corresponds with the dial sections. Laminate the dials. When the incentives needs to be altered, simply wipe off the menu and sections and fill with new one. This tactic is effective and motivating for all age groups, including adults! an individual, whole class, or a group of students.

Consider Level and Student Interest

Motivation is learned, not earned. Students must see the value of their efforts in completing work and the relevance of it to their world of reality. Have you ever noticed how well students work when they know there is something desirable attached to the end product? Or a reluctant, resistant adolescent reader whose skills miraculously blossom when studying for the written test for a driving permit? Effective teachers take these perspectives into account when planning and delivering instruction. They also consider students' ability to persevere in tasks assigned to them. Even under what you consider the "best" conditions for learning and motivation, students may not be able, ready, or willing to engage in the learning process. Unfortunately, learned helplessness is alive and well. Some students have been exposed to so much failure and unpleasant academic experiences that even if they won the "no homework for the rest of your life" lottery, they still wouldn't be able to convince themselves they won it, or even worse, were worthy of it. So they engage in "why bother" behavior—"Why bother to do this, I'll only get it wrong," or "Why bother, I am not smart enough to do this," and the ultimate, "I can't do this!" Educators must motivate and help move students into successful, life-long learning experiences. Students must be taught that they do have control over their successes and failures, and teachers must arm them with the strategies and behaviors to win the fight over the "why bother" syndrome.

Tactic: Help Students Value Schoolwork

Effective teachers know the importance of providing lots of examples and reasons for the assignments they require of their students. Students are more likely to complete assigned work when they understand what is required of them, why it is required of them, and how it relates to past and future learning. It is worth your time and energy to make sure students have a clear understanding of purpose for the assignments, tasks, and projects you require of them. Have students restate in their own words what they understand the purpose to be and how it relates to past,

delivering

current, and future use. This may sound easier than it is because students vary in their ability level and interest in school.

Tactic: Provide a Road Map for What's Ahead

Effective teachers make it part of their daily practice to let students know what they will be learning, how they will learn it, and what they need to do to show mastery. Effective teachers share this information at the start of every unit of instruction. This helps students get the "big picture" of what is required and what they will be doing. It also helps to model how to plan ahead for completing long-range projects and coordinate other school activities and assignments. For example, a student involved the school play or sports team may need to know well in advance when tests and assignments are due in order to plan ahead and manage time for studying and task/project completion. Provide students a "week at a glance" or "month at a glance." Post these for all to see and review them daily. Have students replicate them and keep them in their class folders.

Tactic: Lattice Math

Here is a motivating way to have students practice math facts. It can be used for adding, subtracting, and multiplication. Here's how:

▲ Provide students with a lattice framework suitable for the math problem (see Figure 35).

▲ Model what they are to do using the framework.

Be sure to monitor students when they begin learning lattice math—it can be confusing and students will create errors if they put numbers in the wrong spaces. Correct alignment is critical.

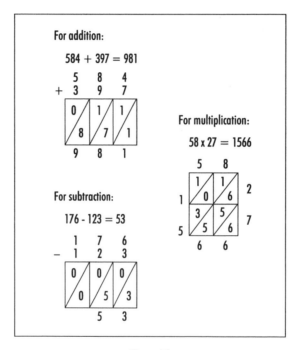

Figure 35

Tactic: Cut 'em Up

For those students who have little tolerance for what they perceive as long assignments, cut them up. Yup, take a pair of scissors and cut the assignments into pieces. It's an oldie but goody. You don't necessarily need to show them how many cut ups they will be doing. All they need to know is when one is complete hand it in and take another. Decide on where students will hand them in and pick new ones up. Some teachers prefer to grade them as they are completed, providing immediate and supportive feedback to students. Students of all ages enjoy this novel tactic. For some it provides them an opportunity to have brief but individual time with the teachers while the cut ups are checked.

note: Be sure to consider whether tasks can be done out of order or not. For example, a math fact sheet can be done in any order. However, a cloze procedure may not. Cut accordingly. Students should be required to complete cut up assignments within the same time periods as those doing the traditional format.

Variation
Have a peer checker or study buddy do the checking of the cut ups.

Tactic: Use Doing the Dots
This tactic is a novel, fun way for students to earn the privilege of doing or not doing work of their choice. It's all in the way they "do their dots." Here's how:

Purchase some peel and stick dots at your local office supply store. Cut them apart so you have all single dots. Tell students they can earn the dots by engaging in expected classroom behavior, for example, doing independent seat work during practice sessions. Tell students they can collect and accumulate the dots or spend them as they wish. On any given assignment they can use the dots to cover up the problem(s) they

choose not to do. If students are working from a text and are to answer chapter questions 1-10, tell them to number their paper and place the dot by the number of the question they choose not to answer. As you can see, students who earn a lot of dots could eventually end up not doing any work, ever. Think about requiring a minimum item completion per assignment. Have students complete these and then decide which of the remaining items they don't want to do. For example, all students must complete questions 1-5. Items 6-10 become dot-able. And if students have five dots, they may choose not to do any of them. You will be amazed how hard students work to get out of work. Think your boss would go for a system like this?

Adapted from: *The Tough Kid Video Series* (1995).

Tactic: Teach Students to Use Affirmations
An affirmation is a statement of fact or belief that is written in a positive, personal, present tense form, as though the goal was already accomplished. For example, "I am a good student." Affirmations are conscious steps at developing positive thinking and self-image. It's "mind over matter." However, too many students give up too easily and need to be taught how to take stock in who they are, their strengths, and their skills. Teach students to create and use affirmations for anything they need to. Explain to students that all affirmations begin with "I" statements, since you can only affirm yourself. Affirmations are always stated in the positive and in the present tense. Tell students to see or visualize them-

delivering

selves completing the task or doing the affirmation. Remind them that lots of sport coaches use this technique with their athletes. Together try some of these out for size:

▲ I am a relaxed and confident student.
▲ I am a good writer.
▲ I am an honest person.
▲ I have confidence in my ability to learn.
▲ I control my anger.
▲ I can do things I set my mind to.
▲ I thrive on beating the bell for class.

For many students this will be a difficult task. Have students brainstorm a list of qualities they see in themselves, then turn them into affirmations. Have students write them on index cards and carry them in a pocket. Or they can type them up on a word processor and put them in a notebook or in their locker. Encourage students to reaffirm themselves daily and whenever they need a little hurdle help.

Tactic: Use Technology

With today's technology how could learning be anything but interesting and fun? There are many ways to engage students in active and motivating learning events. CD ROMs, portable CD players, computers (both personal and laptop), and the Internet are just a few things that spark students' interest. However, many do not have access to these wonderful tools. Get resourceful. Contact your local technology store and ask for a tour or classroom demonstration. Talk

to community groups for donations and fund-raisers to purchase these learning tools. Make it a class or schoolwide goal to raise money for a piece of technological equipment. Remember, these do not have to be new—look into buying used equipment. The market changes on a daily basis, and what was in today will be out tomorrow. There are some who keep up with these changes and would be interested in selling older versions to buy newer ones. Check into educator discounts at computer companies and retail stores. If you do have access to a computer and modem but not the Internet, enlist community support and have businesses adopt the class for the month, paying for the Internet charge for the month. The world of information opens up to you and your class on the Internet.

Tactic: Join the Yagottawana Team!

Coach Yagottawana says, "Realize what you can be!" Effective teachers take time to talk to their students about attitude —what is it, how does it influence us as people, and how can it help or hinder the learning and performance process. Ask students to identify which of the following statements fits them best:

▲ "I can't do it, so I won't even try to do it."
▲ "I could do it if I wanted to, but I don't want to."
▲ "I can do it and would want to do it if it didn't involve so much work."
▲ "I can do it, and I want to do it, and I'm going to use all of my abilities to make sure that I do it."

delivering

Some points to include in your discussion are:

▲ Yagottawana be teachable, and that includes attitude. Talk to your students about starting from where they are. Previous low grades and experiences don't mean stop trying or give up.

▲ Yagottawana set goals. Talk to students about setting goals for themselves. Discuss the purpose of goal setting in a variety of areas.

▲ Yagottawana do the work. This is sometimes the most difficult part of Coach Yagottawana's strategy. Teach and talk to your students about finding time to both work and play hard. Talk about self-discipline and what it means in a variety of contexts.

Adapted from: G.O.A.L.S. (1989).

Tactic: Teach Attitude Choices

Expand students' knowledge and understanding about attitude by having them show what they know and how they would apply themselves in difficult or challenging situations. For example, sometimes when you know you're wrong, it's hard to apologize and act polite. What do you do? Provide students with practice scenarios. Tell them to think of the "best way" to handle the given situation. You can make it more personalized by asking them to identify the way they would handle the situation, and why and what the potential effects could be. Situations can range from be-

ing late to class to letting the teacher know the pace of instruction is too fast.

Tactic: Do It, Solve It, Own It

This is another tactic to provide students an opportunity to check in with themselves on where they stand on issues, attitudes, and challenges they face on a daily basis. School is full of challenges. Some are tougher than others. Teach students how to problem-solve potential situations. Help them become better equipped and automatic with handling touchy situations. Students are individuals. Therefore, what may be a potentially difficult or challenging situation for one may not be for another student. Provide students with an array of scenarios. Have them write three or more ways they would handle the given situation. Then tell them to put a star next to the one they think is the "best" option to use, and be prepared to discuss. Have students develop scenarios to present to the class. Often students will present a current situation they could use some help on (or they "have this friend who …").

Tactic: Teach It's Okay to Make Mistakes, But Be Sure to Learn From Them

Everybody makes mistakes, but smart people learn from them. Effective teachers know that it's okay to make mistakes, and they let their students know it too. For many students, this is just enough to take the pressure off being "perfect" and allows them to engage in learning in more creative and productive

delivering

154

ways. In a sense it gives them permission to take risks they wouldn't otherwise take. Tragically, many students see mistakes as evidence of wrongdoing, stupidity, and even unworthiness. Teach students that mistakes show the way for improvement. Without them, there would be nothing to work on. Teach students to embrace problems and mistakes. Adopt the attitude "problems are our friends!" Teach students to aim for success, not perfection. Teach them never to give up their right to be wrong. Teach them that avoiding situations in which they might err may be the biggest mistake of all. Most of all, practice what you teach!

Tactic: Teach Students About Responsibility

Teach students about taking responsibility for how they act. One of the best ways to do this is to provide students with potential problem-solving situations. Have students take the active first person role and tell how each situation could improve if he/she took responsibility for his/her attitude. Have them discuss and/or write about the better way to act. You may consider having students work in small groups to share problem-solving solutions. Be sure all groups get the opportunity to share how they would handle it. Consider having students reach a consensus on each. This may prove to be a challenge as all people do not see, act, or take responsibility in the same way. Regardless, use this as a way to teach options, solutions, and alternate ways to handle situations.

Tactic: Use the Autograph Hunt

Here's a novel way to perk student interest and activity—create an Autograph Hunt. Make a list of items and require someone to sign off on it. That is, someone must authenticate an item by signing next to it. The list of items can include just about anything. For example:

_____ Sleeps past 10 AM on the weekends

_____ Saw a movie last week

_____ Was born outside this state

_____ Thinks dissecting frogs is cool

_____ Believes in conflict resolution

The ideas are endless and can be tailored to age and interest level as well as course content.

Students are provided the time and opportunity to get up and move about the room looking for someone who can autograph the item. Tell students only one person can autograph one item on their sheet. This restriction allows for students to talk and get around to other students they may not know. The Autograph Hunt is a great ice breaker for a new class or vehicle for students to learn more about each other. Be sure you participate in the Autograph Hunt so you get to know your students and they you!

delivering

Variation

The Autograph Hunt can be quickly converted into People Bingo. It follows the same format, except students sign off in a grid or square. The first person to complete a row, column, or diagonal wins. However, in this case not all the squares are filled, and there-fore students do not interact with each other at the same level as they do when required to have 20 items, for example, signed off to be considered finished with the task.

Adapted from: Kagan, S. (1994).

For Teaching Thinking Skills

Students are expected to come to school knowing how and when to think and process information. But students don't always know how to think things through, or how to strategize actions and options for problems. Many students are good at memorizing rote or isolated facts but cannot integrate them to use in problem-solving or to transfer to other applications. Just like any other skill, thinking skills must be assessed and taught. It's that old prior knowledge thing again. Don't assume all students have had the opportunity to experience creative thinking or problem solving. Thinking skills must be taught.

onstrating processes or steps needed to complete tasks or problem-solve. They also model error correction procedures and how to handle academic and behaviorally frustrating situations. Teaching students how to monitor what they think and how to think through situations and tasks are extremely valuable tools for students, both in and out of the school setting.

Tactic: Teach Think-Aloud Strategies

Modeling expected behaviors is one of the most powerful means of teaching and should be a part of every lesson. Think-aloud strategies provide a wonderful opportunity to model the process and procedures to complete a task, problem-solving situation, or just about anything. For example, when teaching the writing process a teacher may think aloud, "First I have to come up with a topic to write about. Okay, let's see, how about gorillas. Now I need a topic sentence to begin my first paragraph. But I need to have an idea of where I want the paragraph to go. I know I need a be-

strategy

Model Thinking Skills

One of the most effective ways to teach thinking is through modeling them. Effective teachers take time to plan and integrate teaching thinking skills by dem-

delivering

ginning, middle, and end." And so on. This process shows the exact steps the students should follow in their process of writing. A nice feature of this tactic is it shows students that, no matter how old or skilled you are, thinking, planning, problem-solving, preparation, and corrections are all a part of a process to get from one task to the next, in the most linear fashion.

Tactic: Use HDYKT

Here is a tactic that keeps students (and teachers) on their toes. Once introduced to students, no longer will answers be given without someone asking, "HDYKT?" or "How Do You Know That?" Whenever a question is answered simply ask "HDYKT?" The student must back up his/her answer with evidence of what, where and/or how the answer was derived. HDYKT encourages students to back up their answers with supporting facts, theories, and details. In some cases it curtails and encourages students who blurt out answers without thinking to take the time to think through an answer and be prepared to tell about it. HDYKT also provides students the opportunity to listen to the process and procedures of how others arrived at their answers. In addition, it provides a golden opportunity for error correction procedures to be modeled, if needed. One teacher posts a huge HDYKT sign in her classroom as a prompt to herself and students to use the strategy with her and each other.

Tactic: Teach Talk to Yourself

Teach students it's okay to talk to yourself. It is a form of metacognition—a very big word they will be able to use when people ask them, "Why are you talking to yourself?" Response—"I am using a metacognitive strategy to help me think through a process (problem, procedure, etc.)." Very cool. Some students and adults prefer to think in their head rather than aloud, and that's fine. Be sure to model how you use this tactic in your day-to-day thinking, specifically when working in content areas. Talk yourself through a math problem, or getting organized to complete an assignment, or even how you will manage your time in order to get your work done so you can play.

Tactic: Use Checklists to Keep Skills Fresh

Regardless of how you teach thinking skills, some students will benefit from a checklist of steps to follow when thinking through a task or procedure. Help students create their own personal lists, or create one as a class. For example, what thought process should your students use if they arrive late to class and instruction has already begun? Or how should Melea think through the steps of preparing and putting together an oral report? These checklists can be used for developing steps needed to complete guided or independent practice on a particular skill. For example, a checklist for writing could include things like capitalize first words, mark end sounds, dialogue/conversation, check for appropriate punctuation, watch

delivering

endings on action words, etc. Checklists can be devised for math, spelling, and any other task or topic that requires students to think through a routine procedure. Here's how:

1 Brainstorm what steps a student needs to do or must follow to compete a task.

2 Write them down in the order they need to occur (if order of operation applies).

3 Have students copy the checklists into their notebooks or make a class poster.

4 Repeat this process for any task or procedure when students need or would benefit from the use of a checklist.

Tactic: Teach Predicting and Correction Procedures

For many students, the act of predicting is almost impossible. Have you ever worked with a student who, no matter what, cannot manage to make a prediction? Perhaps it's the risk involved, or maybe they don't fully understand the concept or purpose of prediction. Either way, the skill needs to be modeled and taught. One way is to start with a jar of beans, buttons, rocks, or whatever else you can get your hands on. Before you start, count how many objects you place in the jar so you know that number. Throughout the day or week, have students write their guesses on a slip of paper, sign it, and put it in the "Guess Box." This activity provides a grand

opportunity for students to tell how they arrived at their guess. You need to be sensitive to those students who have "predictaphobia." Avoid having those students feel "put on the spot" to tell their predictions. Teach students the many ways you go about creating or arriving at a prediction. Call on those students who are more confident. Generalize predicting behavior to academic task completion and performance. For example, have students predict how long it will take them to complete a task and how well (number of corrects) they will do. After they complete the task, take time to process how they did. How close did they come to their prediction? Many errors could mean the student took a careless and rapid approach to a task, the student needs more skill instruction, or the student needs more practice on predicting.

Tactic: Use PMI

Plus, Minus, and Interesting is a great way to have students synthesize, evaluate, and voice their opinion or thinking on a topic or issue. After modeling the procedure, tell students to think about the Positives (P), less than positives or Minuses (M), and the Interesting things (I) about the posed topic. The Interesting ideas are those things they feel they need more information about, wonder how they would fit or impact the topic, or see as interesting alternatives to consider. Be sure to tell your students that PMI does not have to be completed in any order of sequence (first P, then M, …). Rather, just brainstorm ideas for each and write them down in the category where they think they belong.

delivering

PMI can be successfully used independently by students, in small groups, or with the whole class. Allow students to complete the procedure individually first. Provide students time to think creatively without any pressure before moving to small or large group processing. Whether done independently or in small or large groups, the final product of PMI is a master list that incorporates all group members' ideas. Students are (by consensus if done in a group) to identify the three Ps, Ms, and Is in each category that best reflect the group's thinking on the topic.

Adapted from: deBono, E. (1986).

Tactic: Model Error Correction Procedures

Trial and error are part of learning. When students accept problems as friends, they give themselves permission to learn from their mistakes. Effective teachers value the importance of modeling error correction procedures. It provides an opportunity to show students how to reconsider, compare, contrast, and evaluate what part(s) of a task or procedure were correct, almost correct, or way off. Teach students to take time to maximize their learning from mistakes. Make sure your students observe that you, too, make mistakes and false starts, backtrack, reconsider your course of action, correct, and adjust without worrying about being wrong. Model error correction procedures with a matter-of-fact, try again attitude that encourages persistence and learning.

Teach Fact-Finding Skills

Students are required to engage in critical thinking and problem solving on a daily basis, both in school and social situations. This type of thinking affects the way students gather information for making decisions. While fact-finding seems like a rather straightforward task, many students are clueless about where and how to do it. For example, some teachers assign book reports or papers to students with the assumption they know how to plan the task, where to begin, and how to identify the most important and relevant information. Yes, the procedure for fact-finding must be taught like any other skill.

Tactic: Use I Spy

Here's one that goes way back. Simply pick something in your classroom and begin the process of providing clues or facts about it. Students are to try to guess the object you have in your mind. It can be used as a way to acquaint students with class materials. One middle school science teacher uses it for providing facts or clues that describe different lab equipment. "I spy something flat, circular, with a lid. What is it? Okay, here's another clue: It is usually glass and is used to hold or grow things. Give up? A petri dish!" Get students involved in the act. Find out what they know or don't know by the facts or clues they provide.

delivering

Tactic: Use Hide the Keys

A variation of I Spy, Hide the Keys is a fact-finding, direction-following game where an object is actually hidden in the classroom. Students are provided factual clues as to where the object is. Some teachers simply provide clues of hot, cold, warm, and variations thereof. While verbal clues and facts are readily offered, students must go through a fact-finding and thinking process that is guided by the temperature clues.

Tactic: Teach Students to Do Research

Do not assume students know how to research or plan a project or paper. Model and teach first. Provide students with outlines of what you are looking for in their reports. One teacher starts with a simple list of the "wh" questions (who, what, when, where, why, how, what for, etc.), and then takes her students to the library and actually leads them through the process of finding the answers. Another way to teach research and fact-finding is to have students interview someone for the purpose of gathering information about a topic. For example, interview a grandparent. Find out when they grew up, where they grew up, what it was like, and any other experiences they can offer. Before a field trip or guest speaker, have students write questions about information they would like to know. If the questions remain unanswered, have students further research their answers using a library and other resources. There are many, many resources available, and the sheer vol-

ume can be intimidating. Many times students do not know how or where to gather information, or what resources are available and helpful. Give students a list of resources, their purpose, potential uses, and where they can be located. Better yet, create the list with the students and find out what they already know.

Tactic: Teach Students How to Plan and Organize for Research Projects

Once students have an idea of what their topic is about, they need to plan when and how they will actually do the work, get to the library, and peruse resources. This is often difficult for students, especially when it is a long-term assignment. Effective teachers provide students with schedules and outlines to help students see the big picture and plan needed daily, weekly, and even monthly progress toward the end product.

Tactic: Send Students on a Fact-Finding Mission

Use content area tasks to sharpen students' fact-finding skills. Provide students with sentences, passages, or a paragraph. Instruct students to underline the words that answer a specific question posed. You can provide these questions verbally or in writing. Students are to not only find the answer, but underline or highlight it. If you are using textbooks, have the students write on a separate paper the page, paragraph, and line in the paragraph where the answer can be found. Expand their knowledge application by using worksheets or other material that require them

delivering

to circle the split infinitives, box the dangling participles, and put an X through all interrogative sentences. Fact-finding can be fun.

Tactic: Teach Students to Apply Study Skills

Here's one to use with textbooks. When assigning work, do not give the page number; rather, give factual clues of what and where students are to do the work. For example, instead of telling students the chapter or story name and page number, give only the title. It is up to them to use their study skills to locate the story (e.g., use of the table of contents, index, etc.). To make the task more difficult, give the author name or the topic of the chapter. Students are then required to use the author index and read through the contents in the book to decide what title most closely matches the topic given. Be sure these are fairly straightforward. Some chapters or literature stories have titles that offer few clues to what the story is actually about.

Tactic: Use Inferential Thinking Activities

Provide opportunities for students to practice and develop inferential thinking skills. There are many ways to do this. One way is to provide only some of the facts needed to solve a riddle, answer a question, or make a conclusion. Have students problem-solve aloud. Have them tell the steps they went through to apply the facts given to arrive at a theory or answer. Another way is to use a slide projector to project an object that is badly out of focus. Have the students go about the process of inferring what the picture is. Be sure to provide independent as well as guided practice. Gradually focus the picture, in stages, until it is clear. Once in focus, encourage students to write down and/or evaluate their original inferences. How did they do?

Tactic: Use Maps and Webs

Story mapping and webs are alive and well. They provide students with a structured and organized way to lay out and record facts found in stories, passages, or chapters. They provide students with a visual road map of the facts they are looking for and how they connect or integrate into the story, passage, or chapter as a whole. Decide how much beginning information you will give to the students. Provide them with some information filled in or none at all.

delivering

⏱ Tactic: Use Question Wheels

Here is another way to engage students in a prereading activity. Make or draw a circle on the board or overhead. In the middle write the name or topic of the story (see Figure 36). Draw spokes in the wheel. Have students generate questions they want to know about the topic or story. Then read the story, and use the question wheel to review what was learned about the topic. Were all the questions on the spokes answered? Can any answers be inferred from the reading? If questions remained unanswered after postreading discussion is complete, use these spokes to generate research topics, or launch fact-finding missions.

Figure 36

Variation

Instead of spokes on a wheel, think of sections of a circle. Write the questions on the lines that divide the sections of the circle. Record the answers to the questions inside the sections of the circle. You now have a fact sheet about the story. Not only do you have student-generated questions, you also have the answers to them. If some questions remain unanswered, have students record their answers as they are researched. The question circle can serve as a review tool and prompt for needed research.

⏱ Tactic: Teach Students How to Follow Oral Directions

Teach students the facts about following oral direction: listen for important words, and depend on visual reminders instead of memory only. Provide students with fun opportunities to practice and experience early listening success. Present a list of directions for students to follow. Deliver the directions in a "normal" conversation speaking rate. Use inflection as appropriate, and repeat each direction once. Be sure to pause after each direction to allow students time to complete each instruction before going on. Monitor timing by walking around the room and watching students work.

delivering

162

Teach Divergent Thinking

Teaching divergent thinking skills simply means teaching students to think differently and in different ways by expanding horizons, challenging the practical, and deviating from the norm. Breathe diversity into students thinking by providing them with interesting and expansive thinking tasks. For example, if you were stranded on a desert island and had only one opportunity to communicate with civilization to request two items, how and what would you request, and why? Think of all the consideration and pondering this task requires. Your students will obviously need to do a lot of thinking about a very serious matter—life and death! Have students create divergent thinking tasks. You would be surprised how well they can deviate from the norm.

Tactic: Use Think-Ahead Strategies

Teach students to not only make predictions, but to think ahead to the possible outcomes of a prediction. Have students generate possible outcomes to their prediction and then rank order them in terms of likelihood and/or personal preference. Here's how:

1 Pose a situation. For example, "What do you predict would happen if there was a famine in the United States?"

2 Tell students to list the possible consequences.

3 Then have students number the consequences in order from most to least likely to occur.

4 Finally, when students are ready, have them put an "X" next to the two consequences they personally would prefer or not prefer to occur.

This tactic can be completed independently, in small groups, or as a whole class activity. If done in a group, steps 3 and 4 become tasks of consensus. The group must order the items from most to least likely to occur and agree on the two best consequences.

Adapted from: Harmin, M. (1995).

Tactic: Use Fishboning

Effective teachers know the importance of keeping students actively engaged in content-related discussion. They plan to deliver information in ways that engage all students. Here's one interesting way to get students involved. Draw an outline of a fish on the board or chart paper. Draw a line down the length of the fish signifying the backbone. From the body of the fish draw bones or lines that extend from the backbone on the fish. At the mouth of the fish draw a bubble or circle.

Now you are ready to Fishbone. On the backbone write the topic or theme of discussion. On the bones that extend from the body write supporting facts, items, factors, causes, etc. that relate to the theme of the discussion. At the mouth of the fish write what the desired outcome is or is believed to be. This may need to be done by consensus.

delivering

Students can complete this activity in small or large groups (even independently). It encourages active discussion and debate about items, issues, and topics as only a few thoughts can be recorded on the limited number of fishbones drawn. Fishboning can be used as an initial brainstorm of ideas surrounding a topic and outcome. If needed, subbones can be drawn to allow more space for the recording of ideas.

Tactic: Use Critical and Noncritical Attributes

Teach students to think in ways that examine critical and noncritical attributes, essential and nonessential details or facts, and examples and nonexamples. Provide students with the opportunity to practice skills of discrimination and perception. This can be done by having students find what's the same or what's different about an object, concept, piece of literature, verbs, nouns, and so on. For example, have students tell what the similarities are between a tribe and a community. Or ask them to tell what differences exist between a tribe and a community. Have them discuss suspension and expulsion, reading and writing, happy and surprise, an elephant and a song, a magazine and multiplication. Ask them to tell how they are the same or different, but not both. Many times you can discriminate the differences by reversing the similarities. You can push students to higher levels of thinking and discrimination by the word pairs you pose.

 ## Tactic: Use K-W-L

K-W-L is a strategy that focuses on what students already know about a topic (K), what they want to learn about it (W), and after reading and/or participating in a lesson, what they learned about it (L). Prior to the lesson, provide students with a worksheet, or simply have them draw three columns on a sheet of paper and at the top of the columns write K-W- L, one letter per column. The students fill out the first two columns of the sheet (K-W) before the lesson begins and the third column (L) when the lesson is complete. This procedure can be completed individually, in small groups, or with a whole class. An effective way to use K-W-L is to allow students to record their own thoughts first, then move into small or large group discussion. The purpose of this tactic is to provide students with a structured opportunity to think and evaluate their knowledge on a particular topic or issue. Information gained from the W (want to know) column provides you information to tailor your instruction to meet the interest levels or knowledge gaps of your students. Completing the L (what learned) column serves as a quick evaluation of students' understanding and learning of the content delivered. Plan for following up and/or reteaching if necessary.

Adapted from: Olgle, D. (1986).

Tactic: Use Think-Pair-Share

Here is a another way to provide you and your students a structured way to observe and model thinking skills. It is a way for all students to generate individ-

delivering

ual ideas, practice expressing ideas, and listen and paraphrase others' ideas.

1 Assign students to random heterogeneous learning teams of four. Within the group of four students, students then create two groups of two. Each student is designated as "Number One" or "Number Two."

2 Pose a question, problem, description, comparison, or position to your students.

3 Instruct all students to THINK individually. That means there is no direct eye contact with anyone (to avoid distraction) and no talking. However, it is important to encourage students to write and record their thoughts in any manner for use in later discussion.

4 After an appropriate amount of time (determined by monitoring student action or writing behavior), usually anywhere from two to four minutes, instruct your students to PAIR up with their partner within their original group of four. In pairs, students tell their ideas about the posed topic. Tell them that Number Ones will talk first while Number Twos listen. Tell students you will give them a signal when it is time to switch roles, so that Number Twos talk while Number Ones listen. Again, you decide how long is long enough by monitoring student behavior while in their pairs.

5 After a sufficient amount of time, students are instructed to get back into their original groups of four. Pairs are then instructed to SHARE their ideas with each other.

6 Instruct the teams of pairs to be prepared to share their most interesting and important information about the topic or issue with the class.

This tactic provides you with rich information about what and how students think about a topic. It gives students the opportunity to hear different points of view and thinking on posed items. There are many ways to think, but there is no one right way to think. This demonstrates how different people think the same or differently about issues, and why.

Adapted from: Kagan, S. (1994).

Tactic: Provide Opportunities to Change and Modify Materials

Have students rewrite a story, events in a story, and/or the ending. Provide them the opportunity to change character roles (males to females and visa versa), reactions to story events, settings etc. This task sounds easier than it is. Students must not only comprehend the story in general, but be aware of nuances and subtleties of events, dialogue, characters, and so on. Have students discuss the effects of the changes on the story, play, or piece of literature.

delivering

Tactic: Provide for Divergent Predictions

Have students judge a book by its cover. Have students make predictions based on facts they think are important. For example, have them predict the outcome of the school football game and tell what they based their prediction on (bigger players, more seniors, better equipment). Any sporting event works fine. Or how about the weather. Have students predict what they think tomorrow's and/or the five-day forecast will be. They need to back up their predictions with how and why they arrived at their prediction. Who knows, they may teach the local meteorologists a thing or two. This tactic can be used for class novels and literature books as well. Show the students the book, tell them the title, look at any pictures, and have them predict what they think it is about and why. These tasks teach divergent predicting skills.

Tactic: Provide Opportunities to Generate Character Thoughts

Take an old classic or any reading material you require of students, and have students generate alternate thinking and thoughts for the characters. Discuss TV shows and cartoons that show not only the character acting/speaking, but also the thoughts they are thinking. Assign the creation of a similar format to your students. Have students create cartoons, pictures, or use illustrations from a book to show what the characters are "really" thinking. One teacher uses this tactic by providing cartoon caricatures with empty dialogue bubbles over their heads.

Students are to write in what they think the character is really thinking. Students write the nonverbal thoughts in the dialogue bubbles. This task provides students the opportunity to apply what they know about the plot and characters as well as develop an alternate personality for each one.

Variation

Have one set of students silently role play a scene or act of a play, while another set, assigned one to each character, verbalizes the thoughts. This can be a humorous and entertaining display of creativity and divergent thinking.

Tactic: Teach How to Generate Different Applications for Materials

Here is a quick way to give students an opportunity to practice brainstorming different functions for different materials or inanimate objects. For example, have students generate a list of possible functions for a potato peeler, ruler, eyelet of a sneaker, etc. Look around the classroom—select a familiar object or geometric shape to use in this activity. The purpose of this tactic is to provide students the opportunity to think of any different and creative applications for a common item.

Variation

Show students a geometric shape—it can be one or three dimensional. Have students generate a list of objects and respective uses that could be formed by the shape.

delivering

Tactic: Play the Word Game

Here is an old favorite—simply have students sit in a circle and create sentences one word at a time. Have a student pick a word, any word, to start, and then have the next student add a word. Soon you will have a string of words that are creating a sentence—some of which are creative yet hysterical.

Variation

Give students a topic around which to build a sentence. Offer, for example, the topics of metamorphosis, or having a third arm growing out the middle of your chest. The more creative and expansive the topic, the more interesting the sentences are.

Tactic: Use Free Association: Let It Flow!

Here is a wonderful associative thinking activity that gets the juice going (brain juices, that is). Draw a square on a board, overhead, or chart. Ask students to give you one word for each quadrant. Below the square write a "statement starter." Have students complete the statement starter using one word in each of the four quadrants. For example:

shrimp	chocolate
summer	homework

Statement starters:

▲ Being the "new kid on the block" is like (a) …, because ….

▲ Following our classroom rules is like (a) …, because ….

▲ Apply this tactic to content area issues or topics. For example, "Being a soldier during the Civil War was like (homework), because … you had to prepare for the next day's lesson, but never knew how you would score."

---

strategy

Teach Learning Strategies

The demands on students to learn more breadth and depth of content areas is evident by the current push in academic excellence across the country. While there is good cause for these changes, students have been left with the awesome task of learning to higher standards. While the brain can hold an amazing amount of information, there are ways to make learning and memorization of facts, concepts, and strategies less arduous. Effective teachers build these learning strategies into the delivery of lesson content and use them to suggest ways for students to remember key points of information.

delivering

Tactic: Teach Concentration

Ask students, "What helps you concentrate?" Find out what students know about their ability to concentrate and factors that influence it. Then share that there are at least three things that can help them concentrate.

1 Wanting to Learn—Remind them that no one can learn for them. Our minds are always active and ready to receive new ideas. Wanting your mind to grow will improve your concentration.

2 Becoming Interested—Tell them the more they know about a subject, the more likely it is they will become interested in it. The responsibility is theirs.

3 Being Organized—Help students stay or become organized.

Teach students how to deal with distractions.

1 Daydreaming—Whenever you find yourself daydreaming, make a mark on a piece of paper. Keep track of how much and how often you catch yourself in a daydream. Work to reduce that number. Set a timer, have a buddy check in with you, etc.

2 Being Hungry and Tired—If you are hungry or tired you are at a great disadvantage. Get some sleep and eat some food. Being alert is half the battle of achieving a productive state of concentration.

3 Personal Problems—Believe it or not, being concerned about personal problems postpones your ability to concentrate. Talk to someone to let out some thoughts or steam, especially if you have a test or project due in the immediate future.

Finally, have your students take a little concentration quiz. Find out what they truly know and understand about their own patterns of concentration.

Tactic: Use Mnemonics

Mnemonics are learning tricks or methods used to help improve memory. They involve the use of elaboration strategies. Elaboration refers to activities that link two or more items to be memorized in some meaningful way. A high school science teacher helps her students memorize animal phylums using an elaboration strategy. In order to remember that Annelida was the phylum for earthworm, she teaches her students to visualize a girl wearing a sweatshirt that says "Ann" across the front walking an earthworm on a leash. When the students are asked the phylum name for earthworm, they visualize Ann walking an earthworm on a leash—Annelida. There is overwhelming

delivering

168

support for elaboration strategies for learning facts about natural history, unfamiliar English and foreign language vocabulary, science facts and expository prose. Your students will like this tactic.

Tactic: Use Method of Place

The ability to retrieve information stored in memory depends on the process of encoding, or how the information is filed in people's memory banks. Method of Place involves organization, visualization, and association. It is used when one concept has many items or facts connected to it. Using this learning strategy entails making a mental map of a place that is familiar (classroom, bedroom, baseball diamond, etc.). The items to be remembered are associated with certain landmarks of the room. For example, in teaching students to remember five advantages the North possessed in the Civil War, one teacher has her students

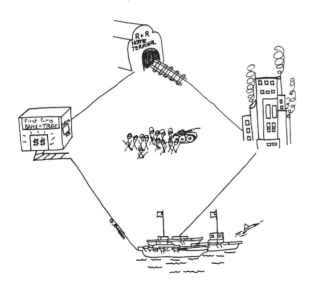

visualize a baseball diamond. The pitcher's mound and the four bases serve as the key reference points. Students make a mental picture of each advantage the North possessed at one of the five locations. Students picture a steam engine chugging across home plate for "the more extensive railways." At first base, they visualize factory exhaust stacks for "a more widely developed industry." At second base, students imagine Navy ships on water for "a large Navy." At third base students picture a bank bursting with $100 bills for "more cash flow." And on the pitcher's mound, students imagine hundreds of pitchers in blue uniforms for "a greater number of soldiers." Method of Place is a powerful learning strategy to teach students.

Tactic: Use the Pegword System

The Pegword System is a fun way for students to remember ordered or numbered information. A pegword is an easily pictured rhyming word for the numbers one through ten. They are:

One is a bun.
Two is a shoe.
Three is a tree.
Four is a door.
Five is a hive.
Six is sticks.
Seven is heaven
Eight is a gate.
Nine is wine.
Ten is a hen.

delivering

Here's one way a high school history teacher uses the Pegword System to teach students abut the Fourth Amendment of the U.S. Constitution. This amendment protects citizens against unreasonable search and seizure. The students visualize a door (the pegword for four) with arms, legs, and a face being frisked by a police officer. When asked about the Fourth Amendment, students think, "four is a door," and visualize a door being frisked by a police officer. This translates into, "The Fourth Amendment protects U.S. citizens against …."

Another middle school teacher uses the Pegword System to remind students of important things that must go home and come back to school in a timely fashion. Her students visualize the item (conference confirmation slips, report cards, etc.) on a bun (a number **1** priority sandwiched in a **bun**). The rate of return has improved substantially.

Tactic: Use the Keyword Method

The Keyword Method can be used with a variety of paired/associated learning tasks such as learning vocabulary, cities and industrial products, states and capitols, to name a few. The keyword method enhances memory and learning by creating an acoustic and imagery link. An elementary teacher uses the following example to teach her students country/product associations. The country of Mozambique is known for its export of peanuts. Students use the sound of "beak" for the acoustic link or keyword. The mental picture or imagery is a bird holding a peanut in its beak. The students are asked, "What is the product of Mozambique?" Students hear the keyword "beak" and they visualize a bird with a beak full of peanuts.

Other examples:

▲ Bolivia is known for its corn product. The keyword is bowl—visualize a bowl full of corn.
▲ Roman numeral D = 500—think of the Indy 500.
▲ The Roman numeral M = 1,000—the Milky Way has thousands of stars.

delivering

Tactic: Use Acronyms and Acrostics

Acronyms and acrostics both make use of the memory method of chunking. Chunking simply reduces the amount of material to be learned into manageable bits or chunks of information. Acronyms provide cues to each word by listing the first letter of each word in the acronym. For example, HOMES is used to remember the five Great Lakes —**H**uron, **O**ntario, **M**ichigan, **E**rie, and **S**uperior. Acrostics, on the other hand, are a series of words, lines, or verses in which the first or last letters form a word, phrase, or sentence. For example, many novice musicians are taught to remember the lines in the treble clef (E, G, B, D, F) as **E**very **G**ood **B**oy **D**oes **F**ine. The classification system of plants and animals becomes **K**ing **P**hilip **C**ame **O**ver **F**or **G**reen **S**tamps and **V**ariety (Kingdom, Phylum, Class, Order, Family, Genus, Species, and Variety). Or, remember the five largest planets in the solar system as **J**ohn **S**mith **U**npacked **N**oodles **E**arly (Jupiter, Saturn, Uranus, Neptune, and Earth). Acrostics and acronyms are learning strategies that are so simple yet so underused.

Tactic: Use Rhymes or Memory Songs

Rhyming and songs are traditional mnemonics that have been successfully used for many years. The act of rhyming and singing appeals to the ear (assuming everyone is on key). Remember these? Thirty days hath September, April, June, and November … or "i" before "e" except after "c"… or the a-b-c- song you learned in Kindergarten. The oldies but goodies stick with us forever.

Tactic: When All Else Fails, Use Repetition

Even repetition needn't be boring. Use repetition games with the entire class as a fun way to learn short facts. For example, here are three games that can be used to teach multiplication facts.

▲ Password for the Day—Select a multiplication problem, perhaps 6 x 7 = ? Then call for the answer at different times of the day—when students leave the room, go to sharpen a pencil, or any other odd times when they aren't expecting it. Encourage students to ask at least three other classmates for the password multiplication fact for the day.

▲ Hand Math—Show six fingers, cross your arms, and then show seven fingers. Students respond by flashing 42 (10 fingers four times, then 2 fingers). Have students partner up and check each other.

▲ Spell It—Spell the problem (s-i-x t-i-m-e-s- s-e-v-e-n), and have the students chorally spell the answer back. Again, have students partner up and check their spelling. Be sure to have the spelling of the numeral in clear view for those students who need it. You are looking for the product, not whether the student can spell it (unless it is a past spelling word).

Adapted from: G.O.A.L.S. (1989).

delivering

Tactic: Use the CAR Method

Here's a quick method for remembering someone's name as soon as you are introduced.

C = CONCENTRATE
   Stop—Stop everything else you are doing.
   Look—Look directly into the eyes of the person
      being introduced.
   Listen—Listen carefully to the person's name
      as it is said.

A = ASSOCIATE
   Try to associate the person's name with
   someone you already know with a similar name,
   or associate the name with something humorous
   or ridiculous.

R = REPEAT
   Repeat the person's name as soon as possible. For
   example, say, "Mary, it is nice to meet you" (and
   think you belong in a zoo). See her
   swinging from something in a monkey cage.

Try this the next time you enter a new class (or a
party) and have just been introduced to a new person. What are some creative associations you can use
to help you remember the name?

Adapted from: G.O.A.L.S. (1989).

Tactic: Use Colors to Aid Memory

It's as simple as taking two colored highlighters, perhaps green and pink. Teach students to read through
passages or directions or whatever and highlight the
main ideas in green and the supporting details in
pink. The facts can then be transferred to an outline
or integrated into an assignment that requires the
highlighted information. Be sure to check district pol-
icy before highlighting textbooks. If in doubt, copy
the pages from the text, then highlight.

Tactic: Teach Students to Generalize Learning Strategies

Many students do not spontaneously generalize what
they learn. This is especially true for less-proficient
learners. Have you ever had the experience of teaching a fact, concept, or strategy to students in one subject area, having them show you they know it, only to
have it pop up in another subject area and have students treat it like new information? Most students
learn best if taught by demonstration, modeling, practice, and other proven methods of teaching. For example, teach students to generalize paired/associated
learning (learning pairs of words) by having them try
the strategy on familiar items (ordinary pairs of
words), not-so-familiar word pairs (countries and
products) and very unfamiliar word pairs (French vocabulary words with their English translation). By providing different practice opportunities, you
strengthen students' proficiency in the initial learning
strategy and skill, while raising their awareness level
of how the strategy can be applied to different subject

delivering

matter requiring similar tasks. You can further help students learn when and how to use learning strategies by having them develop charts that provide cues as to when to use different learning strategies on what types of common tasks.

Tactic: Use the Parking Lot

Here is a functional learning strategy that can be used for independent work or small or large group discussion. The Parking Lot tactic simply takes distracting thoughts, topic, or items in need of additional discussion at a later point and parks them in a lot for safekeeping. In doing this, time is not spent in "bird walks" (those discussion that take you away from the task or objective at hand). Have you ever seen a bird's footprints in the snow—they are not linear but all over the place. Bird walks are classic distraction

and occur in every discussion, meeting, lesson unless closely monitored. To use the Parking Lot, simply write the words "Parking Lot" on the board, overhead, or a chart. Present your lesson or engage in discussion. Whenever something comes up that is of importance, needs further discussion, or is of interest but not at the loss of time to the current discussion, park it in the lot. That means write the issue or topic under the words Parking Lot. The Parking Lot tactic provides both you and your students with a visual reminder of those things that need to be revisited or planned into a discussion. It also shows that no matter what is offered, most everything is heard or processed. Be sure to gain consensus on items put in the parking lot. Take a quick vote on whether things are worthy of being parked in the lot.

delivering

For Providing Relevant Practice

Sometimes one of the most difficult things to provide students is time to practice what they learn. Every student needs to be actively and overtly engaged in learning and the practice process. Effective teachers provide students relevant practice to enable them to reach automaticity of a skill. Providing guided practice and independent practice, both with corrective feedback, is a desirable and monumental task. Even when teachers find time and creative ways to provide students relevant practice on facts, concepts, and strategies, staying with that practice until mastery has occurred is sometimes almost impossible.

Effective teachers recognize the difference between learning and performance efforts and task completion. Learning means that a student is successful when he/she shows progress, improvement, and knowledge. However, a performance orientation means that students believe success is achieved simply by completing assignments. There is no concern whether the work is correct, only that it's done. Have you ever had students who do all the easy tasks first? These students feel good about getting something done and off their desk. But, the harder tasks either are never done, or are partially completed and nonetheless handed in, as is. Effective educators strive to have students engage in learning and the success and failures that inherently occur along the way. Remember, everybody makes mistakes, but smart people learn from them. This section will provide you with

many ways to not only provide your students with relevant practice, but also ensure that students are actively engaged in the process, allowing for skill acquisition to become fluent and automatic.

Develop Automaticity

It is one thing to correctly acquire a skill, and another to be fast and fluent. For example, Rosilyn can read almost anything put in front of her, but in a most painstaking, laborious manner. By the time she gets to the end of a sentence or two she cannot tell what the passage was about. Rosilyn reads too slow to allow her to comprehend what she reads. Then there is Fapatay. Fapatay is a whip at calculating number facts in isolation. However, he does not know when or where to apply them to help solve word problems or formulas. He is not automatic in his ability to integrate his skill of number calculation with problem solving. In these example, both students have acquired the skills in isolation but have not reached automaticity in them. Because there is so much to learn, with so little time to learn it, it is important that students are provided opportunities to practice skills that are needed at the automatic level in order to move through a curriculum at the expected rate of progress.

delivering

⏱ Tactic: Adhere to Stages of Learning

To provide relevant practice and develop automaticity of skill, effective teachers know the importance of assessing what stage of learning a student is at. For example, some students are not ready for the stage of skill automaticity because they have not yet acquired the skill. If a student lacks knowledge of a skill or task, he/she may be at the initial phase of learning called acquisition. Before automaticity can be reached on the skill, the student must correctly acquire it.

Rosilyn is a student who is able to perform the task of reading, but is too slow to effectively complete quality work on time. She needs fluency instruction (e.g., rapid drill and practice) that facilitates mastery—accuracy and speed. A goal of effective instruction is to have students use skills independently and apply them automatically whenever needed. In order to gain automaticity of a skill, students must first acquire the skill, be provided multiple opportunities to practice it, and then directly taught how to generalize and/or apply the skills in larger, novel contexts. Remember, it is good practice to identify the level of proficiency the task requires (accuracy, mastery, automaticity) and the level at which the student is currently performing. Then providing for relevant practice for building automaticity can take place.

Tactic: Use One-Minute Timed Readings

One of the best ways to increase reading fluency is to provide students with one-minute timed oral reading passages. Also known as curriculum-based measures, timed readings or probes are short, fast, and painless to complete. The goal of the one-minute reading probes is to increase the number of correct words per minute (CWPM) while keeping errors to a minimum.

Procedure:

1 The Passage—Create a grade level reading probe from a passage that students have already read. These passages can be taken from a basal reader, anthology, newspapers, magazines, or other content textbooks. The important thing to remember is that these passages represent the material and level of difficulty used in your day-to-day curriculum. Most teachers photocopy pages and then cut and paste them into one complete passage of approximately 500 words. Depending on skill and grade level of your students, you may make longer or shorter passages.

2 Administration—You will need two copies of the passage, one for the student and one for you. You will need a pencil to mark the students errors and where he/she is at the one-minute mark. Administer the oral reading passage individually to students as follows:

When I say "begin," start reading the passage. Read as quickly and as accurately as you can. If you don't know a word, skip over it and keep reading. If you pause or hesitate on a word I will

delivering

tell you the word. The main thing is to read as many words as quickly and correctly as you can. Keep reading until I say "stop." You will have one minute to read. Ready, begin.

3 Error Corrections—When the student errs, put an X over the word. If a student hesitates for more than three seconds, tell the student the word and mark it as an error. Mark with an X any word the student mispronounces. Do not count self-corrections, word insertions, phonetic sounding-out of words, or words the student repeats.

4 The Tally—At the one-minute mark, place a slash or dot where the student is in the passage. Allow the student to keep reading until he/she finishes the entire passage. Do not continue to mark reading errors after the one-minute mark has passed. Simply let the student finish reading the passage. After the student completes the passage, count up the number of errors and subtract them from the total number of words read within the one-minute timing. The result will be the CWPM (correct words per minute).

5 Progress and Practice—Effective teachers have students' record and chart their progress on the one-minute reading probes. Charting their progress keeps students alert to their progress and need for practice. Students are encouraged to increase their CWPM. In order to do that they need to know how they did on each

timed reading. Encourage students to practice the readings as many times as they want in between the official timings. The goal is to provide relevant practice that builds automaticity in reading. Challenge students to increase by at least one to three (or more) CWPM on each successive reading.

6 Changing the Passage—To prevent boredom, change the passages students read after three improvements have been made in the CWPM.

One high school teacher uses one-minute reading probes with her language arts students. Although most of the students are fluent in reading, improvement and the simple act of reading need to be reinforced. There are a few unmotivated readers. Upon introducing the one-minute reading probes, her students are so motivated and challenged by the novelty of the task that they beg to read and reread the stories! Imagine that!

Variation 1
Comprehension Probes

Comprehension probes can be used with one-minute oral reading passage probes. The goal of comprehension probes is to find out what the students understand of what they read. You can also have students listen to a story read and have them use auditory comprehension skills to complete the probe. For nonreaders, pictures can be used to stimulate discussion and comprehension of what is pictured. Action pictures work well.

delivering

1 The Materials—Story passages or action pictures. You will also need a list of elements or concepts expected of the students performance, as illustrated in Figure 37.

Comprehension Probe

Name:_____ Date:_____

Story:_____

    Tells main ideas
    Identifies characters by name
    Mentions the title of story
    Gives at least three facts about the story
    Identifies personality traits of character(s)
    Makes inferences
    Tells or recreates the story in chronological
        sequence

Figure 37

2 Administration—Using a one-minute time limit, give the student the following directions:

> *When I say "begin," I want you to tell*
> *me about what you read (heard, see).*
> *Continue telling about it until I say*
> *"stop." Ready, begin.*

Provide students with verbal prompts such as "what else, keep going, tell me more," etc. Some students will have difficulty filling one minute with details and facts of a passage. Encourage them to continue using verbal prompts.

3 Error Corrections—None, just verbal prompts.

4 The Tally—After one minute has passed, stop recording story elements and let the student finish his/her current thought. Then say "stop." Count up the tally or checks you have given the student according to your sheet.

5 Progress and Practice—See original procedure.

6 Changing the Materials—See original procedure.

Variation 2
Written Expression

1 The Materials—Lined paper, writing utensils, a timer, writing elements sheet, and a story starter. Story starters are one-line sentences that really serve as topic sentences of a paragraph. Story starters can be about any topic. Be sure it is one your students can write about. For example, the following story starter would be inappropriate for many students. "Nuclear power plants can pose a serious threat to society." Be sure to tap into students prior knowledge and experiences.

2 Administration—As with comprehension probes, you will need to make a list of criteria or elements you expect of the students. For example, decide whether or not to count punctuation, spelling, grammar, words not spelled out (1996, 5, etc.), "word salads," or even total number of letters written. For some students sim-

delivering

ply writing words on paper is a major feat. For these students it may be wise to consider exempting spelling from the list of elements.

Written expression probes can be administered individually, or in small or whole class groups. Tell the students they will be practicing their writing using story starters. You may provide them on a piece of paper or write them on an overhead or board. Be sure to keep it covered until the procedure begins. Say:

I will show you a story starter. You will have one minute to think about the sentence and organize your thoughts for writing. After one minute has passed I will say "Begin writing." You will be given three minutes to write as much as you can about the story starter sentence. After three minutes is up I will say "Please put your pens down." I will collect all your papers.

3 Error Corrections—None. You may need to deliver verbal prompts to students such as "keep writing, write more, almost there, keep going," etc.

4 The Tally—At the conclusion of the three minutes of writing, collect student papers. Some teachers prefer to teach students how to tally their own writing. The choice is yours. Either way, count up the number of words written. Be

sure to include the story starter itself if the student wrote it down.

5 Progress and Practice—See original procedure.

6 Changing the Materials—See original procedure.

Variation 3
Spelling Words

1 The Materials—You need a list of grade level spelling words and a timer or a watch with a second hand. Spelling words should reflect the current curriculum the students are learning. They can be taken from textbooks, magazines, and newspapers. Students will need a piece of paper and writing utensil.

2 Administration—Spelling probes can be administered individually, or in small or whole class groups. Tell the students they will be practicing spelling. Say:

I will dictate words to you. Please write each word on your paper. You will have ten seconds to write each word. When I tell you the next word, write it down, even if you haven't finish the word before it. It is important for you to keep up with me. Any questions?

Using your list of spelling words, dictate to students for two minutes. Say each word twice. Be sure to not use any homonyms in a sentence. For younger students (grades 1-3), dictate at a rate of

delivering

one word per ten seconds. For older student (grades 4-8), dictate at a rate of one every seven seconds. Do not dictate a new word if there is less than three seconds left. Approximately 12-13 words should be dictated at the ten-second rate, 17-18 words at the seven second rate.

3 Error Corrections—None

4 The Tally—You may count the whole word as either correct or incorrect, or you may count letter sequences. For example, the word "cat" is spelled k-a-t. The score is too of three. Instead of marking entire words wrong, partial credit and attention is given to letter sequences that are correct. This may take you longer to tally, but for those students who are faced with constant failure and defeat, this is a way to show small incremental steps of progress, instead of total failure.

5 Progress and Practice—See original procedure.

7 Changing the Materials—See original procedure.

Variation 4

For math and other content areas, see Planning: What to Teach; Assess to Identify Gaps in Performance; Use Curriculum-Based Measures Effectively.

Tactic: Provide Practice Frequently and Informally

Similar to curriculum-based measurement, informal, direct, and frequent practice means daily or weekly checks of student performances on instructionally relevant tasks. This includes those tasks students need to be automatic at. Information gained from frequent, informal practice allows for assessment of instructional tasks while providing relevant information or data for planning and delivering instruction.

Informal practice and assessment should occur frequently, be direct, and designed to evaluate precisely what students need to learn, or what students have been learning and are automatic on. To select tasks for informal practice and assessment, be sure to use the curriculum you are teaching from on a daily basis. To build automaticity, effective teachers provide relevant practice often. As a general rule, opportunities to practice should occur daily, especially when introducing a fact, concept, or strategy, for building automaticity and mastery.

Tactic: Set Different Standards for Different Tasks

During the acquisition and automaticity stages of learning, effective teachers know that students need to practice skills more than when practice sessions are part of lesson/skill review. Overall, students need to practice new skills at least 10-15 minutes a day at no less than 80-90% accuracy. Less than five minutes

delivering

is usually sufficient time to review performance of a skill that has already been acquired. This performance should be at or above 90% accuracy.

Tactic: Teach Students to Set Daily Opportunities to Practice

On average, professional athletes practice five to six hours a day—some more, some less. But at a minimum, they practice daily. Students acquiring new skills, building fluency and automaticity, are no exception. In order to improve skill levels students need opportunities to practice under the supervision of a coach or teacher. Effective teachers know the importance of building practice opportunities into the daily schedule of instruction. They also know how important it is to teach students how much and how often they need to practice. Give students an estimate of how much time they should devote to practice both during and after school hours. Give them the materials they need and show them how to practice with them. And, when students are practicing skills during class time, be sure you are either doing the same or actively providing corrective feedback. Remember, you are a role model 100% of the time for your students.

Tactic: Establish a Plan to Help Students Retain Acquired Skills

Often after initial mastery, instruction moves to new skills without accounting or recounting for previously learned skills. Teachers continue instruction and assume that previously learned skills will maintain

themselves with periodic review. This is not always the case. Effective teachers know that when introducing a new skill, it is important to establish a plan that incorporates past and current learning skills by providing for distributed practice. For example, an elementary teacher devised the following plan of practice for students to maintain the acquired skill of two-digit subtraction with regrouping, starting from most intense to more distributed.

Practice Plan

Students will:

- ▲ Practice daily facts to 95% accuracy
- ▲ Practice daily 12 problems correct per minute
- ▲ Practice three times per week as long as an average of 95% accuracy is maintained
- ▲ Practice one time per week with 95% accuracy
- ▲ Practice one time every two weeks with 95% accuracy

Tactic: Play Beat the Clock!

Some students thrive on competition. Students can often be taught how to work toward improving their own personal performance relative to timed standards they have set. Students can work toward building and improving automaticity by setting their own personal goals. Have students record the amount of time it takes to complete a worksheet or task. For example, José can correctly complete 25 two-digit multiplication problems within three minutes. At the next practice session, José's goal is to beat the clock. That

delivering

is, he will try to finish the 25 multiplication problems before three minutes are up. Be sure if you use Beat the Clock that the tasks are timeable. For example, Lucy can write a three-paragraph composition in 20 minutes. Her goal is to at least maintain that rate. There are many variables involved in writing a composition and they may vary according to topic. Some may be easier to write than others. Be sure to consider the task and level of complexity when using this tactic.

Procedure:

1 Record a baseline of a timed performance on a student's skill area.

2 Set a timer for at least that baseline time.

3 Tell the student to begin and start the clock. The student is to work quickly and accurately and finish the task before the clock chimes the time.

4 Count up the number of correct problems completed, or record where the student was in the process of writing when time was up. Record and take note of the performance to beat for the next Beat the Clock session.

Have students keep track of their personal progress and time of accomplishment. Use a record-keeping chart.

Tactic: Use Classwide Peer Tutoring.

Cooperative learning techniques have resulted in many empirically proven ways to actively engage students in learning and practice opportunities. Classwide peer tutoring provides students with an opportunity to practice and build automaticity in several skill areas. Specifically, CWPT provides students multiple alternative opportunities to practice acquisition and fluency of facts. In addition, it provides opportunities for practice and immediate corrective feedback on efforts.

As with other cooperative structures, there are many ways to adapt CWPT to the specific needs of your classroom routine and students. CWPT can be used in any subject area that requires students to acquire important factual information. For example, CWPT can be used to reinforce learning of periodic symbols, second language vocabulary, music notes, letters (printed or cursive), sounds (initial, medial, final consonants), one-to-one number correspondence, identification and use of various formulas, vocabulary/terms, fractions and other measurement, and so on. As a general rule, CWPT should be implemented at least three times per week, daily if schedule allows. Its goal is to provide lots of opportunity to practice and build automaticity of factual information in a way that is engaging, motivating, and fun.

delivering

⏱ Tactic: Teach Students to Include Practice Time in Daily Schedule

Daily classroom schedules include instructional times for content areas and skills. Effective teachers recognize the importance of beginning each lesson with a fast-paced but brief review of previously taught skills. To assure adequate time is allotted for students to practice previously acquired skills, schedule a brief practice time per lesson (approximately five to ten minutes). Post and commit to daily practice time in your lessons. This will provide students the means to retain their skill level and knowledge via distributed practice opportunities. Teach students to commit to and record the time they practice or study a skill or content area.

strategy

Vary Opportunities for Practice

Within a classroom setting practice can occur in a number of formats—independent seatwork, small group work, dyads or pairs of students, and whole class. Effective teachers vary their formats of practice opportunities for their students to help prevent boredom and to allow for different ways to generalize learning and skill development.

Tactic: Use Independent Seatwork Effectively

Independent seatwork, also referred to as independent practice, provides students the opportunity to consolidate and apply prior knowledge and learning to practice tasks. Independent practice or seatwork is not a time when students learn new content material. Effective teachers limit the amount of time students are engaged in independent practice to no more than 20 minutes per day. Seatwork provides a way to monitor and check student understanding and to identify areas that are in need of reinforcement and reteaching. It is important for students to understand the purpose of seatwork. Tell them it is not "busy work," but work with a purpose. Periodically ask students to verbalize the reasons they are doing seatwork. Be sure their responses are on target.

Tactic: Provide Tools Needed for Independent Seatwork

Effective teachers have a variety of resources available for students to use during independent seatwork. The rules and routines for using the resources are taught to students. For example, some students may need to spell-check commonly misspelled words, abbreviations, and other grammatical uses (e.g., synonyms, homonyms). Some students may head for the classroom computer and program, while others will prefer to use a dictionary. One teacher has his students create personalized grammar and spelling resource dictionaries. The students create index cards with rules, examples, and nonexamples of the correct use of selected words. Students are encouraged to ex-

delivering

pand their resource card systems and use them at home as well.

Tactic: Organize Independent Seatwork Practice by Skill Objective

Here's a great way to individualize independent practice for students. Create and maintain a file system organized by instructional objective. Gather resources and develop practice tasks, and file them according to the objective an independent seatwork file. For example, you may have a file labeled quadratic equations, numbers 1-5. In this file will be any and all quadratic equations that have the numbers 1-5. This file is for students who need practice with equations while keeping the complexity of number calculations to a minimum. An elementary teacher created a file for sight words for students to read into a tape player. She has a file for preprimer, primer, grade one, and so one. Students read the lists to another student or into the tape recorder for later review by the teacher. A junior high school teacher uses this tactic to create an independent seatwork file on mathematical word problems, while limiting the level of reading difficulty. He created a matrix with reading levels across the top and mathematic skills down the side. In each cell of the matrix, this teacher lists the name or number of the worksheet he can pull and give a student (see Figure 38).

For example, Zach reads at a fifth grade level but is capable of completing grade nine algebraic word problems. The teacher simply looks up the skill levels

math skill	reading level		
	4	5	6
Algebraic Equations	Worksheets pp. 1-8	Textbook pp. 79-85	Textbook pp. 79-85
3 Digit by 2 Digit Multiplication	Worksheets pp. 1-12	Computer program "Wiz"	Textbook pp. 45-48
Percent	Review Book pp. 27-32	Textbook pp. 110-113	Worksheets pp. 21-25

Figure 38
Word Problem Matrix

on the matrix, cross references, them and pulls a practice sheet for Zach to complete that is tailored to his skill level and can be successfully completed independently.

Tactic: Use Self-Correcting Stations

A goal of independent practice is high rates of accurate responding. It is important that students are provided immediate feedback on their efforts. It is not always possible for you to deliver this supportive feedback. Effective teachers want to avoid having students practice errors during seatwork activities. One option to consider is self-correction stations. There are many ways to use these. Students can compare their answer against a prepared answer key, or the answers can be listened to on a prerecorded tape, or a correction buddy system can be implemented. In this case, a student or group of students is responsible for correcting student independent work. It is recom-

delivering

mended that if you use this method, each student checker be assigned about five students. This way the checker, too, can get his/her work completed and checked by you. Another way to provide answers is to write them on charts or the chalkboard before class and cover them up. When students complete their work they can go to the chart or board and uncover the answer key for their task and correct their work. Regardless of how you choose to provide the answers, try the following procedures for setting up self-correction stations:

1 Establish an area or areas for a correction station. Make sure it is visible by you from every teaching point in the classroom.

2 Provide the station or stations with colored pens for correcting and teacher-made answer keys.

3 Designate a place for students to put corrected and completed work. This can be an "IN" box at the station or a folder on your desk.

4 Rules of the station should be posted for all to see. (Of course, you will have already taught them to your students!) Be sure to set expectations for correct use of the station by reviewing the rules frequently with the students. Initially, review at least daily, and then at least three times per week. Reduce review to the first day of the week, and then whenever students need reminding and review.

> ### Self-Correcting Station Rules
>
> 1. One person may use an answer key at a time.
>
> 2. Take only your work to the station. Leave all writing utensils at your desk.
>
> 3. Silently correct your work.
>
> 4. Put all corrected work in the "IN" box.

5 Demonstrate and model desired use of the self-correcting station. Show students how they are to actually use and correct work at the station. Select students to demonstrate and model the procedures.

6 Do random paper checks for self-correcting accuracy. From time to time pick a paper from each student and check for correctness. If the student has incorrectly checked the paper, review the student's understanding of the procedures. Allow the student one opportunity to correct the error in procedure. Encourage him/her to ask for clarification if needed. If the error occurs again by the same student, a pre-planned consequence should be delivered. It is important that you stress the need for doing a good job at both completing and checking the assignments. As always, deliver positive praise statements to students who accurately complete the self-correcting procedures.

Student Self-Correcting Procedures

1. Before you go to the station, double check to make sure you have completely finished the assignment.

2. Leave all your writing utensils at your desk and go to the self-correcting station.

3. Locate the answer key you need. Circle any errors you have with a colored pen of your choice.

   note: If the answer key you need is in use, return to your seat and begin another seat-work task. When the answer key becomes available, go to the station and check your work.

4. Return to your seat and correct any errors you have made.

5. Once you have completely corrected your paper, return to the station and recheck your work.

6. Continue #5 and #6 until you have 100% accuracy on your paper.

7. Papers that are 100% correct are placed in the "IN" box.

Adapted from: Paine, S. et. al. (1983).

Tactic: Use Guaranteed Work Files

Guaranteed Work Files are files full of work students can successfully complete independently, without teacher assistance or instruction. Guaranteed Work Files (GWF) provide students meaningful practice opportunities that are relevant to current or immediate past lessons and learning. These work files are individually tailored for students. They can be kept in a mutually convenient spot in the class or in a student's desk or subject notebook. GWFs are filled with assignments or tasks students are automatic and proficient at. Activities can be worksheets, page and item numbers of textbooks, cooperative learning activities that can be completed with other students who are finished early or also awaiting assistance. GWFs are not meant to be busy work, but work with a purpose which students wait for assistance. One suggested use of GWF is as a backup system for when students are waiting for teacher assistance or for the availability of an answer key at a self-correcting station. Students know that during these unavoidable wait periods they are to get their own personal GWF and begin working in it until help is available.

Tactic: Ask Three Before Me

For this tactic students need to "ask a friend" for help prior to you (ask three peers before asking the teacher). This activity provides the opportunity to nurture a feeling of support among students and prevent them from depending on you or the classroom assistant for constant help. Here's how: If a student has a question, he or she must ask at least three stu-

delivering

dents for help before asking you. You will need to monitor to make sure that the same students aren't asked for help all the time. You may also need to have students tell you which three classmates they asked for assistance. This serves as a procedure check.

Tactic: Use Small Group Activities Effectively—The Fishbowl

An alternative to independent seatwork is small group practice. There are many methods to use for providing small groups opportunities to practice. A particularly fun one is called Fishbowl. Have students create two concentric circles. The inside circle should be smaller than the outside circle. The size of the circle will depend on the number of students involved in the group activity. Each person in both circles should be seated on a chair, or on the floor if more desirable. Once the circles are established, tell the students the following:

> *I will pose a question to the students sitting inside our fishbowl. Anyone of you sitting inside the fishbowl can respond to the question. Raise your hand and I will call on you to speak. After you are through giving your response, someone from the outside circle looking into the fishbowl will have the opportunity to add and expand on the original response. Raise your hand so that I may call on you. When all the responses to the question have been heard, the first re-*

> *sponder on the outside of our fishbowl will change positions with the original question responder on the inside the fishbowl. After the seat exchange is complete, I will pose another question and we will continue the process in the same manner.*

Continue the Fishbowl tactic at least until all the students on the inside circle have been moved to the outside circle. This tactic encourages all students inside the fishbowl to respond at least once in order to get out of the bowl, while encouraging those outside the fishbowl to respond in order to get in. Fishbowl can be used with discussion questions, debates, comprehension questions, or for any questions that are factual, conceptual, or strategic in nature.

Tactic: Use Jigsaw

Here is an oldie but goodie. Jigsaw has numerous variations and uses. It provides small groups and pairs of students a method to review, apply what they have learned, reinforce past skills, rejuvenate newer ones, and engage in intense discussion about issues, topics, and readings. Here's how:

Procedure:

1 Assign students to base groups. Groups can be from three to five in number.

2 Have students within each group count off, for example, one through five.

delivering

3 Give all the number ones the same question or a task.

4 Give all the number twos a different question or task. All the number twos will be working on the same question or task, but different from the ones.

5 Do the same for the remaining groups. You should have no more than five groups of students. Each group will be working on a different task. However, within each group all students are working on the same task or topics. For example, all the number ones are working on generating ideas about drug use and abuse. The number twos are discussing the effects of living with someone who has a drug problem. The number threes are considering the physical damage that one's body experiences from sustained drug abuse. Number fours are reflecting on the legal ramifications of possession or use of drugs in the state or nation.

6 Tell students to gather in their groups to discuss their topic or question. Set a time limit. This will depend on the breadth and depth of the topic or question posed as well as your objective for having students engage in the Jigsaw structure.

7 When the time is up, tell students to reconvene into their base groups. Once back in base groups, each numbered student (1-5) is to share what they learned about their topic or question. By the end of the share time, all questions or topices you posed to each group will have been shared.

Like a puzzle when it is taken apart, each piece resembles a part of a whole. When reassembled, the pieces are integrated into a whole picture of something. Jigsaw is a wonderful tactic to use for fact-finding tasks, research projects, discussing several layers of issues and topics, novels, and so on. When you want all students to learn about several facets of a topic and do not have the desire or need to have each student complete a research paper or composition on it, and you simply feel a lively discussion from different perspectives on different facets of the project is what you're after—Jigsaw is your answer!

Variation

▲ Instead of each small group of numbered students discussing together, have them create smaller groups of two or three, so each small group will have a smaller working group. For example, if there are five number twos, then have one dyad and one triad of students discuss the question or topic.

▲ After a period of time have the smaller groups merge and discuss as a same-numbered small group.

delivering

▲ After another passage of time, have the base groups reconvene and share what they learned in their group experience.

Adapted from: Kagan, S. (1994).

Tactic: Use Chat-Check-Change

A variation of the Fishbowl, Chat-Check-Change provides groups of students the opportunity to talk with a neighbor, check out their thoughts, opinions, or answers, and then do it again with another person.

1 Have students stand in two concentric circles. Students on the inside circle face outward, while students on the outside circle face inward.

2 When given the signal, students are to chat about a posed question, topic, issue, or dilemma. They are to continue for at least 90 seconds.

3 At the 90-second mark, give students the direction to "Change." This means that students turn to their right and walk in their circle until told to stop. The inside circle changes or walks clockwise and the outside circle clockwise. If this is confusing to students, tell the inside circle to walk to their left, and outside circle to their right.

4 Give a signal to "stop." Pose the same question and have students chat and check with a new neighbor.

5 Repeat steps 2 and 3, except this time, after the students change, pose a new question, issue, or dilemma.

Students find Chat-Check-Change fun and stimulating. It gets them out of their seats, provides them the opportunity to check ideas with more than one person, and challenges them to continue dialogue about a topic for at least 90 seconds. You may choose to alter the time for the chat to better suit the age and needs of your students.

Tactic: Use Dyads Effectively

Pair students occasionally for a change of pace. Many of the same tasks that can be completed independently can be completed using dyads or pairs of students. How and when you use dyads will depend on what your learning outcome is for students. Allowing students to work in dyads encourages cooperation and sharing of ideas and problem-solving strategies. Make sure pairs are relatively equal in skills (or not, depending on what your goal of learning is). Dyads can be used for tutoring activities and for completing assignments where both students must show what they know. Regardless, be sure that both students pull equal weight. That is, one does not do all the work while the other watches or "zones out." Assign students to dyads by lesson, week, day, or unit of instruction. Students know that when you give the direction "Partner Up" it means for them to get with their partner to work on a task.

delivering

Tactic: Have Pairs Check for Understanding

For this tactic, students are paired to check for understanding of directions. First, assign student pairs. Then at random times throughout the day direct the pairs to get together to check each other's understanding. Some teachers set a timer and tell students to do the pairs check any time the timer goes off. It is important to teach and model what you expect to be done during the pairs check. For example, what types of questions should be asked, what is the criteria for understanding, what do students do if neither pair member understands, and so on.

Tactic: Partner Up!

This tactic is one that allows students the learning opportunity to actively engage, with another student, in problem solving; reviewing prior knowledge or facts; practicing facts, concepts, and strategies; answering literal and inferential questions; and so on.

Group composition:

Students are arranged in groups of four. Pairs of students are created within the foursome. Both the foursome and the pairs should be teacher arranged in order to balance ability levels. However, depending on the activity, decide whether to create random or formal groups and pairs (see Planning: Decide How to Teach; Establish Group Structures; Create Random Groups; Create Formal Groups). Once groups and pairs are set up the composition can be maintained for the class period, day, week, or month. Be sure to allow students the

opportunity to become familiar and comfortable with the working dynamics of their partner before changing groups around. Use at random or by direction. At random simply means students can decide when they want and need to use this tactic for a quick check, while by direction is by assignment or verbal instruction directly from you.

Procedure:

In pairs, students decide who is 1 and 2. Once given a task, students engage in Partner Up! as follows:

1 Student 1 works on the task item or problem first, while Student 2 supervises. Student 2 encourages his/her partner to write or think through the process aloud.

2 When Student 1 indicates he/she has completed the task, Student 2 corrects it. If the work is correct, a praise phrase is given by Student 2 ("Excellent job!"). If, however, there is an error, both students problem-solve as a pair, and Student 1 corrects his/her error.

3 On the next item or task, Student 2 works on the task item or problem while Student 1 supervises. The same correction procedures are followed. That is, if there is an error, the pair problem-solves it together, and Student 2 makes the correction to the work.

4 At any time during the procedure you may announce to the pairs, "Pairs Partner Up!" This

delivering

tells the pairs to get with the other pair in their foursome and compare or check their work. You may indicate which problems you want Partner Pairs to check or allow students to choose.

5 Pairs always need to be ready to share what they know or information about the task or assignment at hand. They need to be ready to share it if called upon. You can randomly call on pairs to share, or pull a partner's name from a hat. The student whose name is drawn is the one to share the pair's response.

Tactic: Use Whole Class Activities Effectively

Recent research has pointed out how "class pacers" dictate or cue the rate at which teachers deliver instruction and move through activities. Class pacers are those students who are always "with" the teacher as he/she delivers information, and they often are the ones teachers call upon when asking questions. Why? Because teachers know and can count on these students to have the answer. It is easy to see how class pacers reinforce teachers' teaching efforts. Teachers' behaviors are reinforced when a student or students give the correct answer or insight to a question. However, what about students who are not "class pacers?" When asked about the effectiveness of a lesson, some teachers indicate they know a lesson was successful because the students "liked it." But did they learn anything? Effective teachers know the danger of using class pacers for whole class understanding of ma-

terial presented. Effective teachers use a variety of whole class activities to ensure that all students' understanding is monitored and checked before moving on. And, if needed, material is retaught or small group instructional activities are used to provide additional learning opportunities. Be on the lookout for class pacers and their potential influence on your teaching behavior. Use whole group activities effectively.

Tactic: It's in the Can

Here's a tactic to ensure that all students have an equal opportunity be called on during a lesson. Write each student's name on a slip of paper and place it in a can (a decorated one would be nice). During a question and answer period, pull a name slip from the can and call on that student to answer or offer a response. If the student does not know the answer or you wish to have someone expand on the answer, pull another name slip from the can. Do not put the pulled name slips back in the can until all others have been pulled or a new class or activity has begun.

Tactic: Snowball Your Responses

Effective teachers foster a positive environment for learning and risk taking, but some students are hesitant to respond in whole group settings. The Snowball tactic is a fun and stimulating tactic for all.

1 Pose a question, and have students write their response on a scrap piece of paper.

delivering

2 When they have finished writing, have them crumple the paper into a "snowball."

3 Then say: "When I say 'go,' gently toss your snowball around the room. Pick up the nearest snowball that lands by you and gently toss that one. Continue tossing snowballs that fall by your feet until I say 'stop.'"

4 Continue by saying: "After I say 'stop,' you are to pick up the snowball nearest to you and open it up. Be prepared to read the response written on the paper."

This tactic allows students to freely respond without owning the answer. It provides students to feel comfortable taking a risk in responding. It allows feelings to show and opinions to flow, based on the question or topic of discussion. Your use of this tactic will depend on the type of question and answer format you are using, the sensitivity of the topic, and whether or not you are after individual student accountability for learning specific material.

Variation

Have color snowball wars. Provide students with colored pieces of paper to record their response on. Then, let them fly!

Tactic: Use Outcomes and Snowballs

This tactic builds upon Snowball Your Responses. At the end of a lesson, provide students the opportunity to independently reflect on what they learned. Pro-

vide students with statement sheets or simply write the following on the board:

> ▲ "After this lesson I learned …"
>
> ▲ "I was surprised …"
>
> ▲ "I relearned …"
>
> ▲ "I am feeling positive about …"
>
> ▲ "I need clarification on …"

Have students write a response to one of the statements. When they have finished recording their response they are to crumple their paper into a "snowball." Follow the same procedures as noted in Snowball Your Responses. Outcomes and Snowballs provides you a quick way to monitor and gather immediate feedback on students' understanding and participation in a lesson.

 ## Tactic: Use Cooperative Learning Structures

Cooperative learning grouping arrangements are not only empirical but fun! There are many published materials available on structures that can be used for specific tasks and projects, and that meet diverse learner needs. Some favorites are Numbered Heads Together, Think-Pair-Share, Plus, Minus, and Interesting (PMI), Interview, Corners, and Classwide Peer Tutoring.

delivering

Vary Methods of Practice

Few students thoroughly enjoy practicing many school-related activities. Effective teachers recognize and consider this when delivering instruction. Not only do they deliver relevant tasks, but they increase interest by varying the types of practice activities and materials used. In doing so, students' motivation and effort in completing practice activities is increased. Traditional worksheets hardly cut it anymore with students. They yearn for more active, engaging ways to practice and show what they know.

Tactic: Identify Alternatives for Teaching Skills

There are many ways to teach specific skills. Teaching requires the wearing of many hats, one of which is creativity. Your creativity as a teacher comes into play when you identify different ways to teach a skill. Peer coaching and collaboration have provided opportunities for teachers to share in the tricks of the trade they have developed when faced with a skill students are having difficulty mastering. Be creative. Talk to your students and help them help you determine the points of difficulty or confusion. Consider challenging students to come up with alternative ways to teach or learn a skill. Use cross-aged tutoring or gather ideas from students who have already mastered a skill.

In class field trips provide opportunities for students to practice skills using alternative learning materials. For example, individualized, independent math practice activities can be constructed using mail order catalogs and a field trip sheet (e.g., Find three products with a total cost of less than $10.00. Find two products with a total cost of less than $20.00). Presenting alternate ways to problem-solve also provides stimulating ways to teach skills.

Tactic: Use Games, Manipulatives, and Audiovisuals

Practice does not have to be traditional or boring. Effective teachers use instructionally relevant board games, variations of Bingo, and other means to make learning and practice more exciting. Try having students read into a tape recorder to practice reading, or listen to stories or lessons from tapes. Let them type their work on the computer, write their answers to a task on the overhead transparency, draw in salt, pudding, or whipped cream. Let them use the chalkboard and provide them with colored chalk. Try letting them use a handheld tachistoscope or flash cards—they can even make their own. Students can clip answers or completed tasks to a clothesline, or form answers in clay. The options that will increase student motivation and participation in practice activities are endless. Ask your students to contribute their ideas. You'll be surprised what wonderful and feasible ideas they will offer.

Tactic: Use Creative Manipulatives

Students who require concrete and manipulative objects for math can be reenergized by varying the mate-

delivering

rials you use. For example, use buttons, beans, corks, rocks, birthday candles, keys, lids, flower petals, pieces of rock salt, hard candy, carrots, and any other creative concrete object you can put your hands on. The simple novelty of the manipulative increases the students' interest in the tasks.

Tactic: Use Pass the Mints

Here is a novel way to provide students the opportunity to review, state, or restate what they learned or were surprised by, or to offer any other insight to the discussion. Pass the Mints could be Pass the Gum, Pass the Peanuts, Pass the Colorful Paperclips, Pass the Hard Candy, or even Pass the Lottery Tickets. Decide what you want to pass and implement this tactic as follows:

Procedure:

1 Choose what you will have students pass around the room. Be sure there is an equal number of items to students.

2 Starting anywhere in the class, hand the container of items to a student.

3 Upon receiving the container, each student must make a statement related to what you are asking for comment on (one thing the student learned, feelings about …, opinions about …, etc.).

4 After making a statement, each student may take one item from the container to keep, eat,

use, etc. Then they pass the container to a student closest to them. Students can get the container ony once. Only after everyone has had a turn can the procedure be repeated.

5 As always, it is wise to entertain the option to pass. This, of course, will depend on the sensitivity of the topic or the student's comfort level when speaking in front of peers.

This activity is only effective if the items you are passing in the containers are interesting to the students. If lottery tickets are hot and motivating, students will share their ideas in order to obtain one. Likewise for mints. However, monitor the sincerity of student responses—avoid the use of lip service.

Tactic: Create Open Format Skill Builders

Create worksheets that speak to students' interests. The idea behind Open Format Skill Builders is to make a worksheet framework that can be used over and over with different skill sets. For example, some students are really into skateboarding and in-line skating. Make a worksheet that shows a skateboard ramp and a series of skateboards going up, over, and around the ramp. Now you have a framework that can be used for a variety of skill builders. For example, put misspelled words in the skateboard and have students identify and correct misspellings. Or place algebraic equations in each and tell students to solve them. For music, place notes on the wheels and have students identify their value. Or give the direction, "Write an eighth note," and have students write the

delivering

role inside the wheel. Or place dates in the notes and tell students to identify what historical event took place at that time. (For in-line skaters, place the tasks inside the wheels.) For students who prefer to shop, dress a mannequin (on paper, of course) with "cool" garb and write the task on the funky clothes.

Open Format Skill Builders can take a variety of formats. They provide students the opportunity to practice skills in a relevant, fun way using a familiar format. Ask your students to create Open Format Skill Builders.

Adapted from Algozzine, B. (1994).

Tactic: Make Spelling Fun

Not many students enjoy the task of practicing spelling words. Most often they are given isolated words to spell. Here is a fun way to have students create their own spelling words. Create an open worksheet by drawing a shape and placing circles on it. Put letters in the circles and have students come up with three-, four-, and more-letter words. Another way is to give the open worksheet to the students and have **them** add letters to it. They must create an answer key to show that the words can be found. Make copies of the student-made worksheets and use them in instruction (see Figure 39).

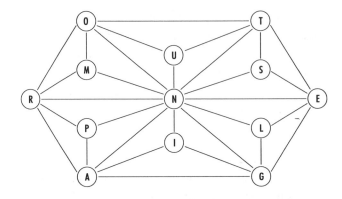

4-Letter Words	5-Letter Words	Longer Words
noun	stone	pronoun
test	mount	morning

Figure 39

Tactic: Use Word Mazes

Here's another adaptation of an open worksheet tactic. Create a maze by drawing a box with, for example, 16 cells. In each cell write words you expect students to know how to spell. When writing the words in the cells, spell some correctly and others incorrectly. Mark the place on the maze where students are to start and where they are to finish. The goal of the maze is to get from the start to the finish by connecting correctly spelled words. Students must decipher if the words in the cells are correctly or incorrectly spelled. You may increase the number of cells in your maze based on the age and skill of your students as well as the number of words on your list.

delivering

Variation

Have students get from the start to the finish by connecting the misspelled words. Once discovered, the students must cross out the incorrectly spelled word and write the correct spelling underneath it, but within the same cell.

Word mazes are fun ways to review previously learned spelling and vocabulary words. They provide students with an opportunity to practice that is challenging and fun.

Tactic: Use Tongue Depressors

Remember tongue depressors? Here is a way to use them in your classroom—for story starters, topical sentences, character identification, role playing, and on and on. For example, say you are staging a debate in your history class about being present at and a part of the War of 1812. Using the tongue depressors, write persons or characters that were present at the time of the war. For example, on one depressor you could write "a Redcoat," on another, "a Minute Man," and on still another, "a civilian." Place the tongue depressors in a can and have students draw their role in the debate.

For a writing activity, simply put a theme, topic, or topical sentence on the depressors. Have students pick their topic or theme from the can.

A high school algebra teacher uses "Tongue Depressor Math." She writes math problems on the tongue depressors, and students have to solve the problem

they pull from the can. Another teacher gives the students instructions on the back side of the tongue depressor as to whether the problem is to be done independently, in pairs, or in a small or large group. Get creative. Have students help devise problems and tasks that can be used with tongue depressors.

Tactic: Use Deep Thoughts

Confusion is created by multiple meanings of words and misuses of punctuation. Here is a fun way to engage students in the act of proofreading for semantics, punctuation, and double meaning. For example, a passage in a novel might read, "When he asked for the pudding, I let him have it!" Ask your students, "What strikes you about this sentence? Can you visualize the scene? How about this one: 'The guy was all over the road. I had to swerve a number of times before I hit him.'"

Students (and adults) love this activity. It is a fun and engaging way to apply knowledge of punctuation and understanding of how to correct double meanings.

Tactic: Use Riddles to Invoke Cooperative Problem Solving

Effective teachers know that students need to be taught how to cooperate. Provide students with tasks where more heads are better than one. Use riddles! For example:

You are walking through a dessert and come across a man (or woman) who is dead. However, you no-

delivering

tice that he has a full canteen of water and a backpack full of food. How did he die?

Have students gather in small groups to discuss options or to collectively problem-solve riddles. Together, discover if there is one "right" answer. Be sure to have groups of students share their ideas with the rest of the class.

Tactic: Use Visual Thinking

Here is another strategy to encourage cooperative problem solving. Use visual thinking tools and have students tell what they see and how they see it. Give students the opportunity to try these independently first, then have them pair up or work in small groups to continue the problem-solving process. For example, how many squares are there in Figure 40? Are you sure of your answer? How do you know? Check it out with someone else—what do they see? Visual thinking is challenging, yet fun. Be sure to have students create some of their own.

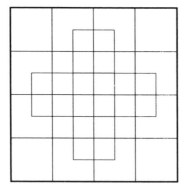

Figure 40

Tactic: Use Super Math Sheets

How many students do you know who absolutely love to practice basic math calculations? Probably not many. In reality, getting students to practice math facts to fluency can be quite a challenge, especially if the students are older. They "wouldn't be caught dead doing this baby stuff!"

Can you blame them? Still, they need to know and be able to do the facts at a relatively automatic level. Super Math Sheets can help.

Adapted from: Algozzine, B. (1994).

Tactic: Chart It!

Effective teachers know the value of providing students with activities that allow them to move around, with structure and a purpose. Chart It provides students with the opportunity to apply and relearn what they know about a topic. The charting exercise allows for relearning, review, or an opportunity to integrate knowledge about several topics. Here's how:

Materials needed:

Chart paper or butcher paper large enough for several groups of students to record their responses.

Procedure:

1 Divide the class into groups of four to five students. There should be as many groups as there are questions or topics. That is, if you have five

delivering

questions, there should be no more or less than five groups.

2 Before class, write a topic or question across the top of each chart paper. Each group gets a different chart. Each chart has a different question or topic.

3 Tell the students:

> *Each group has a chart with a question (or topic) across the top of it. When I say "start," you will have approximately two minutes to write as many responses to the question (or topic) on your chart as you can. After the time has passed, I will say "switch." You are to pass your group's chart to the group on your right.*

note: The direction doesn't matter, just make sure students rotate the charts in the same direction each time the "switch" direction is given.

> *As soon as you receive your new chart, begin working on it. We will continue this process until all the charts have been rotated around to each group once. You should end the activity with your group's original chart.*

4 Once the charts are back to the original owners, give the following instructions:

> *Review the list of items/responses on your chart. Together as a group, select by consensus the top three responses you feel best represent the given topic. You will have about four to five minutes to do this.*

This process entails some discussion and prioritizing of responses.

5 After this is completed, instruct each group to choose a spokesperson to briefly summarize their chart to the rest of the class.

6 After the activity is complete, the charts may be posted in the classroom for later use, additional review, or to help students that missed the lesson.

The information and processing that Chart It calls upon is amazing. Students eventually comment on how hard it is to think of things to add to the chart—most items have been recorded by other groups. The finished product is a student-developed review chart for a test, or an informal assessment of student understanding of a topic.

Variation
Instead of passing the charts to the next group, have the students walk as a group to the next chart.

delivering

The charts can be placed on the floor, a table, or taped to a wall. Be sure to give each group a different color marker to use. It is easier to keep track of groups' responses when they are color coded.

⏱ Tactic: Use In-Class Field Trips

An out-of-class field trip is not to be missed. They enhance and enrich instructional programs. Students love them because they provide opportunities to learn and generalize information to real-life settings or situations. But teachers can't take students on field trips all the time, so here's a way to bring the field trip to the students. Gather some reference materials—magazines, telephone books, retail advertisements, mail order catalogs, TV guides, and the like. Create worksheets that require students to use the resource materials to find the answers. For example, using a dictionary, students could find the answer to: "How many sets of nostrils does an armadillo have?" Students must first find out what an armadillo is (if they don't already know), then explore the answer.

Worksheets can be created that require students to estimate answers as well as calculate them. For example, using calendars students can find a month with a Tuesday date that is a perfect square, or find three dates in a row whose sum is a multiple of 11. Using a T. V. guide, students can find the sports program with the latest broadcast time, or find a movie time longer than 90 minutes but less than two hours.

Have students create their own worksheets to share. Be sure they provide an answer key.

Adapted from: Algozzine, B. (1994).

⏱ Tactic: Shop 'Til You Drop

For those students who spend a good majority of their time "hanging" at the local mall, entice them with mail order catalogs, retail store advertisements, and anything else that relates to the mall or "hang" spot. Write problem-solving questions that require students to use the provided resources. One teacher got so creative that her students actually went to the retail store to check out the bargain they had discovered that day in class. The local record store was selling CDs of the students' favorite rock groups for 25% off the original price. Needless to say, the class enjoyed listening to the bargain purchase the next day in class. Again, have students create their own questions to share. Be sure they provide an answer key.

Adapted from Algozzine, B. (1994).

⏱ Tactic: Use Palindromes

A palindrome is a word, phrase, sentence, or number that is the same when it is written forward or backward. The name Bob is a palindrome. Kayak is a palindrome, and so is the number 6776. In math, palindromes can be produced by repeatedly adding numbers in a prescribed sequence.

delivering

1 Take any two numbers, for example 23 and 45.

2 Add them together. 23 + 45 = 68

3 If the sum is a palindrome, you are finished. If not, reverse the sum and add the numbers together again. 68 + 86 = 154

4 Continue this process until the sum is a palindrome. 154 + 451 = 605, 605 + 506 = 1111

It's not the mathematical principle that is important, but the fact that it will always work out to be a palindrome if you continue the process. Many math haters will work for hours finding sets of palindromes that can be used on their classmates. Give students a palindrome mission—have them find palindrome numbers that can be solved in five steps, eight steps, or more. Now they are ready for the big leagues — have them find a palindrome that when solved in five steps has a sum of 1111, or one that when solved in five steps has a sum of 6779.

Adapted from: Algozzine, B. (1994).

Tactic: Create Vanity License Plates

Effective teachers know the importance of pushing students to use higher levels of cognitive functions or the taxonomy of learning (good ol' Benjamin Bloom). Vanity License Plates is an activity that aids this goal. Vanity license plates are car license plates you see when driving around. They have a catchy riddle or message—portrayed in nine digits/letters or less.

Have your students create vanity license plates around topics, issues, or people recently studied. For example, tell students to create a vanity license plate for a participant of the Boston Tea Party, or one that represents their opinion of nuclear power plants. Sound easy? Try it. Vanity license plates push students to engage in the highest form of thinking and learning. They must synthesize their knowledge about a topic, then apply it to create the plate. A group of teachers created some vanity license plates for the topic of inclusion. Here are a few they came up with:

REGEDNOW
MENEXT
WHYNOTME
IM-IN

Tactic: Use Bingo to Practice Any Content

Information review doesn't have to be boring (and shouldn't be). Use Bingo to stimulate student learning and review. All you need to do is create a Bingo board, provide chips to cover spaces, and gather the facts, concepts, and strategies you want your students to review. Be sure that the answers to your questions are somewhere on the student boards. For example, Bingo can be used to review abbreviations of the periodical table, musical note values, historical dates, products and quotients, vocabulary, grammar, punctuation, and just about anything else! It's fun, easy, and engaging.

delivering

Variation

Vary the cells of the Bingo boards. For students who need more immediate feedback and recognition of efforts, start with a Bingo board that has three cells across and three cells down. Then gradually increase the number of cells to four across, four down, then five across, five down and so on.

You are the master of time, space, and dimension in your classroom. You decide if and what the students will earn for the winning Bingo card. For some students the simple fact they get to yell Bingo first does the trick. Others may desire a more formal record or posting of winning efforts. Be sure to consider asking students what they think when designing the recognition or reward system.

strategy

Monitor Amount of Work Assigned

Many students (and teachers) are overwhelmed by the demands and responsibility school places on them. This becomes compounded large amounts of work are required during and after school hours. Effective teachers are sensitive to these feelings and strive to achieve a balance with the "right" amount of work for students. This is not always an easy task, but it is necessary. There are several ways to do this.

Tactic: Teach Students to Set Personal Standards

Students usually can tell you what is reasonably "doable" and what is not. However, some students are more motivated than others. Perceptions of "doable" will vary. One way to help decipher what is reasonable is to keep track of the amount of work individual students complete during in-class independent work times. You may also want to make note of how the class does as a collective unit. The next day, give an assignment based on the previous day's performance. You may find some students will be doing more than they did the day before, while others do less. Be sure to make it clear how and why you have made alterations. Be on the lookout for students who shift their work efforts in an attempt to artificially alter their workloads. You may want to decide ahead of time what is the absolute minimum of work you will require of all students. In other words, how much work or how many problems do students need to complete to show what they know? You may want to provide the option of extra credit for extra problems completed over the set minimum, or a mystery reward for those who complete extra problems.

Tactic: Chart Progress and Increase Demands

Use aim lines to chart minimum acceptable work production. An aim line is a line connecting current levels of performance to the eventual desired goal. Both goals and objectives are written prior to using aim lines. Make note of the minimum level of proficiency you require as well. Teach students to keep track of how much or many items or tasks they are currently

delivering

completing and where they need to be. The use of aim lines is especially helpful when you have a long-range goal for a student and are interested in progress over time toward the goal. Therefore, once the level of proficiency and time period of learning a skill is determined, aim lines can be planned. For example, Oleema will complete ten sheets a week for the next five weeks, with an average of at least 75% accuracy on each one. Oleema's aim line would look like this:

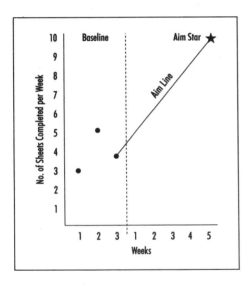

Figure 41

Procedure for creating an aim line:

1 Make a ten-week chart on which student progress can be recorded.

2 Collect at least three baseline data points (or three scores that reflect the student's current level of performance).

3 Using the median or middle score as the beginning point of the line, draw a straight line to the expected date and level of performance. This is called the aim star.

4 Begin instruction or skill practice toward that aim star immediately.

Over the ten-week period both you and Oleema can see the rate and accuracy of work he has completed. Further progress and effort can be driven by the aim line toward the final goal or star. Have students keep track of their performance by marking progress on their aim line. Effective teachers use aim line information to monitor and adjust instruction, and provide immediate performance feedback to students.

For some students, this simple act of monitoring and charting their performance will cause a natural increase in work production.

Variation
Oleema will complete two extra problems per task sheet over the next five weeks, with a minimum of 75% accuracy. So for week one Oleema needs to complete 10 problems per sheet, 12 problems for week two, 14 problems for week three, and so on. This requires students to increase their work productions

slowly and successively. Once the final goal is met, hold a brief conference with the student and decide on next steps. (See Planning: Decide How to Teach; Monitor Performance and Replan Instruction; Use Data to Plan Subsequent Instruction.)

Tactic: Divide Independent Practice Into Phases

Effective teachers know there are students who are self-starters and others who need a jump-start to get in gear for independent work periods. Consider breaking practice sessions into three phases. During the first three to five minutes (Phase I) have students get ready and organized to do their work, gather needed materials, etc. During Phase II allow students to independently work, but have a peer partner or teacher available to provide supervision, support and feedback. The length of Phase II will vary according to the type of assignment and the students' prior knowledge and experience with it. In Phase III, students get reorganized. Have them take note of what they did or did not get done, and decide what needs to be completed by the next day and when and how they will do it. For some students half the battle is getting organized and planning what, where, and how they will complete required tasks. It is not that they don't know the information, they simply don't know how to get it done. Provide students with a sheet to plan practice phases and ultimately the homework that needs to get done for the next day.

Tactic: Teach Students to Set Time Limits for Work Completion

Model the importance of setting time limits for work and sticking to them. Tell students they will have, for example, ten minutes to work on this assignment. Set a timer and stick to the limit. Whether the students are finished or not, transition to another activity. Using this approach teaches students to get to task and work diligently for the set time period. Tell them what they do not finish in class must be finished out of class. This tactic also provides you with a realistic estimate of exactly how much students can complete in a given supervised time period. Of course, time periods can be shortened or lengthened based on task difficulty. Be sure to monitor frustration levels. Transitioning to another activity "finished or not" can cause frustration for some students.

Tactic: Give Students a Choice

Most assignments given in school offer few choices for students. They must complete what is put before them or pay the consequences. Effective teachers know the power of occasionally giving students some say and choice in completing assignments. Teach students the meaning of self-management and personal responsibility. Ask students what they consider reasonable choices, or provide them with any of the following options:

▲ Complete the first 15 problems on page 90 and at least one of the next three problems.

delivering

202

▲ Complete the first 10 problems on page 87 and as many of the next five you choose.

▲ Summarize today's lesson in your notebook in whatever format you'd like (words, pictures, collage).

▲ Answer questions 1-5 on page 32 and then create one you'd use on a test.

▲ Answer questions 1-5 on page 32 and then create one to give to a classmate

▲ For tomorrow, write down one thing you would like to know.

▲ Before we finish reading this literature piece, partner up with a peer and discuss one thing you predict will happen.

▲ Tomorrow is our chapter test, you may sit anywhere you'd like.

▲ Tomorrow is our chapter test, please submit your extra credit questions to me by the end of today. (Here students submit possible questions the teacher may use on the test for extra credit. One teacher had students work in groups to create extra credit questions. At least one question from each group was included on the test. Students were given the choice of answering at least two for extra credit. Most picked their group's question and had to pick another one to answer as well.)

Variation 1

If either extra credit question is correct, extra credit is given.

Variation 2

Both extra credit questions must be answered correctly. This curtails students from answering their own questions, which have been previously prepared, and writing anything down for the second one.

Tactic: Spin for Assignments

This is a novel way to engage students in independent and homework assignments. Make a spinner with sections of varying sizes. In each section put the number of problems students must complete if the spinner lands there. Be sure to reserve the skinniest section for No Homework. Also consider one that says, "You chose any two" (three, four, etc.). Give students the opportunity to spin for assignments. Randomly select students to spin or draw names from a hat. Make sure that no matter where the spinner lands, each student is capable of completing the assignment in the given time frame.

Tactic: Use Doing the Dots

This tactic is a fun and novel way for students to earn the privilege of doing or not doing work of their choice. It's all the way they "do their dots." Here's how:

Purchase some peel and stick dots at your local office supply store. Cut them apart so you have all single dots. Tell students they can earn the dots by

delivering

engaging in expected classroom behavior, for example, independent seatwork during practice sessions. Tell students they can collect and accumulate the dots or spend them as they wish. On any given assignment they can use the dots to cover up the problem(s) they choose not to do. If students are working from a text and are to answer chapter questions one through ten, tell them to number their paper and place the dot by the numbered question they choose not to answer. As you can see, students who earn a lot of dots could eventually end up not doing any work, ever. Think about requiring a minimum item completion per

assignment. Have students complete these and then decide which of the remaining items they don't want to do. For example, all students must complete questions one through five. The items six through ten become dot-able, but if students have five dots, they may choose not to do any of them. You will be amazed how hard students work to get out of work. Think your boss would go for a system like this? Be sure you put some sort of special mark on the dots—students shop at the same stores you do!

Adapted from: *The Tough Kid Video Series* (1996).

delivering

principle

Monitor Presentations

Delivering instruction (teaching) involves monitoring presentations. When monitoring presentations, effective teachers use different strategies for providing feedback and keeping students actively involved.

When providing feedback, effective teachers give immediate, frequent, specific information about performance. They also provide praise and encouragement, model correct performance, provide prompts and cues, and check student understanding.

When keeping students actively involved, effective teachers monitor performance regularly during instructional presentations and practice. They also use peers to improve instruction, provide ample opportunities for success and constructive failure, and monitor engagement rates.

delivering

For Providing Feedback

Learning is enhanced when students are given immediate, frequent, explicit feedback on their performance or behavior. When they do something correctly, students should be told so. Supportive feedback lets a student know that he/she did what was expected; it supports the performance by letting the student know that what was done was done correctly. By the same token, when students do something incorrectly, their performance should be corrected. Corrective feedback lets the student know that he/she did not do what was expected; it provides information to be used to redirect the student toward correct performance and reduces the likelihood of practicing errors. Diffuse, nondirected feedback leaves students wondering, and it should be avoided.

strategy

Give Immediate, Frequent, Explicit Feedback

delivering

Most students enjoy recognition for successful performance. Effective teachers provide supportive and corrective feedback while teaching. Supportive feedback lets students know that what they did was done correctly; it provides support. Corrective feedback lets students know that what they did was done incorrectly, and it provides correction so they will learn and not practice incorrect responses or errors.

Tactic: Dignify Student Responses
Even though students need corrective feedback for wrong responses, the very act of responding can be dignified by the type of statement made by the teacher prior to correcting the error. Some statement examples are: "I can tell you are thinking about the lesson, but let me help you correct your answer," or "Thank you for trying but the right answer is …." An abrupt "No, that's not right!" may cause the student to stop giving any responses.

Tactic: Use Variety When Providing Feedback
Avoid overuse of statements like "Good," "Right," or "O.K." Vary supportive feedback with statements such as "Way to go," "Perfect," "Right on target," or "Correct answer." Use gestures to communicate correctness. A wink or a thumbs up also lets the students know they have responded correctly.

Tactic: Prevent Students From Practicing Errors
It is quite apparent that practice improves performance for desirable skills, but unfortunately, practice also strengthens error responses. If students make an error that appears to be due to an incorrect association, correct the error immediately. Then provide a prompt or cue to assure that when the response is called for again, the correct response occurs, and the error is not practiced. This situation often occurs in

reading when students confuse similar words such as "and" and "sand." Prompting these words with a beginning sound clue can prevent the student from continuing to make errors on the word discrimination. Gradually fade out prompts as success is assured.

Tactic: Systematically Return to Responses

When students make an error on a response, correct the error and then systematically call for that same response until success occurs consistently. A systematic plan could involve returning to the response after one different request, then returning after two different requests, then after three, and so on. Gradually lengthening the time as well as increasing the amount of intervening information between the return will assure that the response has been corrected. For example, if students are recalling math facts and an error is made, give the correct answer, go to the next fact, return to the fact that was missed, then do the next two facts followed by a return to the original fact. Continue to increase the number of facts practiced prior to returning to the original fact. If an error reoccurs on the same fact at some point during this systematic return process, correct the error again and drop back to the beginning of the systematic plan.

Tactic: Check First Responses on Independent Practice

When students begin independent practice, have students do the first item and immediately check all responses. Have them do the second item and again

immediately check all responses. At this point, students who were correct on the first two can continue on their own with some assurance that they will be successful. More guided practice can be provided for students who made errors. This strategy prevents students from practicing errors on several problems before receiving corrective feedback. An important note: Many students require at least 15-20 correct trials before "learning" a new fact or skill. Some students require a few less, but some require many more. It is better to err on the side of requiring more correct responses before moving to new content or assuming mastery.

Provide Specific Praise and Encouragement

Positive responses to work or behavior that go beyond simple affirmation or feedback are called praise. Most students like receiving praise, and although they seldom use it as a reinforcement technique, effective teachers frequently praise their students.

Tactic: Keep Track of Segments of Work, Not Just Final Products

Effective teachers divide complex tasks into smaller units and provide tangible rewards or verbal praise for completion of component parts of longer assignments. Students enjoy collecting these intermediate

delivering

rewards and exchanging them for "grand prizes" when assignments are completed.

Tactic: Focus on Performance

Effective teachers focus feedback on what was done, not simply on the fact that assignments are completed. For example, telling a student that completing an independent worksheet demonstrates skill in adding two-digit numbers is better than simply rewarding the completion of the work (e.g., "I'm glad you are done. You did a good job.").

Tactic: Send Good Work Home

Have students take checked assignments home on a regular basis. Send them home in a folder or large envelope that indicates what the student has mastered (e.g., Super Two-Digit Multiplication) rather than simply providing generic information about the work (e.g., Good Work!). Periodically have parents sign and return the folder as an additional way of motivating students to complete their work.

strategy

Model Correct Performance

Effective instruction begins with a demonstration or explanation of expected behavior. Effective teachers show students what they are expected to do as part of their instructional presentations. Student demonstra-

tions during instruction provide opportunities for supportive or corrective feedback.

Tactic: Display Lesson Materials During Modeling

If a lesson involves a worksheet or printed materials, display those materials on the chalkboard with a clip or tape and actually work problems on the worksheet as students watch. The number of problems that are completed during modeling will depend on the needs of the students. Sometimes, a whole worksheet can be modeled, removed, and then given to the students again for independent practice. If manipulatives are involved in the lesson, display needed materials so that all students can see them, and again actually model their use in front of the students before asking them to use them on their own.

Tactic: Use Overhead Projector for Modeling

An overhead projector is an excellent tool for modeling. Worksheets can be made into transparencies, handwriting models can be projected, pictures can be drawn, and even some manipulative objects can be placed on the surface and their shapes projected onto the wall. In addition to being able to project a variety of materials, the overhead allows the teacher to model tasks while still facing the students.

delivering

Provide Prompts and Cues

Even under the best of conditions, some students need help identifying expected performance. Many teachers account for this by using different types of visual, verbal, and physical prompts or cues during their instructional presentations.

Tactic: Prompt Correct Responses With Associated Signals

If a student is having difficulty remembering a word, say the word repeatedly and tap the desk with a pencil each time. Then as the student reads along in the passage, when he/she comes to the difficult word, tap the desk with the pencil to prompt the correct response and prevent an error from occurring. Hand claps, finger snaps, foot stomps, or other movements can become associated signals.

Tactic: Offer a Variety of Prompts

Words can be prompted by offering beginning sound clues, rhyming words and short definitions. Answers can be prompted by providing incomplete sentences (e.g., George Washington was the first _____.). Math operations can be prompted with physical gestures. For example, a sweeping circular hand motion that appears to enclose a set could be used to denote addition, and a sweeping motion that pushes away from the body could prompt subtraction.

Check Student Understanding

Effective teachers monitor students' understanding of content presented during their instructional units. They use this information to plan future activities or to modify ongoing presentations, and they strive for high rates of understanding when teaching any content.

Tactic: Use Different Methods to Check Understanding

Check students' understanding of lesson content using a variety of formats. Ask questions; have them repeat or explain in their own words; use response cards with every pupil; or monitor individual responses on chalkboards, magic slates, or paper. Sometimes, have your students draw or act out their answers.

Tactic: Monitor Performance Regularly

Effective teachers recognize that student needs vary with regard to learning, and they incorporate a variety of ways of monitoring comprehension in their instructional presentations. For example, if students are learning about metaphors in language arts, an effective teacher might ask students to raise their hands every time they hear a metaphor used in a story, or to write letters in their journals describing metaphors and giving examples, or to prepare a written report of a favorite activity using metaphors in the narrative description.

delivering

For Keeping Students Actively Involved

All students do not learn in the same ways or at the same rates. What works with one student may not work for others. What works one day may not work another. This is what makes teaching exciting for many teachers. While specific rules for keeping all students involved in their lessons are difficult to generate, effective teachers usually monitor the performance of their students regularly. They also use peers to raise levels of student involvement in their classrooms, and they provide opportunities for success, limit opportunities for failure, and keep track of the engagement rates to support the success of all students.

Monitor Performance Regularly

Effective teachers provide immediate, frequent, explicit feedback when they deliver instruction. They monitor their students' performances to determine the extent and content of feedback necessary. They also use this information as a basis for changing content presentations and redirecting a lesson.

Tactic: Check for Understanding Throughout Lesson

Ask questions frequently throughout a lesson to be certain that students are understanding. Students can respond chorally or individually. Be certain that all students are required to give a response at some point during the lesson, and be sure to wait at least three to five seconds before asking another question.

Tactic: Check Levels of Learning With Lowest Student

Although all students should be required to give a response at some point in each lesson, it is a good strategy to check the lowest-functioning students in a class on critical lesson aspects. If the lowest-functioning students understand the critical lesson elements, then there can be reasonable assurance that all other students in the class also understand. However, it is very important that this strategy be applied with care so that students do not feel as though they are being singled out. A quick pace of questioning that involves several students can be alternated between several other students and then a low-functioning student so that the low students do not get the feeling that they are answering everything.

delivering

Monitor Performance During Practice

Effective teachers use independent practice activities to help students become fluent learners. They recognize that practicing errors is counterproductive to learning. They circulate in their rooms, "looking over their students' shoulders" to be sure their instruction has been effective and their students are performing as expected.

Tactic: Check for Understanding During Practice

When students are working on independent practice activities, circulate around the room and ask questions frequently to be certain that students are understanding and completing assigned tasks appropriately. Sometimes, you may want to stop the individual work and obtain group demonstrations of appropriate learning responses.

Tactic: Ask Students to Teach During Practice

Have students explain what they are doing, how they reached an answer, or what expected performance "looks like" while they are completing an independent practice assignment. For variety, have students work independently for ten minutes and then have pairs of them explain the solution to at least one problem or task to each other.

Tactic: Give Students Answers

Prepare an answer key for students to use to periodically check the progress and accuracy of their independent work. Have them share the results of their use of the key. Have them exchange papers and use the key.

Tactic: Don't Keep Them in the Dark

Provide frequent reminders during independent practice to let students know where they should be in an assignment. For example, after two or three minutes say, "Everyone should have started and completed at least the first two problems. If you haven't reached this goal, let me see your hand." Don't assume that because they are sitting quietly they have started their work, know what to do, or can actually do it.

Use Peers to Improve Instruction

Classroom peers often help teachers cope with individual differences in extremely heterogeneous groups of students. Many teachers find that peer helping instructional arrangements are effective regardless of the composition of the student group(s).

delivering

Tactic: Select Helpers From Independent Practice Monitoring

Monitoring total class performance on the first two items of independent practice will enable a teacher to readily identify students who understand the skill and those who do not. Helpers can be selected from those who were successful with the first items on independent practice. Whenever possible, select as many different students as possible to be helpers during the day.

Tactic: Use Peer Tutoring as a Review Strategy

Choose students who are just slightly ahead of other students in skill mastery to do peer tutoring. The tutoring activity will serve as a meaningful review and will also expand the available teaching resources. Have the tutor teach the material to you before releasing him or her to teach classroom peers. Stress the importance of "good teaching" behaviors to all tutors.

Tactic: Use Cooperative Learning Assignments

Have two students work together to complete a worksheet or assignment. Assign specific tasks related to assignment completion to each student (one reads the problem, one records the answer, one checks the answer). With this approach, students can be grouped either heterogeneously or homogeneously. Remind students that they will receive a cooperative score or grade and that they are both accountable for the lesson content. Promote the notion of accountability by spot checking each student individually on performance.

Tactic: Use Peers to Provide Feedback

Have students working in pairs discuss similarities and differences in answers to a quiz or homework assignment. Have them discuss and defend their responses and arrive at one correct solution for answers that differ.

Provide Opportunities for Success

During instructional presentations, teachers present new information, elaborate or extend previously presented content, conduct demonstrations of expected behaviors, or describe how to solve problems. Effective teachers structure these presentations so that students experience success and demonstrate understanding of the content presented.

Tactic: Check Recognition Level Then Production Level

When introducing a new skill or concept, initial questioning should be at a recognition level. At this level, questions are posed by offering multiple choice responses. The response alternatives are manipulated to be initially obvious and then less obvious. After students have demonstrated success at the recognition level, then pose questions that require students to produce the response on their own. If students have difficulty producing answers, drop back to the recognition level.

delivering

Tactic: Model Expected Performance for Students

Modeling the expected response performance for students prior to asking them to respond will increase the probability of their success. Have students demonstrate that they understood what was expected by having them perform the task or complete a portion of the activity. Correct errors quickly to ensure that successive learning experiences will be successful.

Tactic: Alternate Between Group and Individual Responses

Pose questions that require a group response, and then follow by questioning a specific individual. A student may have been unsure of the answer during the group response or may not have answered correctly. Individual questioning immediately following feedback about the group response will assure the student an opportunity to be successful:

Teacher: "Class, what's the capital of New Hampshire?"

Class: "Concord."

Teacher: "Thank you! John, what's the capital of New Hampshire?"

John: "Concord."

Teacher: "Thank you!"

Limit Opportunities for Failure

Many students learn by making mistakes; in fact, trial-and-error learning is a very effective way of acquiring some content. Effective teachers take advantage of students' mistakes and use them as opportunities for corrective feedback, redirection, and subsequent learning.

Tactic: Help Students Accept Failure

Inform students that making errors is part of learning at all ages for all individuals. Teach them that disappointment is an acceptable emotion that occurs in relation to failure but that it can be turned into anger or determination, the latter being the better alternative. Explain that determination means that you will keep trying and you believe you will improve.

Tactic: Provide Feedback That Shows Growth

Using graphs to provide feedback to students about their performance will allow them to see growth and progress even though they may initially perform at low levels of accuracy or rate. Encourage students to chart their own behavior.

delivering

Tactic: Require Continuous Performance Improvement

Set individual student goals that are based on skill improvements and that are dynamic in nature rather than static. For example, requiring that a student show three improvements on reading rate before going on to a new passage requires the student to strive for higher levels of performance based on his/her own best previous score. Frequency data (number of correct words read per minute, number of correct math problems answered per minute) are best suited to the continuous improvement requirement.

strategy

Monitor Engagement Rates

For instruction to be effective, students should be actively engaged in it during content presentations. They should not spend much time waiting for things to happen. Effective teachers keep track of engagement rates and modify their instruction to include students are not involved.

Tactic: Call on Every Student

Be certain that every student in a class is required to respond at some point during a lesson. Asking questions that require a total group response either orally or through signaling is a tactic that maximizes student involvement.

Tactic: Avoid Elimination Games

Playing games that eliminate students who make errors should be avoided. The elimination process often removes students who have the greatest need for practice opportunities. Popular games that typically require elimination can be adapted so that a negative point is scored or a letter is awarded that spells a word that designates the losing team.

Tactic: Avoid Extended Time With One Student

During a group lesson, avoid spending extended time with one student who is having difficulty when it results in idle time for the remainder of the group. Assign peer tutors, prompt responses, or simply say, "I'll help you later," rather than reducing the engaged learning time for the majority of the group.

delivering

principle

Adjust Presentations

Delivering instruction involves adjusting presentations because all students do not learn in the same ways or at the same pace. Feedback from students is generally the best indication of a need to make changes in an instruction presentation. Effective teachers adjust their instruction to meet the individual needs of their students. Strategies they use include adapting lessons to meet student needs, providing varied instruction, and making adjustments in the pace of their presentations.

Component	Principle	Strategy	Page
Delivering Instruction	**Adjust Presentations**	Adapt lessons to meet student needs 216
		Provide varied instructional options 216
		Alter pace 217

delivering

Adapt Lessons to Meet Student Needs

Regardless of time spent planning, instructional presentations sometimes need to be modified to meet the individual learning needs of students. Effective teachers use a variety of tactics when adjusting their instruction.

Tactic: Use Classroom Space Effectively

Seat students who learn better visually so they can easily see the instructional presentation. Use examples and actual demonstrations with these students; sometimes have them act out or demonstrate what is being taught (and learned). Use charts, maps, graphs, and tables as often as possible. Seat students who learn better auditorially so they can easily hear the instructional presentation. Keep directions simple for these students and have them repeat.

Tactic: Provide Alternatives for Evaluation

Some students perform better in one-on-one or small group settings than in a single large classroom group. Providing opportunities for different testing arrangements, including open book, student-designed tests or open notes assessments, fosters student learning and illustrates an easy way to adapt instruction to meet individual needs.

Tactic: Use Organizers and Study Guides

Many students do not need assistance taking notes and focusing on appropriate learning content during lessons. Others profit greatly from instructional adaptations designed to support presentations. Provide study guides, learning outlines, alternative presentations (e.g., tape recorded lectures) and self-monitoring cue cards as adaptations to accommodate these individual differences.

Provide Varied Instructional Options

Effective teachers recognize that their content presentations will not always appeal to every student. They are prepared to use different methods to increase the likelihood that their students will learn. They rely on a variety of instructional options.

Tactic: Vary Format of Instruction

Remember those college courses where the instructor talked and the students listened? Sometimes it was effective and sometimes it wasn't. Usually, it is a good idea to vary the type of instruction being used. Consider using an overhead projector every other day, rather than every day. Use cooperative learning groups, individual learning projects, drama or role playing activities, and simulations to add variety to instruction. Sometimes do the "homework" assignment

delivering

in class with collaborative groups rather than after school as an individual task.

Tactic: Use Technology to Teach

Encourage students to use the Internet and other technology resources to extend information provided in classroom instructional presentations. Have them work together in groups to prepare class presentations extending a topic being studied. Have them share their information using varied instructional methods (e.g., overhead projectors, slide shows, dramatic presentations).

Tactic: Catalog Instructional Modifications

Provide students with a list of instructional modifications and have them select those they believe will be most effective. Encourage them to make their selections based on a particular type of content presentation (e.g., science, social studies).

strategy

Alter Pace

Effective teachers use different strategies to adjust the pace of their content presentations. Most find that it is better to cover material thoroughly rather than quickly. They also plan ample opportunities for practice and check for student understanding more frequently when adjusting the pace of instructional presentations.

Tactic: Minimize Disruptions to Control Pace

Interruptions of instructional activities can greatly influence types and amounts of student responses to instruction. Effective teachers take preventive measures to reduce disruptions during instructional presentations. They establish and enforce classroom rules to reduce or eliminate chronic distractions (e.g., pencil sharpening, trips to restroom). They have all necessary instructional materials ready and available when instruction begins.

Tactic: Use Outlines to Control Pace

Provide students with partial outlines that require minimal information to be completed. Have students follow the instructional presentation and note when new information is to be supplied. Place incomplete information at different points on the outline to control the pace of the instructional presentation.

delivering

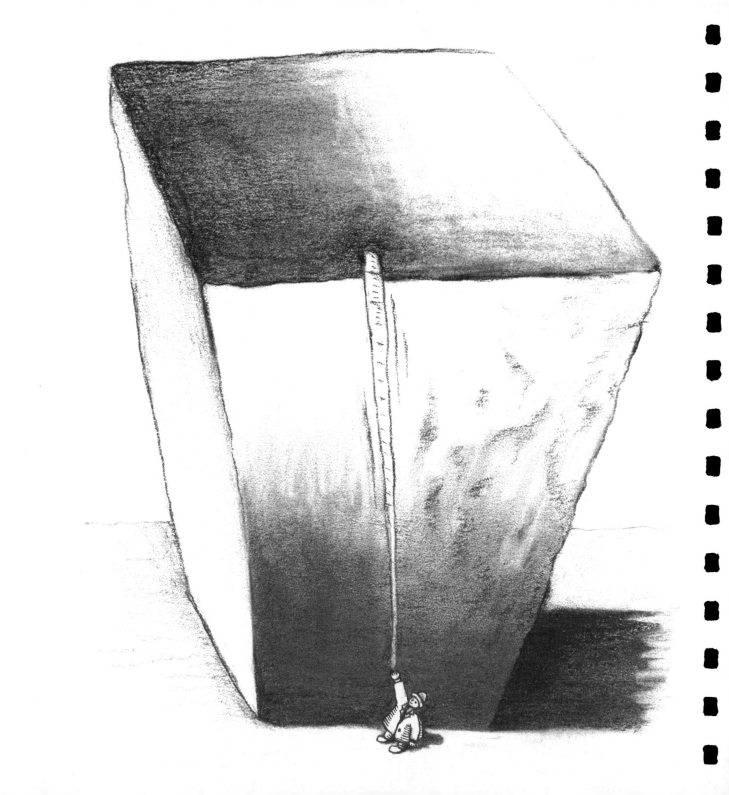

evaluating

Keeping track of the effects of instruction is an important part of teaching. It is the process by which teachers decide whether the approach they are using is effective with their students. Teachers also use evaluation to decide whether the methods and materials they are using are effective. And, evaluation data are used to make important decisions like whether to refer students to specialists, whether to change interventions, and whether (or when) to exit students from programs. Evaluation activities provide a necessary and valuable loop in any effective instructional process. This is why evaluating is a key component of instruction.

Effective instruction requires evaluating. Some evaluation activities occur during the process of instruction (i.e., when teachers collect data during instruction and use those data to make instructional decisions). Other evaluation activities occur at the end of instruction (e.g., when the teacher administers a test to determine whether a pupil has met instruc-

evaluating

tional objectives). There are four principles of effective evaluating:

1 Monitor student understanding

2 Monitor engaged time

3 Keep records of student progress

4 Use data to make decisions.

Component	Principle	Strategy
Evaluating Instruction	Monitor Student Understanding	Check Understanding of Directions Check Procedural Understanding Monitor Student Success Rate
	Monitor Engaged Time	Check Student Participation Teach Students to Monitor Their Own Participation
	Keep Records of Student Progress	Teach Students to Chart Their Own Progress Regularly Inform Students of Performance Maintain Records of Student Performance

	Use Data to Make Decisions	Use Data to Decide if More Services
		    Are Warranted
		Use Student Progress to Make Teaching Decisions
		Use Student Progress to Decide When to
		    Discontinue Service

Figure 42
Four Principles of Effective Evaluating

Each of these principles implies a set of strategies that teachers use when evaluating (see Figure 42).

Monitor student understanding involves checking students to determine if they have understood a classroom instruction presentation and keeping track of their progress as a result of that instruction. The goal is to determine the extent to which students have profited from what has been taught.

Monitor engaged time involves keeping track of student participation rates or having students monitor their own behavior. The goal of monitoring engaged time is to determine the extent to which students are actively engaged in relevant, productive instructional activities rather than irrelevant, unproductive ones.

Keep records of student progress involves keeping track of student performances using a variety of procedures and sharing the results with students regularly. The goal of maintaining records of students' progress is staying informed about performance and sharing that knowledge with students.

Use data to make decisions involves deciding when additional assistance is needed or no longer needed to meet the needs of individual students. The goal of using data to make decisions is identifying the appropriate form of assistance needed to ensure that benefits of instruction are experienced by all students.

These four evaluating principles are addressed in this section, along with a set of specific strategies that effective teachers use when focusing on each one. The main content of the unit is a set of tactics that illustrate specific ways to actively address each principle and strategy when providing effective instruction.

principle

Monitor Student Understanding

Students must understand what teachers expect them to do in the classroom, which means teachers must monitor the extent to which students understand directions. Effective teachers check process understanding by asking students to show them or tell them what they are going to do and by observing the students' response. They also monitor student success rate in deciding whether or not students understand what it is they are to do; low performance may mean simply that students do not understand what they are to do.

Component	Principle	Strategy	Page
Evaluating Instruction	**Monitor Student Understanding**	Check Understanding of Directions 222	
		Check Procedural Understanding 224	
		Monitor Student Success Rate 227	

evaluating

Check Understanding of Directions

Students' understanding and perception of what to do are not always consistent with what teachers intend. Effective teachers use a variety of methods to check for student understanding. Among the most common method is monitoring. Most teachers see monitoring as both feasible and desirable because it does not require extensive planning or preparation.

There are many forms of monitoring. The most familiar include asking students questions, random teacher movement around the room during lessons, and checking students' written assignments, group activities, or tests. Here are some additional monitoring strategies that can be implemented to monitor students' understanding on an ongoing basis.

Tactic: Do Quick Member Checks

This tactic involves teachers checking in with students to make sure they understand what they are learning. These checks should be direct, frequent, and quick. The use of hand signals (e.g., thumbs up or down), writing the answer or concept on a piece of scrap paper and placing it in the corner of the desk, and other creative formative checks are effective.

Tactic: Do Informal Student Summaries

For this tactic, the teacher asks students to summarize what was heard or the main points of material (e.g., reading passages, discussions, videos, etc.). This enables the teacher to do a quick evaluation of whether or not the students have an understanding of the material. As a variation, pairs or small groups of students can retell what was taught to each other.

Tactic: Practice Goal Restatement

Have students repeat the lesson or class goals you have stated. Ask several students to describe what they are expected to do according to stated goals. By checking the congruence between the goal, students' expression of the goal, and students' indication of how they plan to achieve the goal, teachers can effectively monitor and adjust for needed clarification.

Tactic: Practice Quick Direction Summaries

After giving instructions, individual students are asked to repeat instructions in their own words. If multistep directions are given, several students may be asked. For example, Stuart could be asked to tell step one, Sally step two, and so on. Another variation is to ask Stuart for step one and have him call on the classmate of his choice to tell step two. This can also be done using whole class choral responding.

Tactic: Have Pairs Check for Understanding

For this tactic, students are paired with another student to check for understanding of directions. First, assign student pairs. Then at random intervals direct the pairs to get together to check each other's understanding. Some teachers set a timer and tell students

evaluating

to do the pairs check any time the timer goes off. It is important to teach and model what you expect to be done during the pairs check. For example, what types of questions should be asked, what is the criteria for understanding, what do students do if neither pair member understands, and so on.

Tactic: Partner Up!

This tactic is one that allows students the learning opportunity to actively engage, with another student, in problem-solving, reviewing prior knowledge or facts, practicing facts, concepts and strategies, answering literal and inferential questions and so on.

Students are arranged in groups of four. Pairs of students are created within the foursome. Both the foursome and the within group pairs should be teacher arranged in order to balance ability levels. However, depending on the activity, you decide whether to create random or formal groups and pairs (See Plan: How Tactic: Create Random Groups, Tactic: Create Formal Groups) Once groups and pairs are set up they can maintain this composition for the class period, day, week or month. Be sure to allow students the opportunity to become familiar and comfortable with the working dynamics of their partner before changing groups around.

Decide if Partner Up! will be used at random or by direction. At random simply means students can decide when they want and need to use this tactic for a quick check, while by direction is by assignment or verbal instruction directly from you.

Procedure:

In pairs students decide who is 1 and 2. Once given a task students engage in Partner Up! as follows:

1 Student 1 works on the task item or problem first, while Student 2 supervises. Student 2 encourages his/her partner to say, write, or think through the process aloud.

2 When Student 1 indicates he/she has completed the task, Student 2 corrects it. If the work is correct, a praise phrase is given by Student 2 ("Excellent job!"). If, however, there is error, together as a pair both students problem-solve and Student 1 corrects his/her error.

3 On the next item or task, Student 2 works on the task item or problem while Student 1 supervises. The same correction procedures are followed. That is, if there is error together the pair problem-solves it and Student 2 makes the correction to the work.

4 "Pairs Partner Up!" At any time during the procedure you may announce to the pairs, "Pairs Partner Up." This tells the pairs to get with the other pair in their foursome and compare or check their work. You may indicate which problems you want Partner Pairs to check or allow students to choose.

evaluating

5 "Pair Share." Pairs always need to be ready to share what they know or information about the task or assignment at hand. They need to be ready to share it if called upon. You can randomly call on pairs to share or pull a partner's name from a hat. That student whose name is drawn is the one to share the pair's response.

Tactic: Use Lesson Reaction Sheets to Personalize Lessons

Provide students the opportunity to reflect on what they learned during instruction. This facilitates making connections of the newly presented information to other links of previous knowledge and experiences.

Use lesson reaction sheets. For lesson reaction sheets simply provide students with questions such as: (1) One thing I learned today was …; (2) I really enjoyed …; (3) I am still confused about …;)4) I need more information about …; (5) One way this lesson could be improved is …; and so on. You can focus the students any number of ways. Review the sheets for immediate feedback on your lesson and to determine where students are in their understanding of it. Be sure to tell students that any reaction is a good one, and that this activity will not help or hinder grades, status, etc. Some students may only write what they think you want to see. Make sure they understand the purpose of lesson reaction sheets.

Adapted from: Vaughn, D., Schumm, J., & Forgan, J. (in press).

evaluating

Tactic: Reinforce Efforts as Well as Performance

Always reinforce students for their efforts, even if they aren't quite on target with understanding what they are suppose to do. If students' misunderstanding is genuine—that is, they truly don't understand—and this misunderstanding is not due to inattention or misbehavior, reinforce them for their efforts and tell them what they should do. During a lesson teachers often have students monitor their own performance by delivering the simple direction, "Time to check to see if you are following directions. Check your work behavior." This simple effort refocuses students on what it is they are to be doing and provides them an opportunity to independently (or within a pair) check their progress and understanding. Another variation is to have students tell what and how they are proceeding with an assignment or task. This provides teachers and other students a quick in-progress update of understanding and task performance.

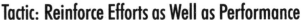

Check Procedural Understanding

It is one thing to check for understanding of directions (factual knowledge); it is another to check for procedural understanding (strategic knowledge). Often students are able to tell in order of sequence what they are to do. However, when they settle into the task they are unsure of exactly how they are to do it. Effective teachers check for process and procedural understanding to ensure that students understand the strategy needed to actually engage in task behavior. They do so by asking students to show them or tell them the process or steps they will use to complete a task. After students complete the task, effective teachers ask them to describe the actual process and procedure they used, noting differences and/or adaptations created by the students. This activity tells teachers a lot about the strategies knowledge base of their students. The information obtained helps teachers proactively plan needed changes so that students continue to learn and understand the procedures.

Tactic: Every Person Responds (EPR)

Here is a fast, fun, motivating way to review material for a quiz, test—or just because.

Procedure:

1 Create a list of questions that reflect the information you want the students to know. They can be factual such as: "What is 5 x 4?"; H2O is the periodic symbol for what?"; and so on.

2 Give each student response strips that correspond with the content you are reviewing. For example:

■ **Math Facts**—Students should have strips of paper with numbers from 0-10 on them (one number per strip). They can combine them to formulate the correct answer. Depending on the level of math problems you

ask, students may need more numbers (0-50 or 100).

■ **Health Facts**—These strips, of course, will depend upon the topic of study. For example, if you are reviewing the cardiovascular system, students can be given strips that have "V" for vein, "A" for artery, "C" for capillary or "?" for "I don't know."

■ **Science Facts**—For the study of rock, use "M" for metamorphic, "S" for sedimentary, and "I" for igneous rock. For the atmosphere, use "trap," "stat," "meso," "iono," "exo." The list goes on and on.

■ **English Facts**—Strips could simply be each of the parts of speech or punctuation marks, one per strip.

■ **History Facts**—Depending on the topic of study, dates, names of wars, important people, treaties, etc. could be written on strips.

■ **Vocabulary and Spelling Words**—These areas of factual information work well too. Decide what words you will review, and make sure students have the corresponding strip.

■ **Question Formats**—Strips can say "T" or "F" for true/false questions; "?," "A," "B," "C," "D" for multiple choice, or numbers 1, 2, 3, 4.

evaluating

Here's how EPR works:

1 Pose a question to the class.

2 Say, "Everybody respond."

3 Students hold up the strip that represents what they think the correct answer is.

4 Scan the room quickly and determine who and how many students got the question correct.

5 The correction or confirmation of the answer can be done two ways. You may choose to simply give the answer, or have another student tell the answer and how they arrived at it (HDYKT—See Delivering: Present Instruction; For Teaching Thinking Skills; Model Thinking Skills; Use HDYKT.). It is good practice, where appropriate, to ask, "Can anyone else expand on the answer just given?"

It is important for students to learn from each other. Therefore, it is important that no judgment about performance be made. Let students know that they are not being graded. Remind them that the purpose of EPR is to show what they know.

Tactic: Use Learning Logs

Learning logs are a type of journal in which students make entries about what they have learned in class. They can be used to pinpoint misunderstandings of content and/or need for reinforcement or clarifica-

tion. Teachers can structure the entries if they wish. For example, "Be sure to include in your learning log entry what process or steps you used to come to your conclusion," or "Describe what you found difficult or easy about today's lesson or assignment."

Tactic: Put Hands in Pockets

This strategy requires students to do nothing but verbalize the process and procedures they will or did use. For some students this is extremely difficult because they want to use their hands or other aids to help in the description. While there is nothing wrong with that method, this one encourages students to talk through the process. With their hands in their pockets, or behind their back, students talk through the necessary steps needed to solve a problem. For example, in math you could put two problems on the board, one that follows a strategy and one that violates it. Then have the student tell how they can or cannot solve the problems. Not only do students enjoy this tactic, they find it easier said than done!

Tactic: Use Two-Minute Papers

This is a fast, informative tactic you can use to find out what students learned and what they need additional clarification on in a short period of time—two minutes! At the end of a lesson have students take out a half sheet of paper and respond to the following questions:

▪ One thing I learned or relearned today is …
▪ An area I need more help in is …

evaluating

These questions can be altered in any way. For example, you might add the following:

 ▌ An area or issue I have concern about is …

Ask students to help generate two-minute questions for general or topic-specific information. At the end of two minutes, collect the papers. You now have up-to-date information or data on where your students are with respect to the lesson or topic of discussion you just taught. You may want your students to write the questions as well as the answers. For some students it may be difficult to remember the second question after they have diligently, but quickly, answered the first.

Tactic: Use Pairs Checks for Process Understanding

Pairs checks can be used for any purpose. Pairs of students are asked to check in with their partner to make sure they both understand the process necessary to compete a task or problem. Pairs checks can either be at random or when a student feels the need to check in with his/her partner.

strategy

Monitor Student Success Rate

Rate of correct work completion is evidence that students understand the goals of instruction as well as the process to use. Incorrect or uncompleted work may be evidence of a lack of student understanding. Effective teachers keep track and monitor student success rates. The types of knowledge (factual, conceptual, strategic) of the task and the level of proficiency (accuracy, mastery, automaticity) of the student will impact both the rate and correctness of task completion.

Tactic: Use Aim Lines and Charts

An aim line is a line connecting current level of performance to the eventual desired goal (see Figure 43). Both goals and objectives are written prior to using aim lines. The use of aim lines is especially helpful when the teacher has a long-range goal for a group of students or student and is interested in progress over time toward the goal. Objectives not only drive instruction but expected student progress. Therefore, once the level of proficiency and time period of learning a skill is determined, aim lines can be planned. For example, Yu's objective is to increase his vocabulary repertoire by learning ten new vocabulary words

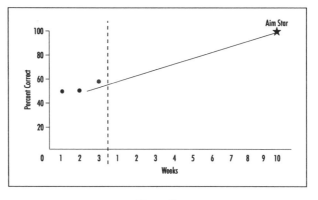

Figure 43

evaluating

at 100% accuracy per week over ten weeks. Based on this objective, the teacher:

1 Makes a ten-week chart on which student progress can be recorded.

2 Collects at least three baseline data points (or three scores that reflect the student's current level of performance).

3 Draws a straight line to the expected date and level of performance, using the median or middle score as the beginning point of the line. This is called the Aim Star.

4 Begins instruction toward the Aim Star.

Over the ten-weeks, both the teacher and student see the rate and accuracy at which these vocabulary words need to be mastered. Using the data gathered, the teacher and/or student mark progress on the aim line. Effective teachers use aim line information to monitor and adjust instruction, and they provide immediate performance feedback to student.

Aim lines can also be developed for class performance. That is, you can decide at what rate you would like to see the class as a whole progress through a unit of instruction or acquire basic facts on, for example, multiplication probes, spelling, or vocabulary probes. Caution is advised in using this format, however. Due to the diverse skills and prior knowledge your students bring to the classroom, high achievers or low achievers can skew or throw off the overall av-

erage class performance. Be sure you are aware of these potential effects. You may find that class or small group aim stars are not worth the information they show because of student diversity. However, students grouped by similar skill level (e.g., reading, math, or writing groups) may provide a better venue to use aim stars as a map for progress.

Variation 1

Teach students to record and chart their own progress by breaking the process into component parts. Perform a quick task analysis of charting, and teach students each of the parts. Students can be taught to create their own aim lines. By involving students in this, effective teachers actively communicate goals, objectives, and standards to students. There are commercially available computerized programs that teach students to chart their own progress and chart the progress for the student.

Variation 2

If it is appropriate for your instructional goal and objective, consider using peer or whole class monitoring of progress. If the class or a group is working toward a common goal, a class aim line chart can be created. This provides the whole class immediate visual feedback and an opportunity to problem-solve ways to improve or maintain progress toward the goal. Or, if the class is in noncompetitive teams, assign different members to be recorders and chart the groups progress. Team charts can be shared within the class.

Adapted from: Wolery, Bailey, & Sugai (1988).

evaluating

principle

Monitor Engaged Time

Effective teachers monitor the extent to which students are actively engaged and participating in class activities and discussions. Keeping track of student performance and progress is a time-consuming activity. Effective teachers deal with this by teaching students to monitor their own participation.

evaluating

Check Student Participation

Academic engaged time refers to the amount of time students are actively engaged in responding to academic content. Research shows that there is a direct relationship between the amount of time students are actively engaged in learning and their achievement levels. The extent to which students profit from instruction is directly related to the degree to which they are actively engaged in learning. However, not to be overlooked is the importance of students being engaged in the *right kinds* of activities. Students learn more when they are provided with multiple opportunities to respond because they practice skills more and participate in discussions and answer more questions during instruction. Effective instructors monitor the extent to which students are actively engaged in the learning process.

Documenting student performance and progress can be an overwhelming and time-consuming task. Effective instructors teach students to monitor their own participation by using a number of tactics. And, effective instructors are vigilant. They continually scan and move about the room in a random manner to reinforce students and spot others who are not actively engaged. Taking steps to reengage students who are not participating can be unobtrusive and relatively easy.

Tactic: Issue Red Flag Alerts

This tactic simply involves making a miniature flagpole and placing it in an accessible and clearly visible place. To use the Red Flag Alert, the teacher begins classroom instruction. Upon noting that a student or students are not engaged in the lesson, the teacher simply walks over to the flag pole and hoists the flag to the top of the pole. The teacher then states, "Someone in this room is not engaged with our lesson," or, being more specific, "Someone in row three is not paying attention." The wording is up to you. The students will automatically check themselves and others around for the noted off-task behavior. The teacher says no more and returns to instructing. Upon noting the correction of the student's behavior, the teacher lowers the flag, without missing a beat of instruction. The students are taken off red alert. Often a feeling of success comes over the class when the flag is lowered, as they have all worked together worked to lower the flag. Some teachers combine time intervals with the red alerts. For example, if the flag is not lowered within one minute, the class is delivered a consequence—loss of talk time at the end of class, etc. This contingency motivates students to assist each other in getting back to task and monitoring their own participation. Other teachers raise the flag without saying a word, leaving students to do a quick monitor and check of their behavior. Once the flag is raised students know someone is off-task. Scapegoating, as always, is not tolerated and is proactively managed by instructing the boundaries of the tactic.

evaluating

Tactic: Use Public Display Participation

A variation of the Red Flag Alert, the teacher, at random intervals, scans the room and counts the number of students who are on-task and writes the number on the board. One teacher puts a masking tape square on the board and titles it, "Are We On It?" For this class and school this is a popular slang for being rather cool and on top of things. The students connect with it immediately. At random the teacher writes the number of students "on it" in the box. Likewise, the teacher erases and changes the number when necessary to reflect off-task behavior. Initially it was easiest for the teacher to write the number of students not "on it." Students, however, were more motivated to know how many of them were truly cool. So the teacher changed to recording on-task behaviors. Either way, students who are not engaged in class learning feel pressure from their peers to "get on it."

Tactic: Use Quick Member Checks

This strategy involves teachers checking in with students to make sure they're engaged appropriately. These checks should be direct, frequent, and quick. Hand signals (e.g., thumbs up or down), writing the answer or concept on a piece of scrap paper and placing it in the corner of the desk, and other creative monitoring checks are effective.

Tactic: Use All Writes

To vary the use of questions during instruction and to check on student participation in the lessons, use this tactic. Pose a question to the group or class of students and pause for 30-60 seconds. During this wait time, students are given a chance to decide on an answer to the question or that they don't know the answer. Ask students to quickly write an answer to the question asked. After observing that a majority have written something down ask, "How many would be willing to share what they wrote?" Since students are asked to simply read the answer they wrote and are not put on the spot, they may feel more comfortable speaking up. Some teachers have students write the answer on a scrap paper and place it on the corner of their desks; the teacher circulates throughout the room checking answers. Others use small slate boards and have students write answers and hold up the boards for the teacher to see. It must be conveyed that this tactic is not to make students feel pressured about writing thorough responses, but to identify students who are on-track, and to identify questions about information that needs clarification. By providing students the opportunity to scribble down a quick response, it provides necessary think time and pushes students to think more precisely about the posed question. After all, there is some accountability to engaged learning time!

Adapted from: Harmin, M. (1995).

evaluating

Tactic: Whip It. Whip It Good!

This tactic provides the opportunity for more students to respond instead of the regulars or a few volunteers. Whip It involves asking each student to speak to an issue or convey their thoughts or responses. At a natural stopping point, the teacher simply states, "Let's whip this around the room," or "Let's whip this down the rows," or "Lets whip this down row two." By varying the method of whips, students never know how the whip will be performed and are more likely to stay engaged in learning. Students are always given the option to say, "I pass." Although some students may continually opt to pass, doing so may put them at greater risk of being discovered by their peers. That is, peers often monitor other peers' behavior and point it out. Either way, allowing students to make the decision to pass or share introduces self-managing behavior to the lesson. Whip It not only gives all students a chance to participate, it also raises the interest level in class. Students listen closely to how other peers respond.

Adapted from: Harmin, M. (1995).

Tactic: Use Chips In

Chips In or Cards In is a tactic that introduces a turn-taking system and limits or increases turns during a lesson. In a small group lesson, students are given any number of chips, for example, eight. The number is based on the number of times students or a target student participates or dominates a lesson. For example, if Ron asks or interjects comments eight times per les-

son, all students get eight chips. Therefore, Ron can still participate but must put a chip in everytime he wants to respond. During a reading or social skills group each student is given eight chips. If and when each student wants to participate, he/she must put in a chip (on the table or in a container). When the student is out of chips he/she is out of turns. This strategy is useful in situations where certain students dominate discussion or responses. It is not meant to limit participation, but to maintain a more equal balance. The object is for each student to end the lesson with few or no chips left. For larger groups this tactic can be modified by using index cards. Each student is given the same number of index cards at the start of the lesson. To respond, the students holds up a card, and when called upon the teacher takes the card from the student. It is important to alternate who you call on so students do not get bored because they are out of cards. One teacher uses bonus cards or chips during a lesson. When students give an outstanding response or effort, including demonstrating appropriate class behavior, participation cards/chips are given to them. This tactic is novel and adds a participatory and self-management flavor to a lesson.

Adapted from: Kagan, S. (1994).

Tactic: Use Instruct-Insight-Internalize

Instruct or lecture until there is a natural stopping point, but not more than five to seven minutes. Then say, "Take a minute to think and record the key ideas or points you've heard so far or any questions you have." Give students an opportunity to jot down

evaluating

some thoughts. Then continue instructions to the next natural stopping point. Repeat the above direction. Continue the instruct-write sequence as appropriate, but stop before students become disinterested in the tactic. Have students pair up and share their insights, key ideas, questions and summary of what they heard. After this, model the most important things that you want the students to know (internalize). Solicit from the students additional reactions, thoughts, or questions.

Adapted from: Harmin, M. (1995).

Tactic: Tally Behavior

Use a class roster to help monitor who you call on and how often. This helps you balance the number of times you call on students during a lesson. You might also have students chart at their desk the number of times they respond. This encourages those students who are less apt to respond to self-monitor their behavior; the simple act of self-monitoring increases (or decreases) the desired behavior. You may want to help some students set personal participation goals for class.

Teach Students to Monitor Their Own Participation

While it is true that students' performances improve when teachers monitor their engaged learning and redirect unengaged students, monitoring can be a time-consuming task. Students can be taught to monitor their own engaged learning time and class participation. Achieving this requires that students be instructed and reinforced for self-monitoring behaviors. Self-monitoring is a technique in which an individual acts as an observer for his/her own behavior and records the observational data. The ultimate goal of effective instruction is to enable students to generalize and function independent of teacher-mediated interventions. Students can be taught to monitor their own engaged time and class participation. Self-monitoring is a useful technique when students are motivated and when keeping track of their own behaviors is socially reinforced. Students who learn how to self-monitor learn how often target behaviors do or do not occur and what may be triggering them. The mere act of self-monitoring has an impact on behavior. Think about the times you have monitored such behavior as what food goes in your mouth or the number of cigarettes you or a significant other has consumed in a day or time period. The thought of monitoring these behaviors in and of itself elevates awareness of their occurrence. Likewise, self-monitoring for students has a similar impact.

evaluating

⏰ Tactic: Check by Chimes

This technique has been used often and successfully with all ages and types of target behaviors. Using a tape recorder, record chimes or beeps at random intervals. Have students chart or mark whether they were engaged in learning when they hear the tone. A simple yes/no checklist works well. Some teachers prefer to use a kitchen timer set at random time intervals. Each time it rings students chart their behavior. Teaching students to quietly ask themselves, "Am I doing what I am supposed to be doing?" is an effective way to frame the idea of self-monitoring engaged learning.

⏰ Tactic: Nag Tapes

A variation of Check by Chimes is using Nag Tapes. This tactic can be more personalized to students and less obtrusive to others in the classroom. Using a personal headset, students listen to a prepared tape of tones or talk. Here a significant other's voice (teacher, principal, parent, guardian, friend) delivers gentle reminders to stay on task (e.g., "Are you working? Check yourself—If you are working, nice job! If you are not, get back to task.") For some students hearing a parent's voice is not only soothing but reinforcing. For others someone else's voice works better. It is a nice idea to ask the student to suggest who he/she would like to be the voice on the tape. Some students have elected to be their own checker. Older students have used voice impersonations to motivate their checking. The sky is the limit.

⏰ Tactic: Give Yourself Five

At random intervals have students give themselves a predetermined number of points if they are engaged in the learning task at hand. Monitoring this tactic will be important. Some students will be tempted to award themselves points when unwarranted. Randomly monitor this behavior and/or use this tactic in small group instruction where scanning is more readily done. Obviously, the points need to mean something to the students. If you use this tactic make sure to connect the points to a positive contingency for the students.

Variation 1

At random intervals, have students check and record another student's or partner's behavior. Again, monitoring will be important so no favoritism or undue influence is delivered.

Variation 2

Assign students to work teams. On cue, the team's captain does a quick scan to check for engaged learning. The captain notes those who are working. Captains and teams should be changed on a regular basis.

Tactic: Use Audio or Video Taping

This technique has proven useful in classrooms for a variety of reasons. A video or audio tape of a lesson provides feedback to the teacher on the effectiveness of instructional delivery to students. Students, on the other hand, are able to see themselves in action (or inaction). They can see or hear exactly how many

evaluating

times they indeed did participate in class (offer responses) and the extent to which they were with the teacher during classroom instruction. One teacher audio-taped a class in which he was having behavioral difficulty. At the end of the class the teacher played back the lesson for the students to hear and to validate that indeed there were problems that needed to be addressed. Students were amazed to hear "how bad we really were." Using this as a teachable moment, the teacher showed students how to chart occurrences of disruptive behaviors. They were able to see that more time was spent managing than teaching. The class as a whole took steps to implement needed strategies to correct what they heard. Following this taping, students were told that on a random basis the class would be audio taped. The fact that they never knew when this would occur helped students work more diligently at correcting their behavior. No one wanted "evidence" of their inappropriate behavior.

Tactic: Structure Cognitive Self-Management

At the completion of a lesson or class, have the student respond to the following questions:

- Was this a productive lesson for me?
- What did I learn?
- What did I do to help myself learn?
- What interfered with my learning?
- What will I do next hour to help me learn better?

Students can log the answers to these questions in a daily journal or class log. And, of course, these questions can be individualized by students and/or the class. By raising their cognitive awareness, students are given an opportunity to think metacognitively and proactively manage their participation and responsibility in the learning process.

Tactic: What Are We Monitoring?

Teach students to create their own monitoring system. Using index cards, have students periodically inventory their behavior and mark their cards indicating whether they were actively engaged in the target behavior or not. This tactic can easily be combined with the use of audio and video tape tactics (see above). Depending on how you decide to implement this, students will need to be cued when and how often they need to inventory their behavior. Some teachers prefer to let students monitor their own behavior and "compare notes" at the end of class. When provided the opportunity to monitor their own behavior, students naturally become more aware of its presence or absence. An interesting phenomenon occurs when students monitor their own behavior—the targeted behavior changes in the desired direction.

Tactic: Use Lesson Reaction Cards

At the conclusion of a lesson, students are asked to write a brief reaction to the lesson by answering direct questions such as: "What did you learn today?"; "How does it relate to other things that you know?"; "What else would you like to know?" This is a quick way to monitor and gather immediate feedback on student learning and understanding.

evaluating

Tactic: Use Outcome Sentences

Outcome sentences are a variation on Lesson Reaction Cards that use statement starters to elicit student responses at the end of a lesson. Teachers can provide students with statement sheets or simply write the following on the board:

■ "After this lesson I learned ..."

■ "I was surprised ..."

■ "I relearned ..."

■ "I am feeling positive about ..."

■ "I need clarification on ..."

This provides teachers a quick way to monitor and gather immediate feedback on students' understanding and participation in a lesson. Information gained enables the teacher to plan and deliver additional information as necessary.

Adapted from: Harmin, M. (1995).

Tactic: Use Acetate Sheets for Completed Assignments

Some students need to keep track of what assignments they have and have not completed. This tactic is just for them! Give students a sheet with a listing of daily classroom routines and assignments. Provide them with an acetate overlay and a grease pencil. Then decide on how to use this tactic. For example, you may simply have students check off a box when they have completed the task. Or, you may have the students copy the assignment on the acetate overlay and then check it off when complete. Teachers can provide an area to record any bonus points or comments to the students for the task. At the end of the day the acetate is wiped clean and ready for next day's use.

evaluating

principle

Keep Records of Student Progress

Effective teachers keep records of student progress in order to know the extent to which students are profiting from instruction. Recordkeeping can be formal or informal. Sometimes teachers chart both student performance and goals. Charting student progress can be a lot of work. Effective teachers teach students to chart their own progress and to keep records of progress. Students perform better in school when teachers keep them regularly informed about their progress. Effective teachers know that for feedback to be effective it must be task specific and explicit.

Component	Principle	Strategy	Page
Evaluating Instruction	**Keep Records of Student Progress**	Teach Students to Chart Their Own Progress . 238 Regularly Inform Students of Performance . . . 239 Maintain Records of Student Performance . . . 242	

evaluating

Teach Students to Chart Their Own Progress

Teaching is a very challenging job. Teachers wear many hats, and diversity in the classroom has never been greater than it is today. Keeping track of student learning proves to be an equal challenge. Effective teachers not only keep efficient records of their students' progress, but they also teach students how to chart their own progress. In doing so, students learn the importance of recordkeeping as well as the value of using progress to guide further achievement efforts. It provides students a sense of acceptability and accomplishment. There are no surprises about grades because students are kept informed. Students can be taught to monitor both academic and behavioral progress.

Tactic: How Am I Doing?

Have students create their own monitoring systems. Students not only can help identify what they feel needs to be monitored but create their own chart for doing so. Using an index card, students can identify what, how, and how often they will monitor their behavior. If counting on a daily basis, it is important for the students to tally and summarize the total number of tallies of the targeted behavior. An important question should be asked—"Did I reduce (or increase) my behavior from the day before?" (or class before, depending on how this is implemented). At week's end, or sooner if

need be, students should chart their progress so that a visual prompt shows the trend in behavior.

Tactic: If You Can Count It, Chart it!

Any behavior that can be counted, can be charted. Teaching students to monitor their own participation and behavior is an important part of generalizing learned behaviors. The ultimate goal of any instruction is not only to have students learn, but spontaneously generalize or transfer the skill to other settings and learning activities. In order to do this several things must occur. Students must learn the fact, concept, strategy, or behavior to an automatic level. That is, they must be able to engage and demonstrate the behavior in the presence of distracters. Many students (and adults) do not spontaneously transfer what they learn and must be specifically taught how to. In instructing students to generalize their learning, start at the level of recognizing the presence or absence of the behavior, demonstrate examples, and model how to apply the knowledge in different situations.

Look back at the tactics discussed under Evaluation: Monitor Engaged Time. Inventory how you can teach students to chart what they monitor. The simple task of teaching students to monitor their behavior has an impact. When students learn to chart what they monitor, they create a visual reinforcement or prompt of their progress. Public display of the charts for accountability and progress in and of itself increases the likelihood that the behavior will be performed. Remember, for some students "public

evaluating

display" can be simply between the student and the teacher. For some students sharing and charting progress data with a teacher or adult may have the same impact as publicly displaying it to the entire class (e.g., posting on a bulletin board) Teaching students to both monitor and chart their behavior makes them more aware of it, so they will take ownership of it, problem-solve to improve or change it, be recognized for it, and generalize it to other settings.

strategy

Regularly Inform Students of Performance

Regular and frequent feedback is one way to keep students informed about their progress. It helps students know what is expected of them and to what extent they are meeting expectations. As always, feedback should be frequent. Some teachers use quick one-minute conferences to personalize immediate feedback to students. Students learn better when they know how they are doing and when errors are corrected immediately. Errors left uncorrected lead to procedural problems.

⏰ Tactic: Be Specific and Frequent

Praise must be task specific. It is not enough to tell Ricardo that he did a "good job." Effective teachers know that students need to be told exactly what "good job" means. For example, "Ricardo, you did a very nice job of filling out the names of the countries on your map—you got them all correct." Do not leave well enough alone. Tell students when they are doing a good job—be specific. "José, thank you for finishing your assignment, I appreciate that." Using specific praise phrases is important. They keep students informed about their progress and let them know you appreciate their efforts. Give at least four praise phrases to students, as a group, per class period.

Feedback must also be specific. For example, "Mareta, you had some difficulty on the third problem. Rework it and see if you can find your error." Having students correct their mistakes immediately is effective practice. To do so requires direct monitoring and delivery of specific feedback on the part of the teacher.

Tactic: Sign Me Up! (Students and Parents)

Provide students the opportunity to "sign up" for quick conferences with the teacher. Effective teachers use this tactic for informing individuals as well as small groups of students about their progress. Small groups may be cooperative teams or students doing project work. These conferences can last from one to five minutes. You decide. It is important that students know what the criteria is for their performance, both academic and behavioral. Some teachers have developed quick conference record sheets that have the criteria used to monitor student/group progress. At the end of the quick conference, students have a record of how they are doing that can be logged into a notebook and/or taken home and shown to parents.

The main objective of this tactic is to allow both you and the student(s) to check in and review progress.

evaluating

This method also works well in making home connections. Give parents the opportunity to call and connect with you anytime. There is a strong correlation with home-school collaboration and its impact on student achievement. By providing parents the opportunity to "sign up," you convey the message, "I care and you count." While parents may not always take advantage of this tactic, they know the option is always there.

Tactic: Publicly Post Progress

Public posting is a tactic that may be used to enhance participation and motivation in the classroom. Public posting primarily involves the visual feedback of academic work and progress. It can be seen from anywhere in the room. Of course, for public posting to have impact, what is posted must be meaningful to the student(s). It is important to not only record progress, but indicate improvement. Bring attention to the postings and make a big deal out of how students are doing. Research has shown that posting improvements is much more effective than posting measures that tell about poor or inappropriate performance.

Anything that can be counted can be charted. Anything that can be charted can be posted. Posting of learning can include scores on assignments, team points, number of assignments completed per week or day, percentage of improvement, and any other measurable target behavior.

Some teachers are reluctant to consider the use of a public posting system in the classroom. The concern is that some students will react or be uncomfortable if

their work is displayed. Of course, this is a possibility. However, research shows that most students (and adults) prefer a public posting system that presents positive information. Think about it—what effect would there be on teacher behavior if the principal posted the names of teachers who enter and leave the building early, even by the number of minutes? And what if this information were posted by the mailboxes for all to see? What impact do you think it would have on those named teachers? In addition, the issue of fairness may arise. "It isn't fair that they come and go and still get a paycheck while the rest of us abide by the rules." The potential backlash could be extensive. In the same manner, if the names of those who are on time (or in compliance with other rules) is posted, then what? A general rule for public posting—post the positive!

Tactic: Plus/Minus Feedback Chart

The Plus/Minus Feedback Chart is a tactic that allows both you and your student(s) to monitor behavior in four specific areas, within and/or over several classes or school settings.

This tactic has several worthy components. First, it provides students with a visual display of their behavior(s). Second, it provides you the opportunity to use it with an individual student or a group of students. Third, it provides you with an opportunity to publicly process and post progress. Fourth, it is a relatively simple way to gather valuable information to help make instructional decisions.

evaluating

Procedure:

Within each quadrant of a box figure, write a specific operationalized behavior. Operationalized means that the behavior is observable and able to be counted. It is important that both you and your students are able to see and account for the specified behaviors. Depending on the schedule of use (by class period or day), record pluses (+) or minuses (-) in each quadrant. These correspond to how the student(s) performed during the class or day (see Figure 44).

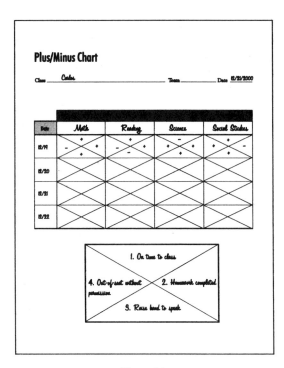

Figure 44

What to Do With +s and -s—Decide what students will be working toward. What will the +s and -s mean? For some the simple notion of having lots of +s and public recognition and praise for them is just fine. Others may need more tangible rewards. The incentive systems can be devised for individual students, the whole class, and/or teams within a class. For example, the entire class can set whole class goals, working to earn an incentive or celebration for the entire class. Individual teams can specify individual rewards, and individual students can set their own personal goals. Whatever method you choose, keep it manageable and simple. Too many teams working toward too many different rewards can soon get unmanageable.

After quadrants are marked, use a tally sheet to record how students performed. Again, pluses do not have to mean anything or trigger a reward, but they should bring lots of attention to the students who earn them. Some teachers choose to create a plus bank. Earning pluses means you can use them as money to trade or buy free time, no homework passes, computer time, or any other incentive students will work toward. Ask them—they will tell you what the pluses are worth to them! No matter what method you choose be sure to emphasis the notion of improvement or "best." Have students identify their "best" day, the biggest improvement, or where they need to focus more effort. Use the data to show trends in behavior, and be sure to change the quadrant behaviors as steady or stable patterns of behavior are maintained over several days.

evaluating

Public Posting—Once again decide ahead of time whether the public posting will be by individual students, the whole class, teams within a class, or all of the above. For individuals, have each student create his/her own plus/minus sheet. Have them tally +s and -s by the class or day. Then have them transfer the points to a cumulative +/- sheet. Each cumulative sheet can be posted on the bulletin board or somewhere students will see it.

caution: Be sensitive to those students who feel threatened by such a display. Find a happy medium that will allow them to continue to work hard for pluses, earn praise, and somehow get displayed.

The same can be created for whole class efforts. Public posting does have a positive effect on all of our behaviors, so post, post, post!

Variation
For older students, individual +/- feedback charts can be reproduced onto 5 x 8 index cards. They can be easily stored in pockets for safekeeping.

Adapted from: Paine, S. et. al. (1983).

Tactic: The Wall of Fame
After grading students' work, those who receive 100% get to post their papers on the 100% bulletin board. At the end of the week, those papers are taken down and redistributed to students who then post them on the Wall of Fame. At the end of the quarter all Wall of Fame papers are taken down and tallied.

evaluating

One teacher gives awards to the top three finishers. All students are recognized by the building administrator. The principal is part of the awards ceremony, and the entire class is recognized for their work. Quarterly tallies are kept and improvements are recognized. Regardless of who the top finishers are or who shows quarterly improvement, all students are praised and recognized for their efforts.

There are a number of ways this tactic can be implemented and rewards and recognition structured. Find out what works best for your students.

strategy

Maintain Records of Student Performance

To know the extent to which students are profiting from instruction, effective teachers must keep records of their progress. Recordkeeping can be formal or informal. A public posting system is an informal method of recordkeeping. Of course, keeping formal records in subject areas is needed to facilitate the process of report card grading. More and more teachers are using computer database programs to keep track of students' scores and print out reports to share with students, parents, and other professionals.

Tactic: Consider Computer Software Programs

The educational market is becoming flooded with computer software programs that enable teachers to keep graphic records of students' progress and performance. Find out what's available and if it will help you in maintaining records of student progress and delivering frequent feedback on performance.

evaluating

principle

Use Data to Make Decisions

There is no way to decide ahead of time the specific instructional approaches and strategies that will work best for all students. Effective teachers use formal and informal records to make important decisions about students. Decisions about whether to refer students for psychoeducational evaluation, whether to change instructional approaches, and whether to keep students in special programs or exit them from programs are made on the basis of data collected by teachers.

evaluating

strategy

Use Data to Decide if More Services Are Warranted

According to Federal regulations, a student cannot be considered for special education classification, placement, or services until a school or district has shown, beyond a shadow of a doubt, that a student cannot succeed in the general education setting given supplemental aids and resources. That is, one must prove that instruction is not effective or needs cannot be met in the general education setting. It is not enough to say that a student is not progressing through the curriculum at the expected rate of progress or that behavior impedes the student's learning. One must be able to prove it. To do so requires that interventions and strategies be implemented and their use documented over a period of time. And, a strategy or intervention does not simply constitute a phone call and/or parent or guardian conference. Too many students have been unnecessarily placed in special education. Use data to track of student progress. Effective teachers know that this is not only best practice but useful in making decisions about when additional help or services are warranted for a student. Gathering data and keeping records are important, not only for charting students' progress, but also for making decisions about their educational programs.

evaluating

Tactic: Consider Normative Peer Comparison

Effective teachers keep track of and document their students' progress. For target students or those with whom there is concern, this has dual importance. Not only does it guide and direct planning and delivering of instruction, but it facilitates decisions about the need for extra help. While it is not uncommon for students to have individual learning goals and objectives, there may come a time when the gap widens to an extreme. Keep records of all student performances in key curriculum areas, and use these data to make informed decisions about when particular students need program changes.

Tactic: Consider Decisions and Data Needed to Make Them

Assessment data and classroom success or failure are used to clarify and verify the existence of educational problems in the areas of academic functioning, behavior, and social and physical development. Data about what has been tried in the classroom are key to making these decisions.

There are 13 kinds of decisions. They are grouped into four broad categories—Prereferral Classroom Decisions, Entitlement Decisions, Postentitlement Classroom Decisions, and Accountability/Outcome Decisions. Each category has its own set of considerations and components for gathering data to make the respective decisions. These categories and the presented framework can be used to make decisions in academic, behavior, social, and/or physical domains.

Many complex social, political, and ethical issues arise when assessment or tests are used to make decisions about students. Assessment and the gathering of classroom data about what works and what doesn't is serious business. It is critical that it be done correctly.

Use Student Progress to Make Teaching Decisions

Effective instruction is about planning, managing, and delivering instruction to students on a daily basis. In order to complete the cycle of effective instruction teachers must evaluate whether students are learning. It is difficult to know ahead of time which strategies and instructional methods will work best for students. The most useful data for making these decisions reflect direct measurements on student progress. These data can be gathered in a variety of formal and informal ways. Create a timeline that indicates the rate at which students should progress through the unit of instruction or curriculum. Gather data on student progress and chart it. Use data to adjust instruction, teacher actions, and materials for students.

Tactic: Use Data to Evaluate Instructional Decisions

Making decisions about instructional techniques and methods requires teachers to consider a number of variables. The most fundamental question is, "Are in-structional methods working?" Using graphs to visually display data communicates quickly the nature and extent of students' progress. A visual data display also facilitates instructional decision making. Although one does not always have to graph data to decide if a procedure is working, the value of such practice has been shown to have a positive impact on student achievement.

There are a variety of ways to use student data to make decisions. Aim lines and 'celeration lines are two that have already been discussed in this book. It is well beyond the scope of this book to provide you with details of single-subject research designs and various multiple treatment designs. Therefore, what follows is a brief list and description of some of the basic designs. But first, there are a couple of fundamentals you should know.

Why Baselines? Baseline data or the frequency and degree to which a student exhibits the target behavior must be collected. It is important to determine the rate or frequency at which students exhibit the selected behavior for at least three reasons:

1 To identify if in fact an intervention is warranted—why put time and energy into influencing a behavior change when it isn't needed? Often target behaviors are targeted because they are driving the teacher crazy and no one else. Take Abbe for example. Abbe had a habit of tapping her pencil during math. Not a malicious act but a habit. The students in the class

evaluating

examples of stable trends in baselines

Stable Baseline Trend

Shows a stable trend—there is no improvement or no decrease in work skill acquisition. Program remains the same.

Ascending Baseline Trend

Shows a steady trend of increase in skill or behavior. This is called an ascending baseline trend.

Descending Baseline Trend

Depicts a steady decline in performance. This may be good or bad depending on what you are measuring. For example, if this data were showing frequency of out-of-seat behavior over baseline collection, this trend would be desirable. However, if the baseline showed scores on physics quizzes, this trend would be negative.

Figure 45

evaluating

were unaware of the behavior, but it drove the math teacher up the proverbial wall. Question—whose problem is it, Abbe's or the teacher's? Clearly a full-blown intervention was

not needed. Abbe's behavior was not impacting the education process of math class, only the comfort level of the teacher. After some discussion and consultation the teacher taught Abbe to tap on her leg or arm (a soft, quiet surface) instead of the desk.

2 To see if an implemented intervention has had an effect.

3 To have something to compare the behavior change to.

How Long Should a Baseline Be? The general rule for baseline data collection is: long enough to get a stable (or variable) trend of behavior. Stable and variable trends can take on different looks. Figure 45 shows examples of stable baselines. Figure 46 shows examples of unstable baselines.

With the fundamentals out of the way, you're ready to examine single-subject designs. Don't be fooled by their names—they are easy to use and generate valuable information for making effective instructional decisions.

Withdrawal Design (ABA or ABAB)

One of the oldest and most frequently used, the withdrawal design consists of three conditions: baseline(A), intervention (B), and baseline (A) (see Figure 47). The two baselines are conducted exactly the same way, and the intervention implemented is what separates them. The first baseline precedes the intervention and documents the current level of performance. After the intervention is implemented and

examples of unstable baselines

Unstable Baseline

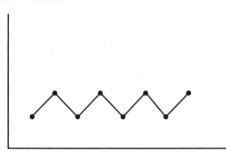

Shows a relatively predictable pattern of an unstable baseline. The student's performance is within the same range. Although it appears to be unstable, it is actually quite stable in showing the range of student performance.

Unstable Variable Baseline

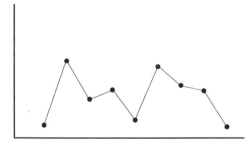

This is a very unstable, unpredictable baseline. The student performance is variable and shows no pattern or range within which performance occurs.

Figure 46

withdrawal design (aba or abab)

Jimmy is an average to below average student in Math 9. Jimmy does not hand in homework. Jimmy's teacher, Mr. Tee, is trying to discern whether Jimmy's homework behavior is due to lack of motivation or skill. Mr. Tee writes the following objective:

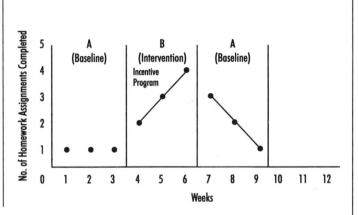

Using an individualized incentive program, Jimmy will increase the frequency with which he hands in his homework from once a week to three times a week with the final goal of 5/5 times per week.

Jimmy's Incentive Program: For every homework assignment he hands in per week he gets 1 point added to the final unit's test score. (5 x 1 = 5 pts per week)

The figure shows that the incentive system worked with Jimmy (B). However, when discontinued during weeks 7-9, Jimmy's behavior dropped. Decision: Continue with incentive program.

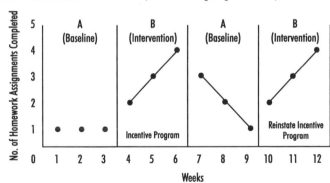

Figure 47

data of progress collected, it is withdrawn and the second baseline is taken. If the intervention has had an impact, after its withdrawal the behavior will begin to return to the original level of performance. This return may be abrupt or gradual.

The ABABA design simply extends the design by a second exact intervention implementation.

note: The behavior you examine in this design must be reversible. That is, it must be likely to return to baseline once the intervention has been withdrawn. Some behaviors are not reversible. For example, the behavior of learning to read a list of words using an intervention is not likely to reverse once the words have been learned; however, homework completion is reversible (i.e., it can revert back or change independent of skill development).

Reversal Design (ABCB or ABC)

This design includes three conditions: baseline (A), intervention (B), reverse application of the intervention (C), and intervention (B). While the reversal design is similar to the withdrawal design, the difference lies in the reversing of the original intervention. For example, Kate swears in class. The teacher wants to examine the effect of teacher attention on her swearing. After an initial baseline (A) is taken, the teacher decides to reinforce Kate when she uses appropriate language and doesn't swear (B). After a period of intervention, the teacher reverses the intervention and attends to Kate every time she swears (C). After a period of time the teacher returns to the original intervention (B). Once again the behavior must be reversible (see Figure 48).

reversal design (abcb or abc)

Decision: As shown by the trend in data, Kate responds to recognition from her teacher when she does not swear. It appears that the act of reprimanding Kate for her swearing triggers its increase. Kate's teacher has decided to continue the use of attention/praise to Kate's appropriate use of language.

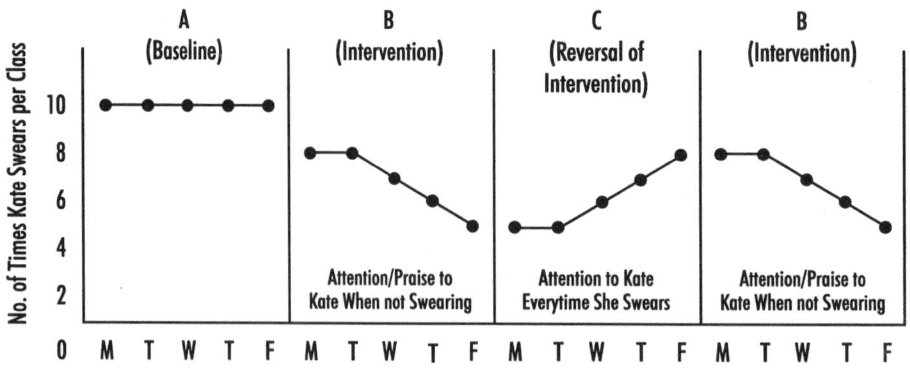

Figure 48

evaluating

Multiple Baseline Design

Multiple baseline designs contain two conditions: baseline and intervention. They require a minimum of three baselines taken at simultaneous times. There are three such multiple baseline variations: across behaviors, across conditions, and across students. Each is briefly described below.

Multiple Baseline Design Across Behaviors—This design examines three independent behaviors of a single student (e.g., out-of-seat, time-on-task, and work completion).

Figure 49 illustrates a multiple baseline design across behaviors. In (A) an original baseline is taken across all three targeted behaviors (out-of-seat behavior, time on task, work completion). Bucky's teacher, has selected a lottery ticket system as the intervention. When Bucky exhibits the desired behavior (in-seat, on-task, work complete), he is given lottery tickets, which in turn makes him eligible for reinforcers.

Bucky's teacher started with the collection of baseline data over the three behaviors and targeted Bucky's out-of-seat behavior first. After a stable baseline was gathered, the teacher implemented the inter-vention of the lottery tickets. Once Bucky's out-of-seat behavior reached the predetermined criteria set for the behavior, the teacher began the intervention for the second behavior, time-on-task. (Note that the baseline on the time on task behavior was continually collected throughout the teacher's intervention on Bucky's out-of-seat behavior.) While reinforcement and rewards were still being delivered to Bucky for his in-seat behavior, the teacher began using the lottery ticket intervention for the time-on-task behavior. After Bucky's time-on-task behavior met the predetermined criteria, intervention on the last behavior was initiated. By the time Bucky's teacher began her final intervention on his work-completion behavior, Bucky had shown improved and stable performance on the first two targeted behaviors.

Two things occurred continuously throughout the various stages of this intervention:

1 Bucky's teacher kept continual baselines of the behaviors that were targeted but not under intervention.

2 Bucky's teacher continued to deliver reinforcement to the behavior(s) that met criterion while she intervened on another.

evaluating

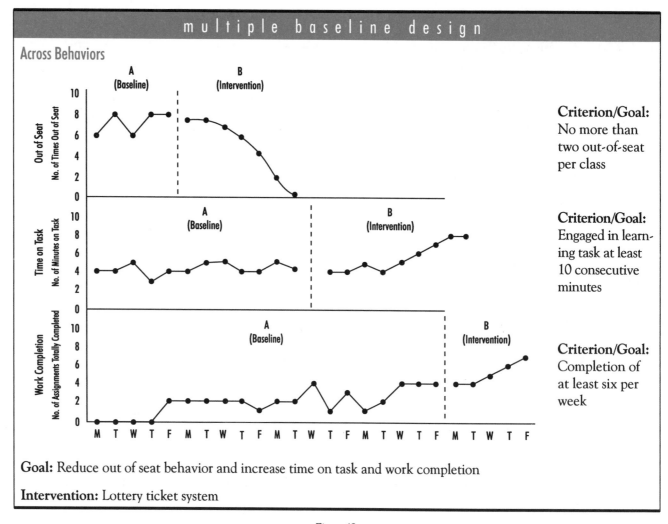

Figure 49

evaluating

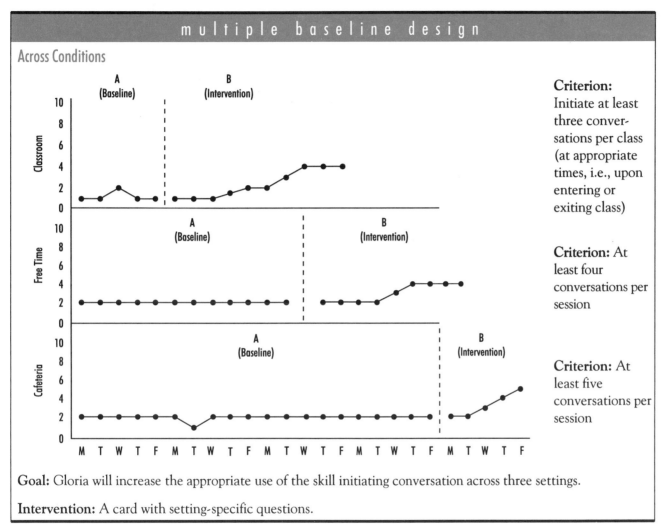

multiple baseline design

Across Conditions

A (Baseline) B (Intervention)

Criterion: Initiate at least three conversations per class (at appropriate times, i.e., upon entering or exiting class)

A (Baseline) B (Intervention)

Criterion: At least four conversations per session

A (Baseline) B (Intervention)

Criterion: At least five conversations per session

M T W T F M T W T F M T W T F M T W T F M T W T F

Goal: Gloria will increase the appropriate use of the skill initiating conversation across three settings.

Intervention: A card with setting-specific questions.

Figure 50

Multiple Baseline Design Across Conditions—Multiple baseline across conditions follows the same procedures as above, however, the settings are different.

Here the example shows baselines and interventions across cafeteria, classroom, and hallway settings. (See Figure 50.)

evaluating

multiple baseline design

Across Students

Criterion: Reduce late behavior to 0 times per week

Goal: Martha, Mike, and Melea will reduce the number of times they arrive late to period 9, the last class of the day.

Intervention: For every time the students are late, they stay one minute after class. Minutes accumulate. For example, on Day 1 they must stay one minute after the bell; on Day 2 they must stay two minutes after the bell; on Day 3, three minutes, and so on.

There is often an interesting effect using multiple baselines across students. As noted in Figure 51, Martha was the first student to be subject to the intervention, which appeared to have an immediate effect on her. In the meantime, Mike continued his late behavior, and after observing the intervention used with Martha (assuming it was consistently used and backed up daily), his behavior changed immediately. Sometimes this effect makes it difficult to know what caused behavior to change—the intervention itself or the observation of the intervention on others. Regardless, in this case the intervention was successful in changing Martha's, Mike's and Melea's late behavior. The teacher has decided to continue with this intervention for all three students.

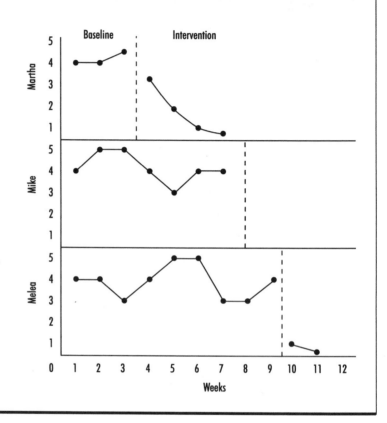

Figure 51

evaluating

Multiple Baseline Design Across Students—This design looks at the same behavior across three different students.

For this design all behaviors, students, and settings (conditions) must be independent. That is, changes in one will not effect changes in the others. (See Figure 51.)

Changing Criterion Design

For this design, a target behavior is selected, for example, class participation. Once the behavior is identified, baseline data is collected. A criterion is set based on the information gathered during the baseline phase. For this design it is desirable that four different criterion levels be established before the intervention is started. They should be distinct from each other, that is, abruptly different. And the demonstrated behavior should be relatively stable before moving to the next criterion level. Note that it is the criteria that change, not the behavior.

For example, Johnny has the habit of getting out of his seat several times, without permission, during a 45-minute instructional lesson. This behavior not only distracts the other students, but keeps Johnny from completing the task at hand. The baseline shows that Johnny gets out of his seat an average of eight times a class period. Using baseline information, Johnny's teacher has set the four criterion levels at 7, 5, 3, 1, with the final level being 1 or zero.

The selected intervention is to give Johnny passes, each one "Good for one out-of-seat." At the start of each lesson Johnny is given the specific number of passes corresponding with the criterion level (see Figure 52). Johnny is instructed he can only get out of his seat by cashing in a pass. If he runs out of passes or gets out of his seat without cashing in (simply by putting a pass in a can with a slotted lid on the teacher's desk), then a preplanned negative consequence is delivered. Not surprisingly, Johnny's out-of-

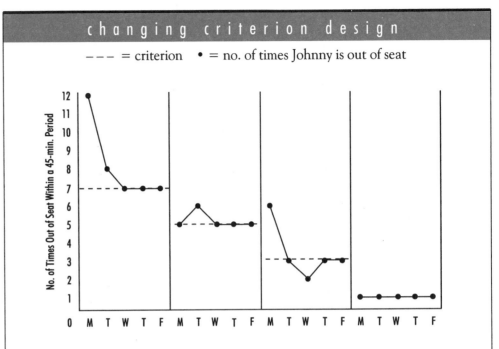

Goal: Reduce Johnny's out-of-seat behavior to one per class period.

Intervention: Deliver preplanned negative consequences if Johnny is out of seat more times than allowed.

Figure 52

seat behavior is closely correlated with the number of passes he is given. Eventually Johnny gets out of his seat no more and no less than the number of passes he has (e.g., three passes, three out-of-seats).

As the graph shows, the teacher should continue use of out-of-seat passes and be prepared to change reinforcer menu and intervention. Perhaps passes can be col-

evaluating

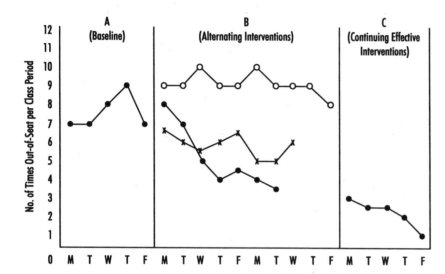

alternating treatment design

For Behavior

• = lottery tickets   x = free time   o = verbal reminder

Goal: Reduce Johnny's out-of-seat behavior to one per class period.

Intervention: Alternate between loss of out-of-seat passes and addition of free time minutes.

Figure 53

evaluating

lected if not used to get out of seat. These can be cashed in for incentives (e.g., five passes, five minutes extra at recess).

Things to keep in mind with this design:

▌ The target behavior must be in the student's repertoire of skills and able to be performed in a step-

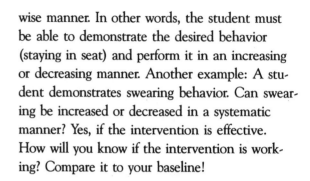

wise manner. In other words, the student must be able to demonstrate the desired behavior (staying in seat) and perform it in an increasing or decreasing manner. Another example: A student demonstrates swearing behavior. Can swearing be increased or decreased in a systematic manner? Yes, if the intervention is effective. How will you know if the intervention is working? Compare it to your baseline!

▌ Finally, although the changing criterion design may take several weeks to complete, it requires only one target behavior, and no withdrawal of intervention is needed.

Alternating Treatment Design
This design is used to determine the effect of two or more interventions on a student's behavior. The primary advantage of this design is a quick assessment of the merits of two or more interventions. A key component to Alternating Treatments is making sure the student discriminates when the intervention is or is not in effect. This can be done by simply telling the student, "Today we will be using out-of-seat passes."

Johnny's teacher is interested in finding out what intervention works best with Johnny's out-of-seat behavior—passes, verbal reminders, or free time (see Figure 53). Johnny is given a total of ten minutes of free time when he enters the class. For every time he gets out of his seat, he loses one minute of free time. Johnny's teacher starts this design by using out-of-seat passes. Johnny is given ten out-of-seat passes when he enters the classroom. Every time Johnny gets out of his seat he must hand in a pass. When he is out of passes he can no longer get out of his seat. After a period of time, the teacher switches the intervention to minutes of free time (and makes this clear to Johnny). After another period of time she switches back to the passes. Then again to the free time minutes. When it becomes clear to the teacher which intervention is more effective, she continues that procedure for a week or two to demonstrate that it alone is having a positive effect on Johnny's out-of-seat behavior.

The data displayed in the graph indicates that the out-of-seat pass intervention is the most effective with Johnny. It may be the simple fact that he holds a number of passes telling him how many times he can get up out of his seat without penalty.

Why not just ask Johnny which he would prefer? Some students will be unable or unwilling to participate in this decision, and the teacher is left to figure it out. Using the Alternating Treatment Design, one can get a clear view of what the student will or will not respond to and what strategies will satiate the fastest. The novelty of some interventions may fade relatively quickly; this design can aid in pinpointing those.

Alternating Treatment Designs are equally useful for deciding what method of instruction is more effective with students. For example, Robin's teacher is interested in examining the effects of classwide peer tutor-

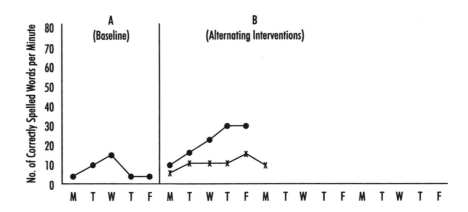

Goal: Improve Robin's spelling accuracy.

Intervention: Alternate between classwide peer tutoring and lecture formats to determine which is most effective.

Figure 54

ing versus lecture formats on Robin's spelling performance. He uses Alternating Treatment Designs to decipher the effect of both (see Figure 54). The graph shows clearly that CWPT has had a significant impact on Robin's spelling behavior. It is apparent she is not learning how to spell as a result of lecture style spelling lessons. The teacher will continue to use CWPT as a means to provide Robin with opportunities to practice spelling.

evaluating

Multiple Probe Design

This design is well-suited for investigating instructional strategies and their effect on learning. A probe is a sheet of facts usually administered in one-minute timings. For example, in teaching multiplication facts a teacher can administer a probe (a sheet of 100 multiplication facts) to a student or students (see Figure 55). The student is given one minute to complete as many multiplication facts as possible; the teacher then quickly ascertains those facts already known and those that need instruction. The teacher can then deliver instruction on those facts and reprobe using the same sheet. If instruction is effective the student should show growth or correct completion of those facts on the probe. The probe-teach sequence continues until mastery of all facts has been reached on the probe. This probe-teach method can be used for teaching spelling words, math facts, vocabulary words, and word recognition or decoding. The probe sheets will vary according to skills. For spelling the teacher can dictate a list of words, review results of the probe, teach the needed rules and probe again. For decoding the students are asked to read as many words on the probe sheet as possible. Instruction follows according to information gained from the probe.

The advantages to the multiple probe design are: (1) Students can chart and see their progress from probe to probe. The slightest improvement motivates the student to work toward continued improvement; and (2) Information about the impact of instruction on student learning is gained immediately.

How Do I Know Which Design to Use? Each of the designs serves a different purpose. All of them can be used to identify effective interventions and cause-effect relationships. However, when selecting the one to use, consider at least two things:

1 Will the design answer the question being asked?

2 Is the design practical to implement?

Only you can answer these questions based on what information you seek. For example, if you want to know if giving out free out-of-seat passes will reduce Malique's out-of-seat behavior, then a number of the designs can be used. If however, you choose to not withdraw an effective intervention, then the design selection has been narrowed. Alternately, if you want to see the effect of this intervention on Malique over three different settings, then a multiple baseline over settings would be most appropriate.

Adapted from: Wolery, Bailey, & Sugai (1988).

evaluating

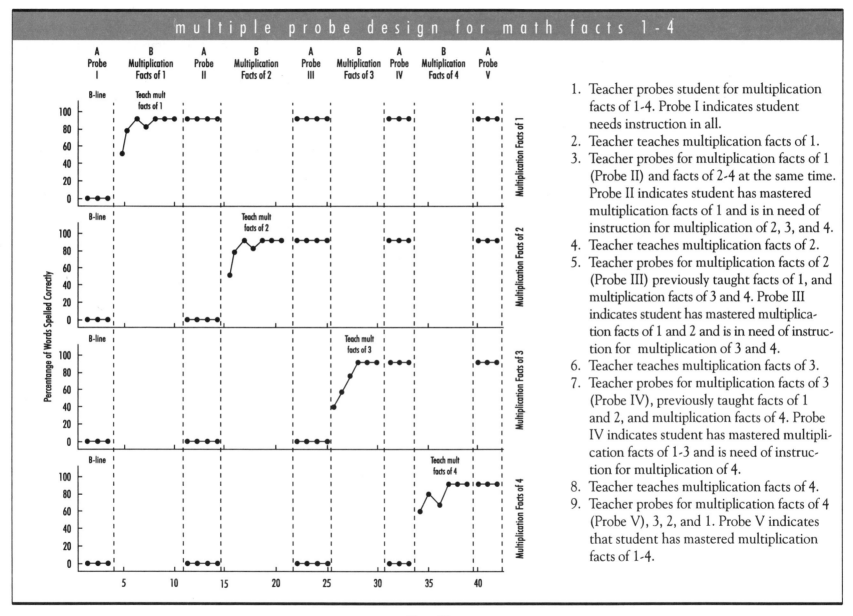

Figure 55

1. Teacher probes student for multiplication facts of 1-4. Probe I indicates student needs instruction in all.
2. Teacher teaches multiplication facts of 1.
3. Teacher probes for multiplication facts of 1 (Probe II) and facts of 2-4 at the same time. Probe II indicates student has mastered multiplication facts of 1 and is in need of instruction for multiplication of 2, 3, and 4.
4. Teacher teaches multiplication facts of 2.
5. Teacher probes for multiplication facts of 2 (Probe III) previously taught facts of 1, and multiplication facts of 3 and 4. Probe III indicates student has mastered multiplication facts of 1 and 2 and is in need of instruction for multiplication of 3 and 4.
6. Teacher teaches multiplication facts of 3.
7. Teacher probes for multiplication facts of 3 (Probe IV), previously taught facts of 1 and 2, and multiplication facts of 4. Probe IV indicates student has mastered multiplication facts of 1-3 and is need of instruction for multiplication of 4.
8. Teacher teaches multiplication facts of 4.
9. Teacher probes for multiplication facts of 4 (Probe V), 3, 2, and 1. Probe V indicates that student has mastered multiplication facts of 1-4.

Use Student Progress to Decide When to Discontinue Service

A driving force behind effective instruction is the degree to which students are benefiting from instruction. Teachers and teams of specialists assess and collect information to decide whether students are making progress and/or in need of additional services. Often this evaluation is conducted when a teacher, parent, or other professional recognizes a need. But it is a sad fact that very few students receiving remedial and/or special education services ever exit the system once they enter it. That is, once they are identified in need of special education services they become "lifers"—less than 5% of students with disabilities ever leave special education. Combine this with the fact that there are many overidentified students and it becomes clear that more needs to be done in the area of using data to make decisions about teaching and the effectiveness of service delivery.

For instruction to remain effective, it is imperative to maintain records of things that work, collect data to support students' progress (or lack of), and promote levels of learning that facilitate student demonstration of what they know and can do in the least restrictive environment.

Tactic: Keep Records of Goal Attainment

In making eligibility or entitlement decisions, collect data about student learning, strengths, needs, and problem areas. This information is used to tailor planning and delivery of instruction, regardless of where and under what program it is provided. Accordingly, this initial student information should be used in documenting whether there is improvement or a need for remediation. Maintaining accurate and specific records is of utmost importance. When students meet criteria for goal attainment, decisions about the need to continue, monitor, and adjust should be made. Obviously these decisions cannot be made unless there is a baseline on what students know and can do (initial screening and evaluation) and accurate records of instructional interventions and methods are kept. Portfolios are one way to document student growth.

evaluating

Algozzine, B. & Ysseldyke, J.E. (1981). Special education services for normal students: Better safe than sorry? *Exceptional Children.* 48, 238-243.

Algozzine, B. & Ysseldyke, J.E. (1982). Classification decisions in learning disabilities. *Educational and Psychological Research.* 2, 117-129.

Algozzine, B. & Ysseldyke, J.E. (1986). The future of the LD field: Screening and diagnosis. *Journal of Learning Disabilities.* 19(7), 394-398.

Algozzine, B. & Ysseldyke, J.E. (1992). *Strategies and tactics for effective instruction.* Longmont, CO: Sopris West.

Algozzine, B. (1993). *50 simple ways to make teaching more fun.* Longmont, CO: Sopris West.

Algozzine, B. & Ysseldyke, J.E. (1994). *Simple ways to make teaching math more fun.* Longmont, CO: Sopris West.

Bateman, B. (1967). Implication of a learning disability approach for teaching educable retardates. *Mental Retardation.* 5, 23-25.

Christenson, S.L. & Ysseldyke, J.E. (1989). Critical instructional factors for students with mild handicaps: An integrated review. *Remedial and Special Education.* 10, 21-31.

deBono, E. (1986). *CoRT thinking:* Book 1. Des Moines, IA: Advanced Practical Thinking Training.

Fuchs, L. & Deno, S. (1991). Paradigmatic distinctions between instructionally relevant measurement models. *Exceptional Children,* 57, 488-500.

G.O.A.L.S. (1989). Guide to organization, achievement, and learning skills. Exceptional Education Department, Frontier Central School District, Hamburg, NY: Federal Grant 89.313.

Harmin, M. (1995). *Strategies to inspire active learning.* Edwardsville, IL: Inspiring Strategy Institute.

Howell, K.W., Fox, S.L., & Morehead, M. (1993). *Curriculum-based evaluation: Teaching and decision making.* Pacific Grove, CA: Brooks/Cole Publishing.

Kagan, S. (1994). *Cooperative learning.* San Juan Capistrano, CA: Kagan Cooperative Learning.

Lovitt, T., Fister, S., Kemp, K., Moore, R.C., & Schroeder, B.E., (1992). *Translating research into practice (TRIP): Teaching strategies.* Longmont, CO: Sopris West.

Ogle, D.M. (1986). K-W-L: A teaching model that develops active reading of expository text. *The Reading Teacher, 39,* 564-570.

Paine, S.S., Radichhi, J., Roselini, L.C., Deutchman, L., & Darch, C.B. (1983). *Structuring your classroom for academic success.* Champaign, IL: Research Press.

Rhode, G., Jenson, W.R., & Reavis, K. (1992). *The tough kid book.* Longmont, CO: Sopris West.

Sacca, K.C. & Elliott, J.L. (1994a). Workshop materials adopted from a series of workshops conducted for the American Association of school Administrators, National Academy for School Executives.

Sacca, K.C. & Elliott, J.L. (1994b). Workshop materials adapted from institute training. Cherry Creek, NJ.

Salvia, J. & Ysseldyke, J. (1995). *Assessment.* Boston, MA: Houghton Mifflin.

Schloss, P.J. & Sedlak, R.A. (1986). *Instructional methods for students with learning and behavior problems.* Newton, MA: Allyn and Bacon.

Sopris West. (1996). *The tough kid video series.* Longmont, CO: Sopris West.

Tucker, J.A. (1987). Curriculum-based assessment is no fad. *The Collaborative Educator, 1*(4), 4-10.

Vaughn, S. Schumm, J.S., & Forgan, J.W. (in press). *Instructing students with high incidence disabilities in the general education classroom.* Alexandria, VA: ASCD.

Wolery, M., Bailey, D., & Sugai, G. (1988). *Effective teaching: Principles and procedures of applied behavior analysis with exceptional students.* Needham, MA: Allyn and Bacon.

Ysseldyke, J.E. (1973). Diagnostic-prescriptive teaching: The search for aptitude-treatment interactions. In L. Mann & D. Sabatino (Eds.), *The first review of special education.* New York: Grune & Stratton.

Ysseldyke, J.E., Algozzine, B. & Mitchell, J. (1982). Special education team decision making: An analysiss of current practice. *Personnel and Guidance Journal.* 60, 308-313.

Ysseldyke, J.E. & Christenson, S.L. (1987). *The instructional environment scale.* Austin, TX: Pro-Ed.

Ysseldyke, J.E. & Christenson, S.L. (1993). *The instructional environment system -II.* Longmont, CO: Sopris West.

Ysseldyke, J.E. & Thurlow, M.L. (1984). Assessment practices in special education: Adequacy and appropriateness. *Educational Psychologist. 19,* 123-137.

Additional Resources for Instructional Intervention

Algozzine, B. & Ysseldyke, J.E. (1995). *Tactics for improving parenting skills.* Longmont, CO: Sopris West.

Beck, R., Conrad, D., & Anderson, P. (1995). *Basic skill builders.* Longmont, CO: Sopris West.

Benninghof, A. (1994). *Ideas for inclusion.* Longmont, CO: Sopris West.

Campbell, P. & Olsen, G.R. Improving instruction in secondary schools. *Teaching Exceptional Children.* 26(3), 51-54.

Fister, S. & Kemp, K. (1995). *TGIF: But what will I do on Monday?* Longmont, CO: Sopris West.

Fister, S. & Kemp, K. (1995). *Making it work on Monday.* Longmont, CO: Sopris West.

Great Falls Public Schools (1990). *Project RIDE: Responding to individual differences in education.* Longmont, CO: Sopris West.

Rhode, G., Jenson, W.R., & Reavis, K. (1994). *The tough kid tool box.* Longmont, CO: Sopris West.

Sheridan, S.M. (1995). *The tough kid social skills book.* Longmont, CO: Sopris West.

Sprick, R., Sprick, M., & Garrison, M. (1992). *Interventions: Collaborative planning for students at risk.* Longmont, CO: Sopris West.

Other Sopris West Publications of Interest

Time Savers for Educators
Judy Elliott, Bob Algozzine, and Jim Ysseldyke

The companion book to *Strategies and Tactics for Effective Instruction*, Second Edition, *Time Savers for Educators* provides hundreds of reproducible blackline masters that will help implement these valuable tactics that are proven to save time and get results.

The Instructional Environment System-II (TIES-II)
A System to Identify a Student's Instructional Needs
James Ysseldyke and Sandra Christenson

Based on the belief that student performance in school is a function of an interaction between the student and the learning (instructional) environment, *TIES-II* provides a set of observational and interview forms, administration procedures, and an organizational structure that allows educators to both identify and address the instructional needs of individual students. While *TIES-II* can be used to assess the learning needs of all students, it is especially potent when

applied to the needs of the tough to teach. *TIES-II* enables education professionals to identify ways to change instruction or the learning environment so that the student will respond to instruction more positively, and thus more successfully. *TIES-II* provides education professionals with essential information for: prereferral intervention; instructional consultation; student/staff support teams (SSTs, TATs, etc.); intervention assistance; and collaborative intervention planning. 180 pages.

50 Simple Ways To Make Teaching More Fun
If You're a Teacher You Gotta Have This Book!
Bob Algozzine

50 Simple Ways To Make Teaching More Fun, written for both beginning and experienced teachers at all grade levels, provides suggestions and practical tips that can be used right away without special preparation or materials. This book is full of down-to-earth know-how and practical hints they didn't provide in college like how to use Bingo and other games to help students practice any content, or how to reduce bothersome behaviors with a simple recording system. It

To order or for more information call:

1-800-547-6747

also provides practical information and sample worksheets you search for in teacher workshops like how to use palindromes to help students practice math, or how to encourage students' creative thinking. Humorous examples and real-life stories illustrate these simple ways to make teaching more fun. 150 pages.

Simple Ways To Make Teaching Math More Fun
Elementary School Edition
Bob Algozzine and James Ysseldyke

Simple Ways To Make Teaching Math More Fun is loaded with innovative, practical ideas for both novice and seasoned teachers to use in planning, managing, delivering, and evaluating their math instruction. Included are teaching tips illustrating ways to: arrange a classroom to facilitate interactions; phrase questions to elicit greater student response; prevent and handle disruptions in order to improve instructional efficiency; use alternative algorithms and games to motivate students to complete assignments … and much, much more. Show your students new ways to use and look at numbers and treat yourself to a successful and enjoyable way to teach with *Simple Ways to Make Teaching Math More Fun*. 88 pages.

Tactics for Improving Parenting Skills (TIPS)
99 reproducible brochures to distribute to parents
Bob Algozzine and James Ysseldyke, Editors

Tactics for Improving Parenting Skills (TIPS) contains brief, easy to implement tactics to help parents meet the complex daily challenges they face in parenting. The ideas in *TIPS* are drawn from a broad range of proven practices and address diverse, topical parenting issues: 28 tips on Home/Family Involvement; 17 tips on School Performance; 16 tips on Social Skills/Self-Esteem; 13 tips on Discipline/Motivation; 10 tips on Personal Health/Safety; 9 tips on Independent Living; and 6 tips addressing Bilingual/Multicultural issues. Supported by a grant from the National Center for Learning Disabilities, *TIPS* contains 99 one-page informational brochures handy for distribution to parents. The format is simple: Each tactic page can be photocopied, folded, and given to parents as an attractive three-panel brochure. The tactics can be used by school counselors, teachers, psychologists, physicians, and others who may need to deliver information quickly and easily to parents or initiate discussions with them about these timely issues. 100 pages.

To order or for more information call:

1-800-547-6747